WADDINGTONS®
ILLUSTRATED
ENCYCLOPAEDIA
of
GAMES
THE
DIAGRAM GROUP

WADDINGTONS®
ILLUSTRATED
ENCYCLOPAEDIA
of
GAMES
THE
DIAGRAM GROUP

PAN ORIGINAL
PAN BOOKS LONDON AND SYDNEY

First published in different form as part of The Way to Play.
Copyright © 1975 Diagram Visual Information Ltd.

First published 1984 by Pan Books Ltd,
Cavaye Place, London SW10 9PG
© 1984 Diagram Visual Information Ltd,
11½ Adeline Place, London WC1
WADDINGTONS is the registered trade mark of
Waddingtons Games Ltd
ISBN 0 330 28477 0

Printed and bound in Great Britain by
Collins, Glasgow.

The Diagram Group

Managing editor	Ruth Midgley
Editors	Susan Bosanko, Paulin Meier, Angela Royston
Contributors	Windsor Chorlton, Jean Cooke, Kathryn Dunn, Peter Eldin, Joan Faller, Peter Finch, Bridget Gibbs, David Heidenstam, Barbara Horn, Ann Kramer, Jenny Mussell, Susan Pinkus, Allyson Rodway, Theo Rowland-Entwistle, Gina Sanders, Joan Ward
Art director	Jerry Watkiss
Artists	Neil Copleston, Robin Crane, Mark Evans, Brian Hewson, Richard Hummerstone, Ann Lumley, Kathleen McDougall, Peter Meadows, Gary Parfitt, Philip Patenall, Graham Rosewarne
Art assistant	Tony Moore

Foreword

This illustrated reference book brings together more
than 400 games and variations that can be relied upon to
provide many hours of entertainment for family and
friends. Some of these games are old favorites, others
are examples of interesting and challenging games from
foreign countries and from ancient times. There are
games to suit players of all ages and abilities – from
simple party games for young children to the
complexities of Chess and Go. Board games, dice
games, party games and races, games using pencil and
paper, dominoes, coins, marbles, jackstraws – or no
equipment at all – are among those included in this
fascinating compendium. Card games have not been
included but can be found in the companion volume,
Waddingtons® Illustrated Card Games.
Detailed rules of play are given step-by-step for each
game. The clear, concise language of the instructions is
complemented by explanatory diagrams. The number of
players and the equipment needed for each game are
also listed, with suggestions for improvised equipment
for the less familiar games.
The order in which the games appear in the main part of
the book is basically alphabetical. Alphabetical
ordering, however, has not been applied to variants of
games; these are included under the same main heading
as the parent game (although they are listed separately
in the index).
Useful information on selecting a game is to be found in
the second section of the book. This includes cross-
referenced lists of games using different kinds of
equipment and for different numbers of players, as well
as a comprehensive index. It is therefore easy to find the
correct rules for a familiar game or to attempt an
unfamiliar game for the first time.

Contents

Section 1
How to play

Section 2
Finding a game

Section 1
How to play

Alleyway

Alleyway is a family game popular in Eastern Europe. It is
great fun to play, because although its rules are simple,
winning is tantalizingly difficult! There can be any number of
players.

Equipment A semi-circle is drawn on a piece of paper or cardboard, and marked with 25 numbered spaces as shown. The thirteenth space or "alleyway" is left open.

Each player has a counter of a different color. One die is used.

Play Each player throws the die and sets his counter on the space with the corresponding number. Players then take turns to throw the die and move their counters the number of spaces indicated by the die.

If at any time a player's counter lands on a space that is already occupied by an opponent's counter, the opponent's counter must be moved back a certain number of spaces, as follows:

a) If the opponent's counter was on any of the spaces from 1–12 or in the alleyway, it must go back to the beginning.

b) Once past the alleyway, however, a counter need only be moved back two spaces – and should that space also be occupied, that counter also must move back the appropriate number of spaces.

c) If the opponent's counter is on space 14 or 15 and has to retreat two spaces (ie to the alleyway or space 12), it has to go right back to the start. If it encounters an "enemy" counter in the alleyway or on space 12, that piece, too, has to go back to the start.

End play If a player's counter lands on space 25, it has to retreat to space 14 (**d**). Thus the winner is the first player whose throw gets him beyond space 25.

Layout

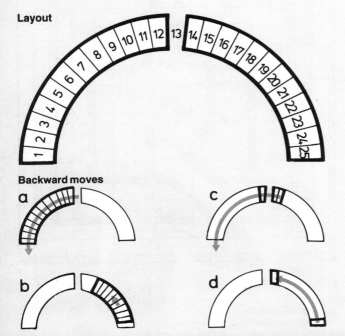

Backward moves

Ashte kashte

Pieces

This ancient board game is of Eastern origin and has similarities with Ludo (p. 184) and Pachisi (p. 216). It is a race game for two, three, or four players.

Board This usually has 49 squares, in seven rows of seven. The square at the center of the board (the finish) and the middle square along each side row (starting and resting squares) are colored differently from all the other squares.
Pieces Each player has four shells, stones, counters, or other objects that must be clearly distinguishable from those used by the other players.

Board

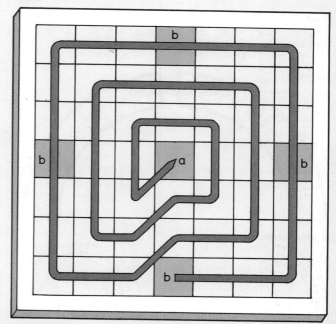

a) Finish
b) Starting and resting squares

Route for one player

Dice Four cowrie shells are used to indicate the number of squares to be moved, as follows:
a) all four shells with openings uppermost, four squares;
b) three shells with openings uppermost, three squares;
c) two shells with openings uppermost, two squares;
d) one shell with opening uppermost, one square;
e) all four shells with openings face down, eight squares.

Dice

Objective Each player aims to be first to move all his pieces from his starting square to the finish. The route for one player is shown on the illustration below left; other players follow a similar route but with a different starting point.

Play Each player selects a different starting square and places his pieces outside the board beside it. Players then take turns to throw the cowrie shells and move one of their pieces the appropriate number of squares onto their starting square and on around the race route.

After their first throw players can choose to bring a new piece into play or may move a piece that is already on the board. Splitting throws between pieces is not allowed (eg a four cannot be used to move one piece three squares and another piece one square).

Taking If a player's piece is on any square but a resting square and another player's move causes one of his pieces to end up on the same square, the first player's piece must be taken off the board to begin again. Pieces on any resting square, not only on a player's own starting square, are safe from taking.

Double pieces If a player moves one of his pieces so that it ends up on the same square as another of his pieces, these two pieces become a "double piece" and are moved together on subsequent throws. A double piece can be taken only by another double piece. No single piece – even one belonging to the same player – can ever overtake a double piece.

End of play The finish can be reached only by throwing the exact number needed to land on the center square. If a player throws a higher number than he needs to finish he must either move one of his other pieces or wait for another turn. A piece that lands exactly on the finish square is immediately removed from the board.

The winner is the first player to move all his pieces from start to finish. The game may be carried on to determine the finishing order of the other players.

Backgammon

Backgammon is an ancient board game developed in the
Orient and now played all over the world. It is an excellent
game in which the opportunities for strategic play add to the
excitement of a race around the board. The fine calculation of
odds involved in skilled play has a strong attraction for the
player who is prepared to gamble.

Players Only two players compete, but others may participate
in the betting when games are played for money.
Pieces Each player has 15 pieces, similar to those used in
Draughts. One player has dark pieces (Black) and the other
light pieces (White). The pieces are variously known as
"counters," "stones," or "men." In the modern game "men" is
the commonly accepted term.
Dice Each player has two dice and a cup in which to shake them.

Doubling cube In a game where players agree to bet on the outcome (there is no need to play for anything but fun), a doubling cube is used. This is a large die on which the faces are numbered 2, 4, 8, 16, 32, 64. (Its significance is explained in the section on gambling, p. 27.)

Board and notation

White

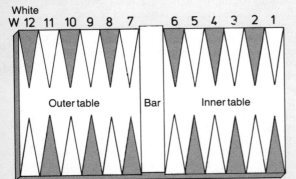

Board Backgammon is played on a rectangular board divided into two halves by a "bar." One half of the board is called the "inner table" or "home table," and the other the "outer table."

Along each side of the board are marked 12 triangles, alternately light and dark colored (this coloring has no special significance.) Each triangle is called a "point." For the purpose of notation, points are numbered 1–12 as shown in the diagram on this page. (No numbers actually appear on the board.) Points 1 (the first points in the inner table) are called "ace points"; points 7 (the first points on the outer table) are called "bar points." No other points are specially designated.

The board is placed between the two players (called Black and White) so that Black has his inner table to his right. The points on Black's side of the table are known as Black points; those on White's side as White points. In simple notation, points are indicated by their number and the initial B or W.

Objective According to the numbers thrown on the dice, each player moves his men toward his own inner table.

Once all a player's men are located in his own inner table he attempts to remove them – by a process called "bearing off." The first player to bear off all 15 of his pieces wins the game. Although the basic objective of the game is simple, the rules and strategies governing a player's moves are much more complex.

Start of play Players draw for color and then place their men in their prescribed starting positions. White places two men on B1; five men on W6; three men on W8; and five men on B12. Black places two men on W1; five men on B6; three men on B8; and five men on W12.

Having placed their men on their starting positions, each player throws a single die to determine the order of play. The player throwing the higher number has first move. If both players throw the same number they must throw again. For his first move the opening player moves according to the numbers on both his own and his opponent's dice. Thereafter, play alternates and each player moves according to the numbers on both his own dice.

Play A player throws both his dice to determine how many points he can move. For a valid throw the dice must be:
thrown from the cup;
thrown in the player's own half of the board;
thrown so that one face of each die rests wholly on the board;
thrown only when an opponent has completed his turn.
The player then moves according to the numbers thrown on the dice.

The direction of play for each player is always from his opponent's inner table, through his opponent's outer table, through his own outer table, and into his own inner table. Thus White always moves his men clockwise and Black moves counterclockwise.

Start of play

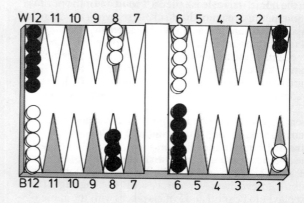

22

Moving men

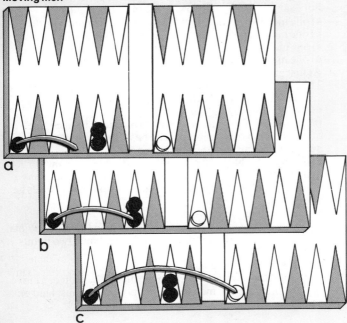

Moving men A player attempts to move the number of points shown on each of his die. He may not merely add them together and move the combined total. The position of the men on the board may affect a player's choice of moves or may even prevent him from moving at all.

Provided that none of his men is off the board, a player may move to any point that is:

a) clear of any other men;
b) occupied by one or more of his own men; or
c) occupied by only one of his opponent's men.

When there is only one man on a point, this man is called a "blot."

A player who moves a man to a point on which he already has one man is said to "make" that point, as his opponent cannot then land on it.

(Also see sections on play after a mixed throw and play after a double, p. 24.)

Play after a mixed throw If the numbers on the two dice are different, the player may make one of four possible moves. For example, a player throwing a 2 and a 6 may move:

a) one man two points, then the same man six points further;
b) one man six points, then the same man two points further;
c) one man two points, and another man six points;
d) one man six points, and another man two points.

At first glance alternatives a) and b) appear to be the same. This is not in fact the case, since the order in which the numbers are taken can affect whether or not a man may be moved (see the section on moving men).

If he can use only the number shown on one of his dice, the other number is disregarded. If he has a choice of two numbers, he must use the higher one.

Play after a double If a player throws a double, then the number shown on both dice is played four times (or as many times as possible up to four). Thus if a player throws two 2s he may move:

a) one man four times two points;
b) one man twice two points and another man twice two points;
c) one man twice two points and another two men two points each;
d) four men two points each.

As before, the number shown on the dice is the limit of a move. A player moving one man four times two points must land on open points at the end of each two point move.

Play after a mixed throw

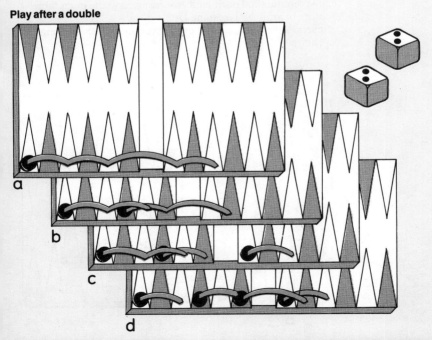

Play after a double

©DIAGRAM

25

Hitting a man If a player moves a man onto a point on which his opponent has only one man (**a**) he is said to "hit" that man. The hit man is removed from play and placed on the bar (**b**). A player who has any hit men on the bar must re-enter them before he can move any of his men on the board.

Re-entering men To re-enter a hit man, a player must throw the number of an open point on his opponent's home table. He may then use the number on his second die to re-enter another man, or, if all his men are on the board, to move any of his men the number of points shown on that die.

Bearing off men Once a player has succeeded in moving all his men into his own inner table, he bears them off by removing them from those points corresponding to the numbers thrown. For example, if White throws a 4 and a 2 when he has men on both W4 and W2 he may bear off a man from each of these points.

If he throws a 4 and a 2 when he has a man on W4 but not on W2, he may bear off a man from W4 and must then move another man two points down from his highest occupied point.

If he wishes, a player may always move men down the board from his highest point rather than bearing off from the points corresponding to the numbers on the dice.

If both numbers thrown are higher than the player's highest point, the player bears off from his highest point.

If a player's man is hit after he has started bearing off, that man must re-enter and be moved around again to the inner table before bearing off is resumed.

Bearing off continues until one player succeeds in bearing off all his men.

Hitting a man

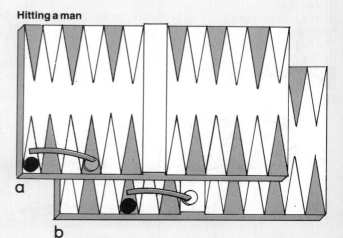

Fouls and penalties In addition to the rules on throwing the dice, players must observe the following:

a) a player may not change his move after taking his hand from a moved piece;

b) if a player makes an incorrect move, his opponent may insist that the error be corrected provided that he has not made his own following move;

c) a game must be restarted if the board or pieces are found to be incorrectly set up during play.

Scoring The game is won by the player who first bears off all his men. The number of units scored depends on the progress of the loser:

a) if the loser has borne off at least one man and has no men left in the winner's inner table, the winner scores one unit;

b) if the loser has not borne off any men, the winner has made a "gammon" and scores two units;

c) if the loser has not borne off any men and also has a man on the bar or in the winner's inner table, the winner has made a "backgammon" and scores three units.

Gambling Backgammon is often played for an agreed base stake for each game. This stake may be doubled and redoubled during play (in addition to the double payment for a gammon and treble for a backgammon). A doubling cube is often used to show the number of times that the stake has been doubled. (At the start of play it should be placed with the number 64 face uppermost.)

Unless players previously agree otherwise, stakes are automatically doubled if the dice match at the first throw of a game. In this case both players then throw again. The number of automatic doubles is usually limited by agreement to one or two per game. There is no limit to the number of voluntary doubles.

Either player has the right to offer the first voluntary double – after which the right alternates between players. A player who wishes to double the stake must offer to do so before throwing the dice when it is his turn to play. His opponent then has the choice of accepting the doubled stake or of forfeiting the game and the stake.

DUTCH BACKGAMMON

This is the same as the basic game except that:

a) all the men are placed on the bar for the start of play and players must enter all 15 before moving any man around the board;

b) a player may not hit a blot until he has advanced at least one of his own men to his own inner table.

Dutch backgammon: start

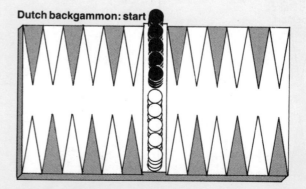

ACEY DEUCY
This is an elaboration of Dutch backgammon and is popular in the US Navy. It differs from the basic game in the following ways:

a) men are entered from the bar as in Dutch backgammon;

b) if a player throws a 1 and a 2 (ace-deuce), he moves his men for this throw and then moves his men as if he had thrown any double that he chooses;

c) the stake is usually automatically doubled when an ace-deuce is thrown;

d) some players give each man an agreed unit value and the winner collects as many units as the opponent has left on the board.

GIOUL
This popular Middle Eastern form of Backgammon is played in the same way as the basic game except that:

a) each player positions all his men on his opponent's number 1 point for the start;

b) a blot is not hit but is blocked and cannot be moved while an opposing man is on the same point;

c) when a player throws a double, he attempts to move for the double thrown and then for each subsequent double in turn up to double 6. (For example if he throws double 4 he goes on to move for double 5 and double 6).

d) if a player is unable to use any of his moves from a double, all these moves may be taken by his opponent.

PLAKATO
This form of Backgammon is widely played in Greek cafes. It is the same as the basic game described here except that:

a) each player positions all his men on his opponent's number 1 point for the start of play;

b) a blot is not hit but is blocked and cannot be moved as long as an opposing man is on the same point;

c) a player must move all his men all 24 points instead of bearing them off when they reach his inner table.

Plakato: start

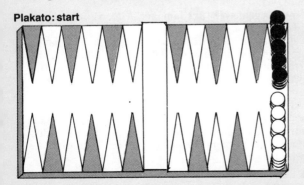

29

Ball games

Although ball games are usually associated with outdoor play, there are many enjoyable games that can be played indoors. A table tennis ball is recommended for minimum damage!

Cup and ball

CUP AND BALL
Cup and ball is a game for one person that was first played several hundred years ago. It was especially popular among children in the late nineteenth century and can still be bought today. The cup and ball are made of wood and joined by a length of string. Sometimes the cup is replaced by a wooden spike and the ball has a hole bored through its center.
The player holds the cup around its base and stretches out his arm so that the ball hangs toward the ground. He then swings his arm and tries to catch the ball in the cup – with a little practice this can be done almost every time. The version with a spike is more difficult to accomplish, as the ball has to be impaled on the spike.

JAM JARS
This is a game needing only a few table tennis balls and some jam jars for equipment. Five or six jam jars are placed close together on the floor or on a table.
Players stand a few feet away and take it in turns to throw a set number of table tennis balls (usually two or three) in an attempt to get them into the jars. As table tennis balls are extremely bouncy, this task is more difficult than it might at first seem!
The player who manages to get the most balls into the jam jars after each round of play is the winner. (Any number of rounds may be played.)

IN THE BOWL
In the bowl is a game very like Jam jars. A deep bowl or bucket is placed on the floor.
Each player in turn tries to throw a table tennis ball so that it lands (and remains!) in the bowl. If the player is successful he may throw again. At the end of a set time, the player with the most successful throws wins the game.

CONTAINERS
This game is played in the same way as In the bowl, except that players try to get a ball into one of several containers – each with a points value depending on its size. The player with most points wins the game.

© DIAGRAM

BLOW FOOTBALL

Blow football is a game played at a table by two players or by two teams of two or three. Each person blows through a drinking straw at a table tennis ball, and tries to get the ball into the opposing goal. The player or team that scores the most goals after a given time wins the game.

Equipment Blow football is best played at a long table, although it can also be played on the floor. A goal must be marked at each end of the table – using pencils or other suitable objects.

It is a good idea to make a wall around the edges of the table to help keep the ball in play. (Strips of wood or cardboard can be used.)

Each player is given a drinking straw, and the only other equipment needed is a table tennis ball.

Play The table tennis ball is placed in the middle of the table. At a given signal, the players start to blow through their straws in an attempt to get the ball into the opponents' goal – while at the same time defending their own goal from attack.

Whenever a goal is scored (ie the ball passes between the "goalposts"), the ball is repositioned at the center of the table and the game is restarted.

If the ball is blown off the table, the opposing side places the ball on the table at the spot where it came off and then takes a "free" blow before the other side may continue blowing.

Blow football

THROUGH THE TUNNEL

Through the tunnel is similar to Archboard – a game played with marbles (see p. 208). Playing procedure is exactly the same as for Archboard, but table tennis balls are used instead of marbles, and the arches through which they are rolled are correspondingly bigger.

HOLEY BOARD GAME

This is a target game in which players score points by throwing a table tennis ball through a "holey board."

The holey board can be made quite easily out of stiff carboard. A random number of holes is cut out, each one a different size. (The smallest hole should be just big enough for a table tennis ball to pass through it.) A scoring value is written above each hole – the bigger the hole, the lower the value.

The board is held or propped up in an upright position – books can be used to keep it in place. Players stand as far away from the board as possible and take turns to throw the ball.

Each time a player gets the ball through a hole, he scores the number of points written above the hole. (The smaller the hole, the more difficult it is to get the ball through it!) The player with the highest score after a set number of throws is the winner.

Once players have become quite skilled, they can try throwing the ball so that it bounces on the floor before going through a hole.

Holey board game

Checkers/Draughts

Known as Checkers in the USA and Draughts in the UK, this is a popular board game for two players. It was played in southern Europe in medieval times and appears to have been derived from much older games played in the Middle East. Each player attempts to "take" (capture and remove) his opponent's pieces or to confine them so that they cannot be moved.

Board The game is played on a board made of wood, plastic, or cardboard and 14½–16in square.
It is divided into 64 squares, eight along each side. The squares are alternately a light and a dark color (usually black and white, or sometimes black and red or red and white). Play is confined to squares of only one color – usually the darker color.

Start of play

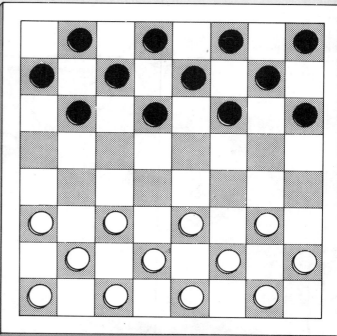

Pieces Each player has a set of 12 pieces – wooden or plastic disks 1¼–1½in in diameter and about ⅜in thick. One set is usually white, and the other red or black.

Objective A player aims to "take" all his opponent's pieces or to position his own pieces so that his opponent is unable to make any move.

Start of play The players sit facing each other, and the board is positioned so that the players have a playing square at the left of their first row. Lots are drawn to decide who will have the darker pieces for the first game. Each player has the darker pieces for alternate games.

For the start of play each player positions his pieces on the playing squares in the three rows of the board nearest to him. The player with the darker pieces always makes the first move in a game.

Moving A player may make only one move at a turn. As play is confined to squares of only one color, all moves are diagonal. Individual pieces or "men" may only be moved forward (**a**); double pieces or "kings" may be moved either forward or backward (**b**).

A piece may only be moved into a square that is vacant.

Moving

a 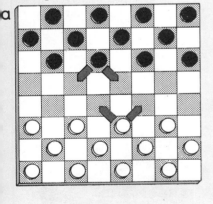 b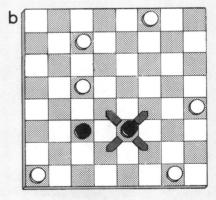

Touch and move Except when he has given notice of his intention to arrange pieces properly in their squares, a player whose turn it is must when possible make his move with the first piece that he touches.

If he first touches an unplayable piece, he is cautioned for a first offense and forfeits the game for a second offense.

Time limit for moves If a player fails to make a move within five minutes, an appointed timekeeper shall call "time." The player must then move within one minute, or forfeit the game through improper delay. (At master level in some tournaments, players must make a prescribed number of moves within set time limits.)

A non-taking move Except when "taking" an opponent's piece, a player may only move a piece into a touching playing square.

A taking move One of the game's objectives is to "take" (capture and remove) the opposing pieces.

A piece may be taken if it is in a playing square touching the taker's square when there is a vacant square directly beyond it (**1**). Several pieces can be taken in one move provided that each one has a vacant square beyond it (**2**).

Whenever possible, a player must make a taking move rather than a non-taking move (even if this means that his own piece will in turn be taken). If a player has a choice of taking moves he may take a smaller instead of a larger number of pieces (**3a**), but if he begins the move enabling him to take the larger number he must continue until he has taken all the pieces possible (**3b**).

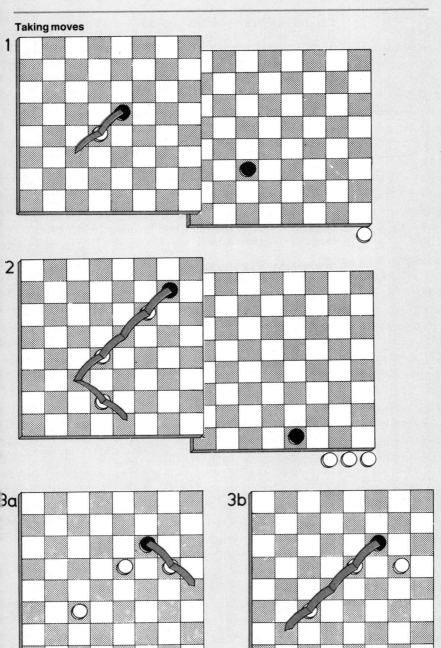

1

2

3a 3b

©DIAGRAM

Failure to take If a player fails to take a piece when he is able (**1a**), modern tournament play rules state that his opponent should point this out and so force him to take back the wrongly moved piece and make the taking move instead (**1b**).

This ruling has replaced the old "huff or blow" rule, by which a player who failed to make a possible taking move forfeited the piece moved in error.

King

Crowning When a man reaches the farthest row on the board (known as the "king row" or "crownhead"), it becomes a "king" and is "crowned" by having another piece of its own color placed on it (**2**). A player's turn always ends when a man is crowned.

A tied game occurs when neither player can remove all his opponent's pieces or prevent him making a move (**3a, 3b**).

If one player appears to be in a stronger position, he may be required to force a win within 40 of his own moves or else place himself at a decided advantage over his opponent. If he fails, the game is counted as tied.

TOURNAMENT CHECKERS

To reduce the number of tied and repeated games at expert level, a system of restricted openings is applied at major championships and tournaments in the United States and elsewhere.

The first three moves of each game are determined by cards bearing the various openings and subsequent moves. The cards are shuffled and cut, and the top card is turned face up. Opposing players then play two games with the prescribed opening, each player making the first move in one of the games.

LOSING/GIVEAWAY CHECKERS

This is played under the same rules as standard British or American checkers. The tactics, however, are very different, as the objective is to be the first player to lose all his pieces.

Failure to take

1a

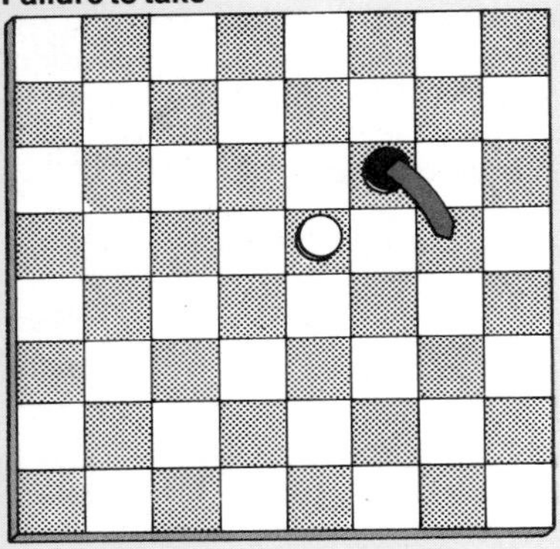

1b

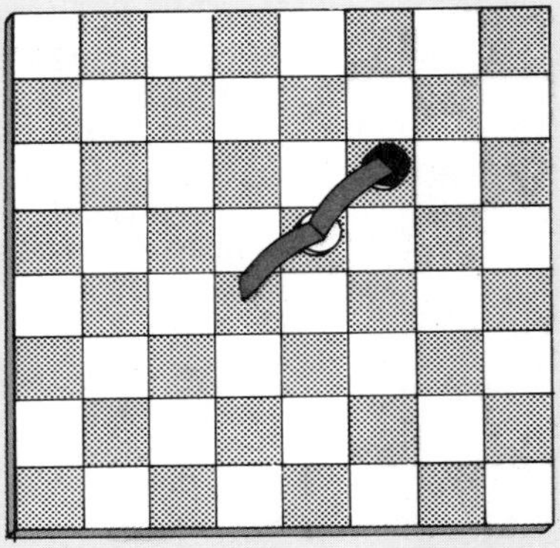

Crowning

2

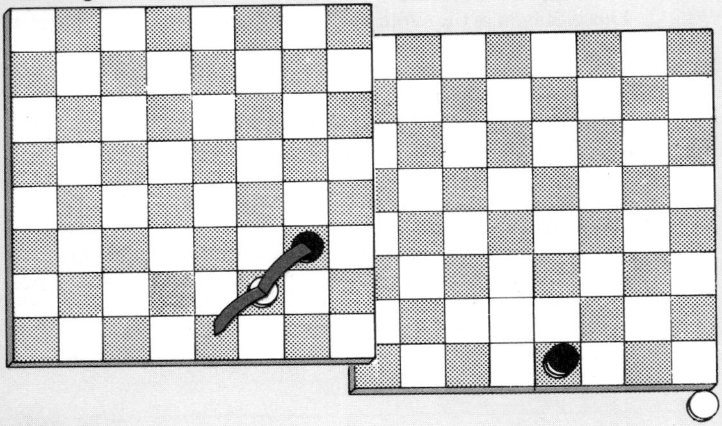

Tied games

3a

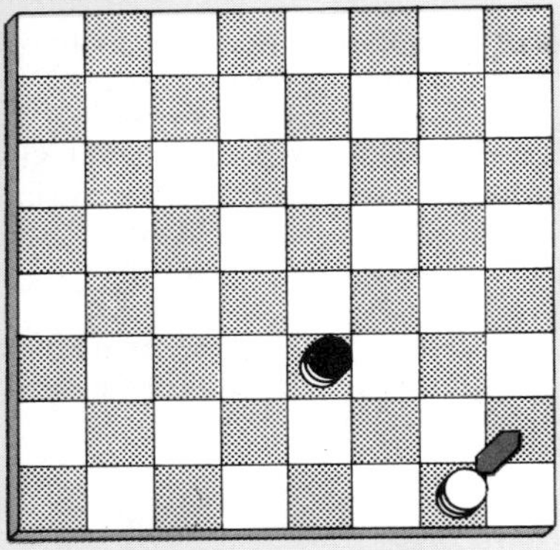

3b

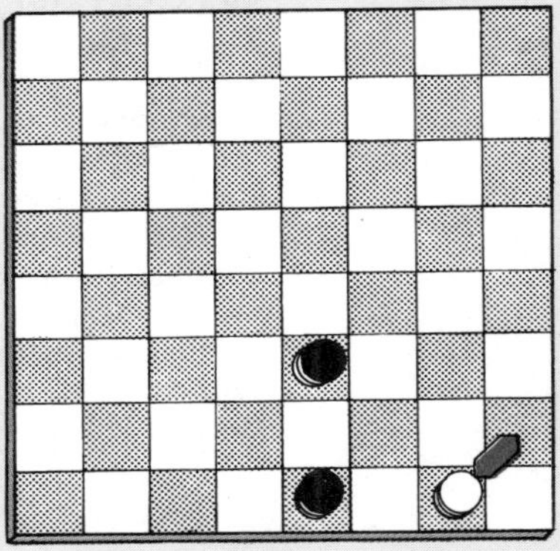

©DIAGRAM

39

DIAGONAL CHECKERS

This is an interesting variant of the standard game. It can be played with 12 pieces per player, in which case starting position (**a**) is used, or with nine pieces each if starting position (**b**) is used. Men are crowned when they have crossed the board to reach the opponent's corner squares (marked K in the diagrams).

Otherwise, rules are the same as for standard checkers.

ITALIAN CHECKERS

This is played in the same way as standard British or American checkers except that:

a) the board is positioned with a non-playing square at the left of each player's first row;

b) a player must make a taking move whenever possible – or forfeit the game;

c) a man cannot take a king;

d) if a player has a choice of captures he must take the greater number of pieces;

e) if a player with a king to move has a choice of capturing equal numbers of pieces, he must take the most valuable pieces (ie kings rather than men).

SPANISH CHECKERS

This is played in the same way as Italian checkers, except that kings are moved differently. A player may use a king to take a piece anywhere on a diagonal, provided that there are no pieces between and there is an empty square beyond it. (This is sometimes called the "long move.") The jump need not end in the square immediately behind the taken piece, but may continue any distance along the diagonal if there are no intervening pieces (**a**).

A king must make all its jumps before any taken pieces are removed, and these pieces may not be jumped a second time in the same move (**b**).

Diagonal checkers: alternative starts

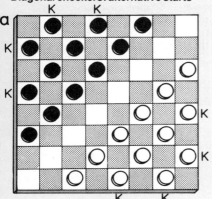

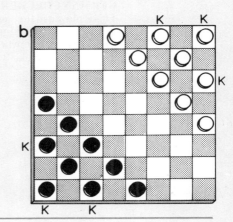

Italian checkers: start

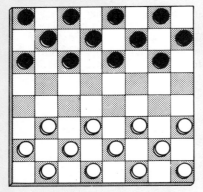

Spanish checkers: taking with a king

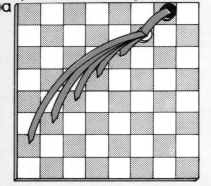

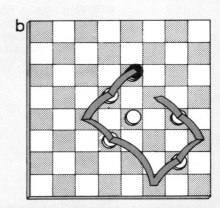

©DIAGRAM

GERMAN CHECKERS

This is played in the same way as Spanish checkers except that:
a) men can make taking moves either forward or backward;
b) a man is only crowned if its move ends on the far row – if it is in a position to make further jumps away from that line it must always take them.

RUSSIAN CHECKERS

This is played like German checkers except that:
a) a player with a choice of captures need not take the larger number of pieces;
b) a man is made into a king as soon as it reaches the far row and then jumps as a king for the rest of the move.

CONTINENTAL CHECKERS

Also called Polish checkers, this is played on a board with 100 squares, 10 along each side. Each player has 20 pieces – positioned on the first four rows for the start of play. The game is played under the same rules as German checkers.

German checkers: moving

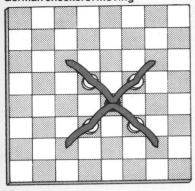

a

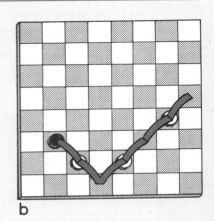

b

Russian checkers: moving

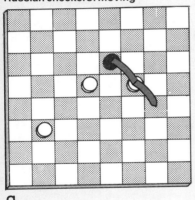

a

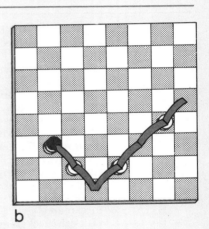

b

Continental checkers: start

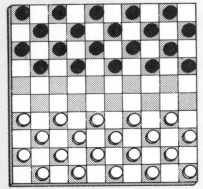

©DIAGRAM

43

CANADIAN CHECKERS

This is another variant of German checkers. It is played on a board with 144 squares, 12 by 12. Each player has 30 pieces – positioned on the first five rows for the start of play.

TURKISH CHECKERS

This may be played on a standard checker board, but the traditional Turkish board has squares all the same color. Each player has 16 pieces – positioned on each player's second and third rows for the start of play.

Men move as in British or American checkers, but directly forward or sideways and not diagonally (**a**). Kings move any number of squares directly forward, sideways, or backward. Multiple captures by kings are made as shown (**b**) – as for Spanish checkers except that moves are not diagonal and pieces are removed as soon as they are jumped (instead of staying on the board to prevent further jumps).

A player must make a capture whenever possible, and must always take the greater number of pieces when he has a choice of captures.

Turkish checkers may be won in the usual ways, and also by a player with a king when his opponent has only a single man remaining on the board.

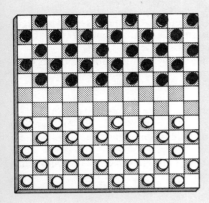

Turkish checkers: start

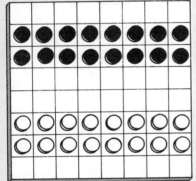

Turkish checkers: moving

a
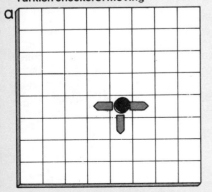

b
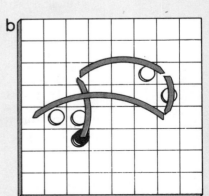

©DIAGRAM

CHECKERS GO-MOKU

This is an adaptation of the Japanese game described on page 166. Play is on all the squares of a standard checker board, and the two players have 12 checkers each.

The board is empty at the start of a game, and the players take it in turns to place one checker on any square. After all the checkers have been placed, a player uses his turn to move one checker into any vacant, adjoining square.

If, at any stage of the game, a player succeeds in placing five checkers in a row (horizontally, vertically, or diagonally), he is entitled to remove any one of his opponent's checkers from the board.

The game is won when a player has removed all his opponent's checkers.

CHECKERS FOX AND GEESE

Two versions of Fox and geese (p. 154) are often played on a checker board and are particularly popular with children.
In both checkers versions, one player has one dark checker (the "fox") and his opponent has several white checkers (the "geese").

Play is only on the black squares of the board. A player moves only one checker at a turn. The fox wins the game if it can break through the line of geese. The geese win if they can trap the fox so that it cannot move.

FOUR GEESE VERSION

At the start of play, the player with the geese positions them on the four playing squares of his first row; the player with the fox positions it wherever he chooses.

The geese move diagonally forward one square at a time like the men in British or American checkers. The fox moves diagonally forward or backward; it is not permitted to jump over the geese, so there is no taking in this version.

TWELVE GEESE VERSION

This version is sometimes played with a "wolf" and "goats." At the start of play the geese are positioned on the first three rows, as for British or American checkers; the fox is positioned on one of the corner playing squares on the opposite side of the board. The geese move like the men and the fox like a king in British or American checkers. (Jumping and taking geese is permitted in this version.)

Checkers go-moku: won game

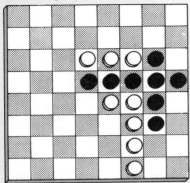

Checkers fox and geese: alternative starts

Four geese version

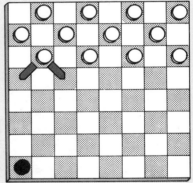

Twelve geese version

Chess

Originating in the East over a thousand years ago, Chess has developed into one of the most popular of all games. Despite being highly complex and sophisticated, it can also be enjoyed at a simpler level by inexperienced players. It is a game of strategy for two people, with each piece – from the king to the pawn – representing units in an army.

The board is a large square divided into eight rows of eight squares each. The squares are alternately dark and light colored (usually black and white).
The board is placed between facing players so that each has a white square at the near righthand corner.
The rows of squares running vertically between facing players are called "files"; those running at right angles to the files are called "ranks." Rows of squares of the same color that touch only at their corners are called "diagonals."

Start of play

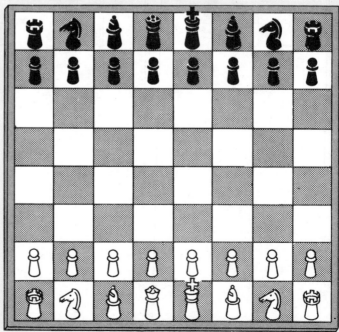

Pieces At the start of a game 32 pieces are positioned on the board. 16 of these pieces are dark in color, 16 light. They are called black and white respectively and make up the two sides. A player's side is made up of six different kinds of pieces. These are – in descending order of importance: king, queen, rook (castle), bishop, knight, pawn. Each player has one king and one queen; two rooks, bishops, and knights; and eight pawns.

Objective The objective of each player is to capture his opponent's king. Unlike the other pieces, the king cannot be removed from the board; it is held to be captured when it has been "checkmated" (see section on check and checkmate, p. 58).

The player forcing checkmate wins the game – even if the pieces he has left on the board are outnumbered by the opponent's pieces.

A player seeing the imminent checkmate of his king or recognizing a losing situation will often resign. The player forcing the resignation wins the game.

Moves Each kind of piece can move a certain distance in one or more directions. Moves are limited by conditions on the board at the time of play.

A piece may move to any square within its range, provided that:

a) the square is unoccupied by a piece of its own color;

b) if the square is occupied by an opponent's piece, that piece is first "captured" and removed from the board;

c) it does not, with the exception of the knight's move, cross a square that is occupied by a piece of either color.

Names of rows

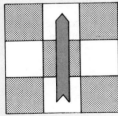

File

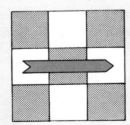

Rank

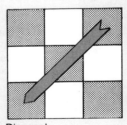

Diagonal

The king is the most important piece on the board, and its capture by checkmate ends the game. It is represented diagrammatically by a crown.

The king can move one square in any direction, provided that this square is not one where it can be taken. Opposing kings can never stand on touching squares.

Castling The only time that a king may move more than one square is in the "castling" move involving the rook. A player can make a castling move only once in a game.

The move is made to produce a defensive position around the king and to allow a rook to come into play. It comprises:

1) moving the king two squares to left or right from its original position and toward one of the rooks; then

2) transferring that rook to the square over which the king has just passed.

Castling is permitted only if:

a) neither the king nor the rook involved has moved from its original position;

b) no piece of either color is between the king and the rook involved in the castling move;

c) the square that the king must cross is not under attack by an opponent's piece.

The queen, represented diagrammatically by a coronet, is the most powerful attacking piece. It can move to any square on the rank, file, or either of the two diagonals on which it is placed.

King's moves

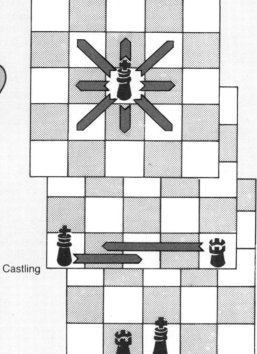

Castling

Queen's moves

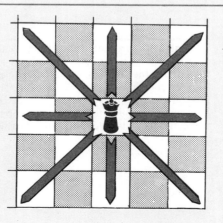

©DIAGRAM

51

The rook, sometimes called the castle, is represented diagrammatically by a tower. It can move to any square on the rank or file on which it is placed. In addition, either one of the rooks in each side may be involved with the king in the castling move (p.50).

The bishop, represented diagrammatically by a miter, can move to any square on the diagonal on which it is placed. Thus each player has one bishop that can move on a black diagonal and one on a white diagonal.

The knight is represented diagrammatically by a horse's head. In a single move it travels two squares in any direction along a rank or file, then one square at right angles to that rank or file. Thus whenever a knight moves from a black square it must land on a white square – and vice versa.
In moving, a knight may cross a square occupied by any other piece; it is the only piece allowed to do this.

Rook's moves

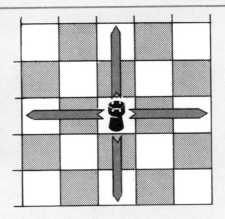

Bishop's moves

Knight's moves

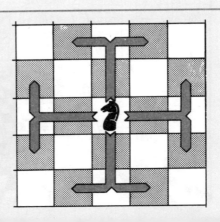

53

The pawn, represented diagrammatically by a small ball on a collared stem, has the most restricted movements of any piece: it can only move forward.

In its opening move, a pawn may be moved forward either one or two squares on the file that it occupies. Thereafter, a pawn can only move forward one square at a time, except when capturing.

Unlike other pieces, a pawn does not capture in the same way that it moves. Instead of capturing in a forward direction, it does so diagonally – taking a piece that occupies either of the two squares diagonally next to it.

In addition, a pawn may capture an opposing pawn *"en passant"* (in passing). If the opposing pawn moves forward two squares in its opening move, the square it crosses is open to attack as though the pawn had only advanced one square. Thus the capturing pawn may make its usual taking move (ie one square diagonally forward) onto the square just crossed by the opposing pawn – the opposing pawn is then considered "captured" and is removed from the board. (The *en passant* capture must be made immediately the opposing pawn has moved forward two squares.)

Pawn promotion Whenever a pawn reaches the end of the file on which it is moving (ie it reaches the far side of the board) it must – in the same move – be exchanged for a queen, rook, bishop, or knight.

The choice of piece is made by the player promoting the pawn, and is made without taking into account the number and kind of pieces on the board. Theoretically, therefore, a player could have up to nine queens on the board.

The effect of the promoted piece on play is immediate.

Pawn's moves

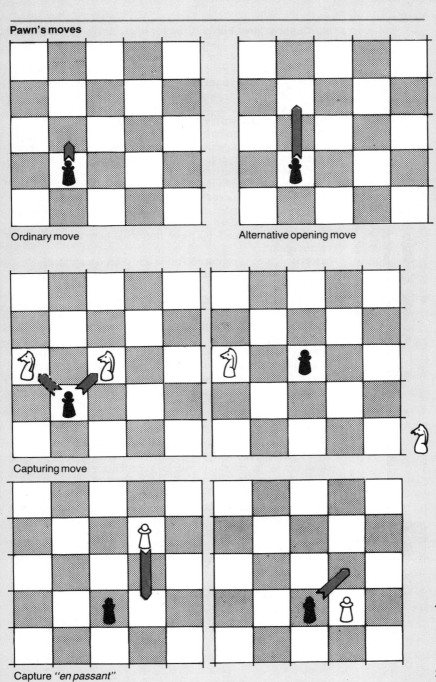

Ordinary move

Alternative opening move

Capturing move

Capture "en passant"

©DIAGRAM

55

Starting procedure Players draw for sides, and position their pieces on the board. The player drawing white makes the first move, and thereafter the players move alternately.

Play The position of the pieces at the start of play is such that each player can move only a knight or a pawn. After the first move by each player, more pieces can come into play.

In moving their pieces, players are governed not only by the movements laid down for each piece but also by rules that affect how pieces can be handled.

If a player touches a piece that can legitimately be moved, then he must move that piece – unless he has previously warned his opponent that he is adjusting the piece on its square. The usual warning used is *"J'adoube"* (I adjust). Similarly, if a player touches an enemy piece that can be taken, the touched piece must be captured unless the player has given a prior warning.

Capturing move

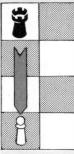

A move is completed when:

a) a player's hand has left a piece after it has been moved to a vacant square;

b) a player, having captured a piece and placed his attacking piece on the captured square, removes his hand from the piece;

c) in castling, a player's hand has left the rook (once the king has been moved, the castling move must always be completed);

d) in pawn promotion, a player's hand has left the piece that replaces the pawn.

Phases of play Chess players commonly divide a game into three phases: opening game, middle game, and end game. These phases are not clear-cut divisions – they simply reflect the strategies and tactics employed.

1) In the opening game, both players position their pieces into what each considers to be an advantageous situation. Castling moves are usually made during this phase.

2) In the middle game, players attempt to capture enemy pieces, thereby reducing the opponent's attacking ability. However, as the main objective is to checkmate the opponent's king, moves or captures should not be made unless they weaken the opponent's defense of his king. The player should also beware of making moves that jeopardize his own position.

3) In the end game, players attempt to checkmate the opponent's king. If, during this phase, a player has few attacking pieces, he will attempt – where possible – to promote a pawn to a more powerful piece.

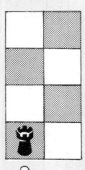

©DIAGRAM

57

Check and checkmate Whenever a king is attacked by an opposing piece, the king is said to be "in check." The check must be met on the following move by either:
a) moving the king one square in any direction onto a square that is not attacked;
b) capturing the piece that is checking the king; or
c) interposing a piece between the king and the attacking piece (if the king is checked by an opponent's knight, it is not possible to intercept the check in this way). A piece that intercepts a check can – in the same move – give check to the opposing king.

Meeting check

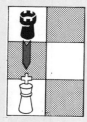

Check

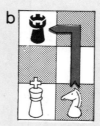

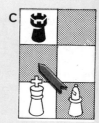

If the check cannot be met then the king is deemed "in checkmate" or simply "mate." When a checking or checkmating move is made, it is customary for the player making such a move to declare "Check" or "Checkmate" as appropriate.

Winning A player wins if he:
a) checkmates his opponent's king; or
b) forces his opponent to resign.
Checkmate may be made, or a player may resign, at any time during the course of the game.

Examples of checkmate

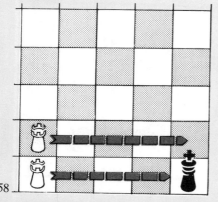

Drawn game Many games of chess do not end in a victory for either player. A game is drawn in any of the following cases.

a) When the player whose turn it is to move can make no legal move (a situation known as "stalemate").

b) When neither player has sufficient pieces to force checkmate.

c) When a player can check the opponent's king indefinitely but cannot checkmate it (a situation called "perpetual check").

d) When no capture or pawn move has been made by either side during 50 successive moves of each player.

e) When the same position recurs three times, always when it is the same player's turn to move. The right to claim a draw then belongs either to the player who is in a position to play a move leading to such repetition (provided that he declares his intention of making this move), or to the player who must reply to a move by which the repeated position is made.

f) When both players agree to call the game drawn.

Illegal positioning If an illegal move is made during the course of a game, the pieces are set up as they were just before the illegal move. If this is impossible, the game is annulled.

If pieces are accidentally displaced and cannot be correctly repositioned or if the initial position of the pieces was incorrect, the game is also annulled.

If the chessboard is found to have been incorrectly placed, the pieces on the board are transferred to a correctly placed board in the same positioning as when the error was discovered and play then continues.

Competition chess is strictly controlled. It differs from the informal game in the following ways.

a) Each player must write down every move made.

b) Each player must make a certain number of moves in a given time (time is kept by a special control clock).

c) If a game is adjourned, the player whose turn it is must write down his move and place it in a sealed envelope, together with his and his opponent's scoresheets. The sealed move is made on the resumption of play.

d) It is forbidden to distract or worry an opponent; ask or receive advice from a third party; use any written or printed notes; or to analyze the game on another chessboard.

e) A designated person must direct the competition. The competition director must ensure that the rules of play are strictly observed – he may impose penalties on any player who infringes these rules.

(These notes on competition chess are an outline only. The official international governing body – the Fédération Internationale des Echecs (FIDE) – lays down the full rules and interprets any problems arising in the game. Its decision is binding on all affiliated federations.)

Chess notation is the method by which moves in a game are recorded. Two of the systems officially recognized are: the descriptive system and the algebraic system.

Descriptive system

Each piece is represented by its initial letter, but the knight may be represented by either Kt or N.

With the exceptions of the pawns and the king and queen, pieces are further distinguished by the side of the board on which they stand:

pieces to the right of the king take the prefix K;

pieces to the left of the queen take the prefix Q.

Thus the rook to the left of the queen is a queen's rook and is represented as QR.

Each file is represented by the initials of the pieces that occupy the squares at either end. The eight files (from left to right for white, and inversely for black) are represented as follows: QR, QKt, QB, Q, K, KB, KKt, KR.

Each rank is numbered from 1 to 8; both players count from their own ends of the board. Consequently each square has two names: one name as seen from white's side, and one from black's. For example, QKt3 (white) equals QKt6 (black).

A move is described by the initial letter of the piece moved and the square to which it moved. For example, the king's knight move to the third square of the king's rook file is represented by KKt – KR3.

If two pieces of the same kind can move to the same square, both the square from which the piece moved and the square it arrived at are given. For example, KKt (KB4) – KR3 means that the knight on the fourth square of the king's bishop file made the move, although another knight on the board could have reached the same square in the same move.

Other explanatory abbreviations are:

O – O or Castles K denotes a castling move involving KR;

O – O – O or Castles Q denotes a castling move involving QR;

x denotes captures;

ch or + denotes check;

! denotes well played;

? denotes a bad move.

QR1	QKt1	QB1	Q1	K1	KB1	KKt1	KR1
QR2	QKt2	QB2	Q2	K2	KB2	KKt2	KR2
QR3	QKt3	QB3	Q3	K3	KB3	KKt3	KR3
QR4	QKt4	QB4	Q4	K4	KB4	KKt4	KR4
QR5	QKt5	QB5	Q5	K5	KB5	KKt5	KR5
QR6	QKt6	QB6	Q6	K6	KB6	KKt6	KR6
QR7	QKt7	QB7	Q7	K7	KB7	KKt7	KR7
QR8	QKt8	QB8	Q8	K8	KB8	KKt8	KR8

QR8	QKt8	QB8	Q8	K8	KB8	KKt8	KR8
QR7	QKt7	QB7	Q7	K7	KB7	KKt7	KR7
QR6	QKt6	QB6	Q6	K6	KB6	KKt6	KR6
QR5	QKt5	QB5	Q5	K5	KB5	KKt5	KR5
QR4	QKt4	QB4	Q4	K4	KB4	KKt4	KR4
QR3	QKt3	QB3	Q3	K3	KB3	KKt3	KR3
QR2	QKt2	QB2	Q2	K2	KB2	KKt2	KR2
QR1	QKt1	QB1	Q1	K1	KB1	KKt1	KR1

©DIAGRAM

61

a8	b8	c8	d8	e8	f8	g8	h8
a7	b7	c7	d7	e7	f7	g7	h7
a6	b6	c6	d6	e6	f6	g6	h6
a5	b5	c5	d5	e5	f5	g5	h5
a4	b4	c4	d4	e4	f4	g4	h4
a3	b3	c3	d3	e3	f3	g3	h3
a2	b2	c2	d2	e2	f2	g2	h2
a1	b1	c1	d1	e1	f1	g1	h1

Black

White

Algebraic system

Each piece, with the exception of the pawns, is represented by its initial letter (and the knight by Kt or N). The pawns are not specially indicated.

The eight files (reading from left to right for white) are represented by the letters from a to h.

The eight ranks (counting from white's first rank) are numbered from 1 to 8. Initially, the white pieces stand on ranks 1 and 2, and the black pieces on ranks 7 and 8.

Thus each square is represented by the combination of a letter and a number.

A move is described by the initial letter of the piece moved and the square from which it moved, plus the square at which it arrived. For example, a bishop moving from square f1 to square d3 is represented by Bf1 – d3 or in a shortened form Bd3.

If two pieces of the same kind can move to the same square, both the square from which the piece moved and the square it arrived at are given. For example, two knights stand on the squares f3 and g4; if the knight on f3 makes the move to h2, the move is written Ktf3–h2 or in the shortened form by Ktf–h2.

The other abreviations used in the algebraic system are the same as those for the descriptive system, with the following additions:

: or x denotes captures;

‡ denotes checkmate.

Chinese checkers

Chinese checkers is a modern game derived from Halma (p. 168). It can be played by two to six persons, playing individually or with partners.

The board is made of metal, plastic, wood, or heavy card. The playing area is a six-pointed star, with holes or indentations to hold the pieces. Each of the star's points is a different color.
The pieces There are six sets of 15 pieces. Each set is the same color as one of the star's points. The most common types of pieces are plastic pegs or marbles.

Start of play

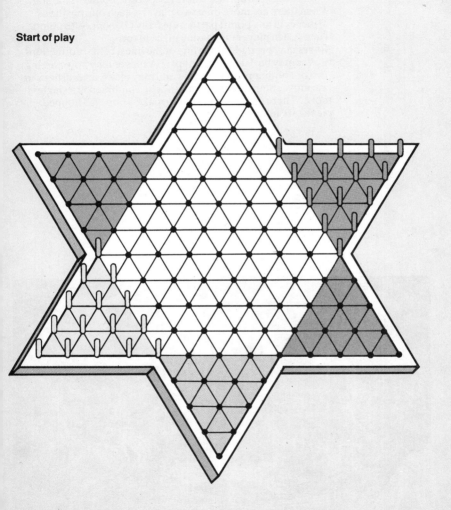

Objective Players attempt to move their pieces into the opposite point. The game is won by the first player or pair to do so.

Start of play For a game between two players, each positions 15 pieces of appropriate colors in opposite points of the star. When there are more than two players, each one positions 10 pieces in any point; partners usually take opposite points.

Turns Each player moves one piece in turn.

Moves may be made along any of the lines, ie in six directions. Moves may be "steps" or "hops." A player may hop over his own or another player's pieces and may make several hops in one move. Steps and hops may not be combined in a single move. There is no compulsion to make a hop. All hopped pieces are left on the board.

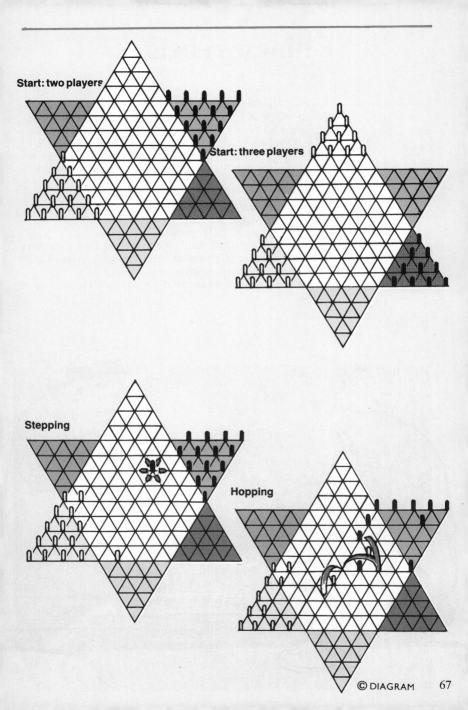

Start: two players

Start: three players

Stepping

Hopping

Chinese rebels

Similar to Fox and geese (p. 154), this game is thought to have originated in China. One player (the "general") attempts to evade the rebelling soldiers that have surrounded him. Although the general is heavily outnumbered, he has the advantage of being able to "kill" the soldiers and remove them from the board.

The playing area may be drawn on a sheet of paper. It consists of a rectangle enclosing 39 small circles. One circle is distinctively marked and represents the "camp."
Pieces Counters or other small objects may be used. One piece represents the general and must be different in appearance from the 20 pieces representing the soldiers.
Start of play The soldiers are positioned around the general, as shown.

Play The players decide which of them is to play the general and which the soldiers.

The general has the opening move, and thereafter the players take alternate turns. In a turn, a piece may be moved one circle forward, backward, or sideways onto an adjoining vacant circle (**a**). Diagonal moves are not permitted.

The general is allowed to "kill" a soldier by jumping over him from an adjoining circle to an empty circle beyond (**b**). That soldier is then removed from the board. (The general's opening move is always a taking move.)

Result If the general kills so many soldiers that not enough remain to trap him, or if he manages to return to camp, he wins the game.

The soldiers win if they manage to immobilize the general by surrounding him or crowding him into a corner.

Alternative result Once players are familiar with playing tactics, they will find that the general invariably loses the game. For this reason, two or more games can be played in succession, with players changing roles after each game.

The person playing the soldiers must note how many moves it takes him to trap the general.

At the end of a set number of games, the players compare results, and the winner is the player who trapped the general in fewest moves.

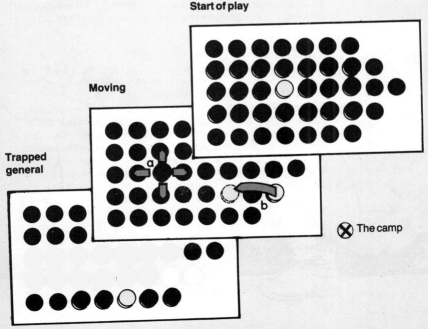

Start of play

Moving

Trapped general

⊗ The camp

©DIAGRAM

69

Coin throwing games

Money has been changing hands in games of chance and skill since time immemorial. In another, much smaller group of games it is the coins themselves that play the principal role.

COVER IT

Cover it is a game for two or more players. The first player throws a coin against a wall and leaves it where it comes to rest on the ground.

Then each player in turn throws a coin against the wall. If his coin is touching another coin when it comes to rest, he picks up both coins. If it is not touching another coin, he leaves his coin on the ground.

HITTING THE MUMMY

This is a variation of Cover it in which the first coin thrown is designated the "mummy" and players aim only to cover this one coin.

A player whose coin is not touching the mummy after being thrown against the wall must leave his coin where it lies.

A player whose coin is touching the mummy is entitled to pick up all coins on the ground except the mummy. If he mistakenly picks up the mummy, he must pay one coin to each of the other players.

BROTHER JONATHAN

This coin throwing game originated in North America in the eighteenth century. It is a game for two or more players, playing for themselves or in teams.

The board may be marked on the ground, or drawn on a large sheet of paper laid on the floor. It is a rectangle divided into sections, with a scoring value marked in each one. Note that the larger sections bear the lower scores whereas the smaller sections contain higher numbers.

Play Each player takes it in turn to pitch a coin from a previously designated spot onto the board. If a coin touches any of the dividing lines it does not count toward the player's score.

The winner may be decided in one of two ways:
a) the first player or team to score an agreed total; or
b) the player or team with the highest score after an agreed number of throws.

WALL JONATHAN
This game is played in the same way as Brother Jonathan except that players must throw their coins against a wall in such a way that they rebound onto the board.

CRACK LOO
In this game, players score points by throwing coins onto numbered cracks on a wood floor (or onto lines drawn on a large sheet of paper). Otherwise play is the same as for Brother Jonathan.

Catch

a

b

PENNIES ON THE PLATE

A metal plate or lid is placed on the ground. At his turn a player throws an agreed number of coins at the plate. The coins must be thrown one at a time from an agreed distance of several feet.

The player who gets the most coins to stay on the plate wins the game. (It is usually quite easy to hit the plate, but much more difficult to ensure that a coin falls in such a way that it does not immediately bounce or roll off it.)

HOLE IN ONE

For this game players need a coin and a plastic tumbler or similar receptacle. The tumbler is placed on its side on the floor and the players take it in turn to try rolling a coin into it. The winner is the player who gets the coin into the tumbler most times, out of an agreed number of shots.

ROLL A GOAL

This game is played in the same way as Hole in one, except that players attempt to roll a coin between two "goalposts" made from folded paper, books, or other objects.

COIN ARCHBOARD

This is a coin version of Marbles archboard (p. 208). Players attempt to roll coins through arches in a board and, when successful, score the number of points indicated above the arch.

PENNY ROLL

This game is popular at fairgrounds in many parts of the world. It can easily be played at home with improvised equipment. Players roll coins down a metal and wood chute onto a board divided into numbered squares. If a player's coin stops completely within a square he receives a sum of money in accordance with that square's number.

CATCH

The skills of juggling and coordination play an important part in the game of Catch.

For the first round, each player:

a) balances one coin on his elbow;

b) drops his hand and tries to catch his coin as it falls.

For the second round, players balance and attempt to catch two coins together, and the number of coins is then increased by one for each further round.

Any player who fails to catch the required number of coins for a round is eliminated from any further rounds, and the winner is the last player left in the game.

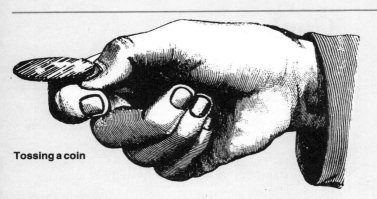
Tossing a coin

TOSSING A COIN

Tossing a coin is a widely known method of deciding the order
of play for many games between two players or teams.
The coin is tossed by a player or non-player, who:
a) flicks the coin into the air by releasing his thumb from
between his clenched fingers;
b) catches the coin in his other hand;
c) quickly turns this hand over to lay the coin on the back of his
tossing hand.
If a non-player makes the toss, he asks one of the players to
"call." If a player makes the toss, his opponent should call.
A player calls either "heads" or "tails" in an attempt to
forecast which side of the coin will be face up after the toss. He
should make his call while the coin is in the air.
A player who "wins the toss" (ie makes a correct forecast)
generally has the right to choose the order of play for the game.

HEADS OR TAILS

Heads or tails is an adaptation of Tossing a coin to make a
game for any number of players.
Each player tosses a coin in turn, and all players, including the
thrower, guess whether it will fall with the head or tail up.
The winner is either:
a) the first player to make an agreed number of correct
guesses; or
b) the player with the most correct guesses after an agreed
number of throws.

SPINNING A COIN

Spinning a coin

This game is played in the same way as Heads or tails, except
that the coins are spun instead of tossed.
(Probably the easiest method of spinning a coin is to hold it on
its edge on a smooth, hard surface and then spin it between the
thumb of one hand and the forefinger of the other, as shown.)

Conkers

Conkers is a popular game with British children. Two players each have a "conker" threaded on a knotted string. Players take alternate hits at their opponent's conker and the game is won when one player destroys the other's conker.

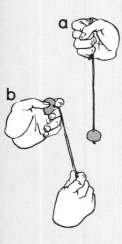

The conkers The game is usually played with nuts from the horsechestnut tree, but is sometimes played with hazelnuts (often called "cobnuts").

When preparing their conkers, players make a hole through the center with a sharp instrument such as a meat skewer or a pair of geometry dividers.

Many players then harden their conkers by soaking them in vinegar or salt and water and/or baking them for about half an hour. Excellent conkers are obtained by storing them in the dark for a year.

When the conker is ready, a strong piece of string or a bootlace is threaded through the hole and knotted at one end. The string should be long enough for about 9in to hang down after it is wrapped once or twice around the hand.

The game Players take alternate hits at their opponent's conker.

The player whose conker is to be hit first, holds his conker as shown (**a**) – with the string wrapped around his hand. He must adjust the height of his hand to suit his opponent, and must then keep his conker perfectly still for the hit.

The striker takes his conker in one hand and holds the opposite end of his string in the other hand (**b**). For the strike, he first draws the conker back and then releases it in a fast swinging motion in the direction of his opponent's conker (**c**).

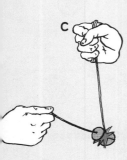

If the striker misses his opponent's conker he is allowed a maximum of two further attempts to make a hit. If the players' strings tangle, the first player to call "strings" can claim an extra shot.

Play continues until one of the conkers is destroyed – ie until no part of it remains on the string.

Scoring Conkers are usually described according to the number of victories won with them – eg "oner," "fiver," "seventy-fiver."

A conker adds one to its title each time it destroys a conker that has never won a game. A conker that defeats a conker with previous wins claims one for defeating it plus all the defeated conker's wins – so a "fiver" that defeats another "fiver" becomes an "elevener."

© DIAGRAM

CONQUERORS

This is a similar game to Conkers and seems to have been very popular in the eighteenth and nineteenth centuries. Two players press empty snail shells tip to tip until one of them breaks. Scoring is the same as for Conkers.

SOLDIERS

This game is now usually played with lollipop, or ice cream sticks. One player holds his stick with both hands, one at each end. The other holds his stick in one hand and gives his opponent's stick a sharp blow.

Turns at striking alternate as in Conkers, and the game continues until one of the sticks breaks. Scoring is as for Conkers.

The game used to be played with stalks from the ribwort plantain – the winner being the first player to knock the head off his opponent's stalk.

Soldiers

Conquest

Conquest is an interesting game that can be played with checkers pieces on an improvised board.

Board The game is played on a checkered board with 81 squares (nine squares by nine).
The central nine squares, called the "fortress," are enclosed within a thick or colored line.
Pieces There are two sets of pieces, one for each player. Each set is of a different color and comprises eight ordinary pieces and one specially marked king.

Start of play

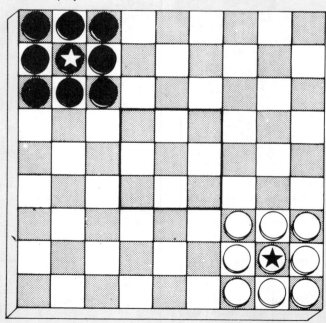

Objective Players attempt to capture the central fortress according to one of the four possible plans of occupation (see illustration). The plan for a particular game must always be agreed before play starts.

Start of play Players position their pieces as illustrated: in diagonally opposite corners of the board and with the kings surrounded by the ordinary pieces.

Turns alternate, and each player makes only one move at a turn.

Moving The only permitted move for any piece is one square diagonally forward or backward (so that each piece stays on squares of the same color throughout the game).

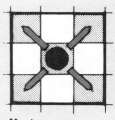

Moving

Exiling If a player traps an opponent's piece between two of his own pieces in a diagonal line (so that all three pieces are on the same color square), the player may "exile" the trapped piece to any other square of the same color.

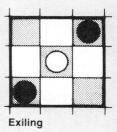

Exiling

Plans of occupation

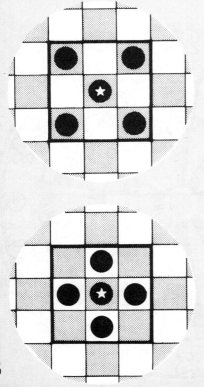

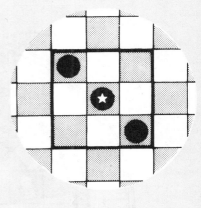

77

©DIAGRAM

Darts

A traditional English "pub" game, Darts now has enthusiasts in many different countries. Players throw darts at a circular target divided into different scoring areas. Games are played by individuals, pairs, or teams. In the standard game, players aim to reduce a starting score exactly to zero. Other games provide a great variety of objectives designed to test the players' skill.

Standard dartboard Most dartboards are made of cork, bristle, or elm, with the divisions and sector numbers marked by wires.

The standard tournament board is 18in in diameter and has twenty sectors, an outer "doubles" ring, an inner "trebles" ring, and an inner and outer "bull" in the center. Adjacent sectors are differentiated by color.

Standard board

Darts Each player has a set of three darts. Designs vary, but most darts are about 6in long. All darts have:
a sharp point, usually made of steel;
a barrel, made of metal (usually brass), or plastic weighted with metal, or wood;
a tail, "flighted" with feathers, plastic, or paper.

The scoreboard is a slate or blackboard, usually positioned to one side of the dartboard. Each side's score is recorded in chalk.

Playing area The dartboard is hung on a wall, with the center 5ft 8in from the ground. Toe lines may be marked on a mat or on the floor, at distances of 8ft, 8ft 6in, and 9ft from the dartboard.

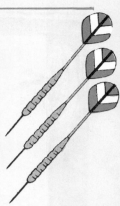

Playing area

8ft (2.4m)
8ft 6in (2.6m)
9ft (2.7m)

©DIAGRAM

79

STANDARD TOURNAMENT DARTS

Players Games are played by individuals, pairs, or teams of any fixed number of players.

Starting Each player, or one member of each pair or team, must get a dart in the doubles ring to begin scoring. The starting double is scored, as are darts thrown after but not before it in the same turn.

Turns In singles games, opponents take turns to throw three darts each. In pairs and team games, one player from each side throws three darts in turn, with members of each side playing in the order established at the start of the game.

The first turn goes to the player, pair, or team that wins the toss of a coin or gets a dart nearest the bull in a preliminary throw.

Scored throws A throw is invalid if the player is not behind the toe-line when throwing.

Only those darts sticking in the board at the end of a player's turn are scored. Thus darts are not scored if they rebound, stick in another dart, fall from the board, or are knocked out before the player ends his turn.

Re-throws are not permitted. (Also note starting and finishing procedures.)

Scoring Scored throws are deducted from a starting total – usually 301, 501, or 1001.

Darts in the inner bull score 50, and in the outer bull 25. Darts in a sector score according to the sector number – unless they are within the outer (doubles) ring (**a**), when they score double the sector number, or the inner (trebles) ring (**b**), when they score three times the sector number.

Finishing The game ends with a double bringing the score exactly to zero. If the scores in a player's turn take him past zero, or to one, he goes back to the score before that turn and forfeits any darts remaining in that turn.

Scoring

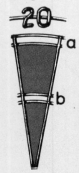

AROUND THE CLOCK

This is a singles game for any number of players. Each player throws three darts in a turn.

After a starting double, each player must throw one dart into each of the sectors, in order, from 1 to 20. Darts in the doubles or trebles rings of the correct sector are usually allowed. The winner is the first player to finish.

As a variation, players may be awarded an extra turn for scoring with the last dart of a turn.

SHANGHAI

Shanghai is another "around the clock" game for any number of players with three darts each.

In his first turn, each player throws all his darts at sector number 1. Singles, doubles, and trebles all score their value. In his second turn, each player throws all his darts at sector number 2 (even if he made no score in his first turn).

Play proceeds in this manner right "around the clock," and the winner is usually the player with the highest total score.

In a popular variation of this game, a player may win by going "Shanghai," ie by scoring in one turn a single, double, and treble of the required number.

CLOSING

This is a game for two players, each with three darts. Each player aims to make as high a score as possible while seeking to prevent his opponent from making a high score.

As soon as one of the players has scored three times from any one sector, that sector is "closed" and no further score may be made from it by either player.

Doubles and trebles score their value; and count as two and three scores respectively. The winner is the player with the highest score when the last sector is closed.

**Closing:
sample scoreboard**

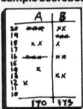

SCRAM

Scram is a game for two players throwing three darts in each turn.

The player with the first turn is the "stopper," and any sector he hits with a dart is closed to his opponent.

The second player is known as the "scorer," and he aims to score as many points as possible before all the sectors are closed.

When all the sectors are closed, the two players change roles. The winner is the player who scores most when playing scorer.

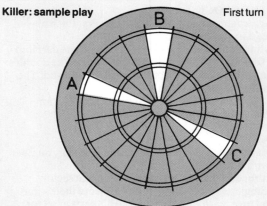

Killer: sample play First turn

KILLER

Killer is probably best with four to eight players, but can be played by either more or less.

In his first turn, each player throws one dart with the hand that he normally does not use for throwing darts. This throw decides a player's own sector for the rest of the game. Unless a very large number of people are playing, it is usual for a player to throw again if a sector has already been given to another player.

In every other turn, each player throws three darts with his usual hand. The game has several versions, but in all cases the winner is the player left in the game when all other players have lost all their "lives."

First version In one version of the game, all players begin with no lives and a player's first objective is to acquire three lives by throwing three darts into his own sector (two lives for a double and three for a treble).

Once a player has three lives he becomes a "killer" and starts throwing darts at other player's sectors. (In the example illustrated, players B and C become killers after their second turns and player A after the first throw of his third turn.)

If a killer throws a dart into the sector of a player with three or two lives, that player loses one life (or two for a double or three for a treble).

If a killer throws a dart into the sector of a player with one or no lives, that player is out (player B after C's third turn in the example illustrated).

A killer who loses a life loses his right to kill until he makes up his lost life by throwing another dart into his own sector.

Second version All players start with an agreed number of lives – usually three or five. To start killing, a player has to throw a double of his own number. Kills are made by throwing doubles and trebles of other players' numbers – one kill for a double and two kills for a treble. Lost lives cannot be won back again.

Second turn

A

B

C

Third turn

A

B

C

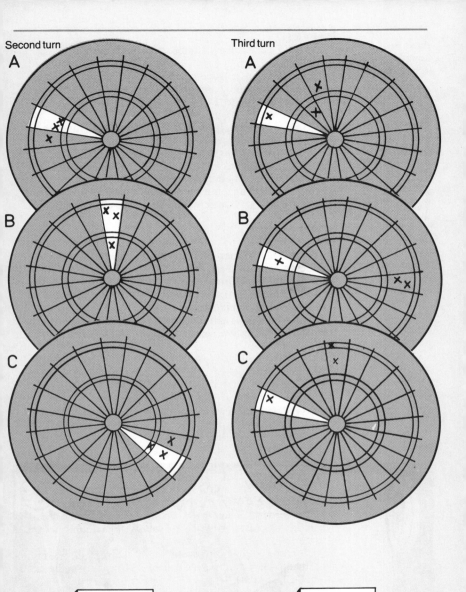

A	x x
B	x x x
C	x x x

A	x x x
~~B~~	x x x
C	x x x

	A	B
20	/	20
19	19	39
18	37	75
DOUBLE	18	105
17	2	127
16	N	31
15		30
TREBLE	4	40
14	4	45
13	30	71
12	18	45
DOUBLE	7	49
TREBLE	3	44
11	25	60
10	35	80
BULL	17	40

HALVE IT

Halve it is a game for any number of players, each throwing
three darts in a turn.

Before play begins, players select a series of objectives and
chalk them up on the scoreboard. A typical series would be:
20, 19, 18, any double, 17, 16, 15, any treble, 14, 13, 12,
double, treble, 11, 10, bull.

In his first turn, each player aims for 20 and scores for each dart
in that sector (doubles and trebles count their value).

Players then take turns to make their way through the list of
objectives, scoring for each dart in the correct sector or halving
their total score (rounding down) whenever none of their darts
scores. There are no minus scores, and a player whose score is
reduced to zero stays at zero until he throws a dart that scores.

FIVES

Fives can be played by two players or sides using a standard
dartboard. The winner is the first player to reach an agreed
number of points, usually 50.

Each player throws three darts in a turn. He scores only if the
sum of his three darts can be divided by five – in which case he
scores the result of this division.

A player who throws a dart out of the scoring area when he has
a total divisible by five, scores no points for that turn.

SORRY—
I THREW
YOUR PEN

DARTS FOOTBALL

This is a game for two players, each throwing three darts in a turn.

A dart in the inner bull "gains control of the ball." This player can then start scoring "goals" – one for each double.

He continues scoring until his opponent "takes the ball away" by scoring an inner bull. The first player to score ten goals wins the game.

DARTS CRICKET

Darts cricket is a game for two teams of equal size.

The team that wins the toss of a coin decides whether to "bat" or to "bowl." Turns alternate between teams, and each player throws one dart in a turn.

When "batting," a team aims to score as many "runs" as possible; when "bowling," to "take wickets" by scoring inner bulls.

The teams change roles after five wickets are taken. The team with the highest batting score wins the game.

DARTS BASEBALL

This is a game for two players, each representing a baseball team.

There are nine innings, and each player has a turn at "bat" in each inning. A player's turn consists of three throws.

In the first inning players throw darts at sector 1, in the second inning at sector 2, through to sector 9 in the ninth inning. Extra innings are played if there is a tie.

A single "run" is scored by getting a dart into the correct sector for the inning (with two runs for a double and three for a treble). Getting a bull at any stage of the game is a "grand slam home run" and scores four runs.

DARTS SHOVE HA'PENNY

This game for two players or pairs is based on the rules of the board game described on p. 330. Each player throws three darts in a turn, and the objective is to score three times in each of the sectors numbered 1 through 9. The scores may be made in any order, and doubles count as two scores and trebles as three.

If a player scores more than three times in any one sector, the extra scores are given to the opposition. The score that wins the game, however, must always be actually thrown by the winner. The game is won by the first side to finish.

Dice games: family

Plan of die faces

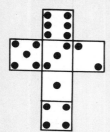

Dice games were played in ancient times and remain universally popular. Here we look first at family games – ways of passing a happy hour with little or no gambling involved. (A selection of private gambling games begins on p. 98.)

Dice A standard modern die is a regular cube, with the six sides numbered with dots from 1 through 6. Any two opposing sides add up to 7.

Odds With one true die, each face has an equal chance of landing face up. With two dice thrown together, some scores are more likely than others because there are more ways in which they can be made.

Possible throws with two dice

2	3	4	5	6	7	8	9	10	11	12

FIFTY

This game, for two or more players, is one of the simplest dice games. It requires two dice, and the winner is the first player to score 50 points.

Each player in turn rolls the two dice, but scores only when identical numbers are thrown (two 1s, two 2s, and so on). All these doubles, except two 6s and two 3s score five points. A double 6 scores 25 points; and a double 3 wipes out the player's total score and he has to start again.

ROUND THE CLOCK

This is a game for three or four players, using two dice.
Objective Players try to throw 1 through 12 in correct sequence. The winner is the first to complete the sequence.
Play Players throw both dice once on each turn.
From 1 through 6, a player can score with either one of the two dice or with both of them – eg a throw of 3 and 1 can be counted as 3, 1, or 4. It is also possible at this stage to score twice on one throw – eg if a player needs 2 and throws a 2 and a 3 he can count both of these numbers.
From 7 through 12, however, a player will obviously always need the combined spot values of both dice to score.

SHUT THE BOX

This is a game for two or more players.

Equipment:

1) two dice;

2) a board or sheet of paper with nine boxes numbered 1 to 9;

3) nine counters used to cover the boxes in play.

(In some parts of the world, specially made trays with sliding covers for the numbers are available.)

Objective Players aim to cover as many of the numbers as possible, in accordance with the throws of the dice. The winner is the player with the lowest penalty score from uncovered boxes.

Play The player taking first turn throws the two dice and then decides which boxes he will cover. He may cover any two boxes that have the same total as his throw – eg a throw of 10 would allow him to cover 6 and 4, 7 and 3, 8 and 2, or 9 and 1.

The same player then throws the two dice again and tries to cover another two boxes. He is not allowed to use combinations involving numbers that he has already covered. After covering boxes 9, 8, and 7 a player may throw only one die on a turn, but he must still cover two boxes at a time.

A player's turn continues until he is unable to make use of a combination from his latest throw. All the uncovered numbers are then added up and become his penalty score.

Play then passes to the next player.

**Shut the box:
sample play**

6+4=10 thrown

8+2=10 covered

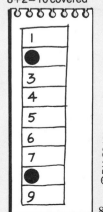

87

DROP DEAD

This is an exciting game for any number of players.

Equipment:

1) five dice;

2) a sheet of paper on which to record players' scores.

Objective Players aim to make the highest total score.

Play At his turn each player begins by rolling the five dice. Each time he makes a throw that does not contain a 2 or a 5, he scores the total spot value of that throw and is entitled to another throw with all five dice.

Whenever a player makes a throw containing a 2 or a 5, he scores nothing for that throw and any die or dice that showed a 2 or a 5 must be excluded from any further throws that he makes. A player's turn continues until his last remaining die shows a 2 or a 5 – at which point he "drops dead" and play passes to the next player.

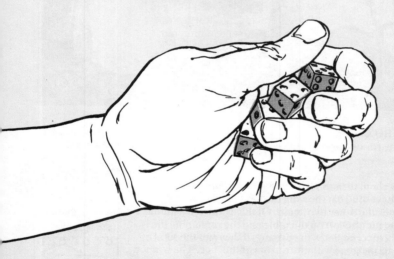

CHICAGO

Chicago, also called Rotation, is a game for any number of players. Two dice are used. The game is based on the 11 possible combinations of the two dice – 2, 3, 4, 5, 6, 7, 8, 9, 10, 11, and 12 – and so consists of 11 rounds.

The objective is to score each of these combinations in turn. The player with the highest score is the winner.

Play Each player in turn rolls the dice once in each round. During the first round, he will try to make a total of 2, during the second, a total of 3, and so on up to 12.

Each time he is successful, that number of points is added to his score. For example, if he is shooting for 5 and throws a total of 5, he gains five points. If he fails to make the desired number, he scores nothing on that throw.

PIG

This simple game, for any number of players, requires only one die. The winner is the first player to reach a previously agreed high score (usually 100).

Order of play is determined by a preliminary round. Each player throws the die once and the player with the lowest score becomes first shooter. The next-lowest scoring player shoots second, and so on. The order of play is important because the first and last shooters have natural advantages (see below).

Play begins with the first shooter. Like the other players, he may roll the die as many times as he wishes. He totals his score throw by throw until he elects to end his turn. He passes the die to the next player, memorizing his score so far.

But if he throws a 1, he loses the entire score he has made on that turn, and the die passes to the next player. Play passes from player to player until someone reaches the agreed total. Given a little luck, the first shooter is the player most likely to win. But his advantage can be counteracted by allowing other players to continue until they have had the same number of turns. The player with the highest score is then the winner.

The last shooter still has the advantage of knowing the scores made by all his opponents. Provided he does not roll a 1, he can continue throwing until he has beaten all those scores.

The fairest way of playing the game is to organize it as a series, with each player in turn becoming first shooter.

GOING TO BOSTON

Also known as Newmarket or Yankee grab, this game is ideal for three or four players, although more can play.

Equipment: three dice.

Play Each player in turn rolls the three dice together. After the first roll, he leaves the die showing the highest number on the table, then rolls the other two again. Of these, the die with the highest number is also left on the table and the remaining die is rolled again. This completes the player's throw and the total of his three dice is his score.

When all players have thrown, the player with the highest score wins the round. Ties are settled by further rolling.

A game usually consists of an agreed number of rounds: the player who wins the most rounds is the winner.

Alternatively, each player can contribute counters to a pool that is won at the end of each game.

MULTIPLICATION

This game is played like Going to Boston, but with one important difference. When each player has completed his turn, his score is the sum of the spot values of the first two dice rolled, multiplied by that of the third. For example, if his first throw is 5, his second throw 4, and his final throw 6, his score will be 54: (5+4)×6.

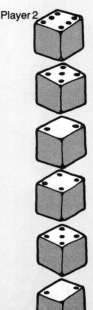

Pig: sample play
Player 1

Out

Player 2

©DIAGRAM

Stops, scores 24

89

BEETLE

This is a lively game for two or more players – more than six tend to slow down the game.

Equipment:
1) one die, either an ordinary one or a special "beetle die" marked B (body), H (head), L (legs), E (eyes), F (feelers), and T (tail);
2) a simple drawing of a beetle as a guide, showing its various parts and (when an ordinary die is used) their corresponding numbers;
3) a pencil and a piece of paper for each player.

Objective Each player, by throwing the die, tries to complete his drawing of the beetle. The first to do so scores 13 points and is the winner. The 13 points represent one for each part of the beetle (body, head, tail, two feelers, two eyes, and six legs).

Play Each player throws the die once only in each round. Each player must begin by throwing a B (or a 1); this permits him to draw the body.

When this has been drawn, he can throw for other parts of the beetle that can be joined to the body.

An H or a 2 must be thrown to link the head to the body before the feelers (F or 5) and eyes (E or 4) can be added. Each eye or feeler requires its own throw.

A throw of L or 3 permits the player to add three legs to one side of the body. A further throw of L or 3 is necessary for the other three legs.

Sometimes it is agreed that a player may continue to throw in his turn for as long as he throws parts of the body he can use.

Continuing play When a series of games is played, each player counts one point for every part of the beetle he has been able to draw and cumulative scores are carried from round to round. The winner is the player with the highest score at the end of the series, or the first to reach a previously agreed total score.

HEARTS

Hearts, or Hearts due, is a game for two or more players.

Equipment Six dice are used. Special dice marked with the letters H, E, A, R, T, S instead of numbers are sometimes used, but the game is now more commonly played with ordinary dice.

The objective is simply to score more than your opponents over an agreed series of rounds, or a single round, or to be the first to reach an agreed total.

Play begins after a preliminary round has decided the first shooter (usually the player with the highest score).

Each player in turn rolls the six dice once and calculates his score according to the following ratings:
1 (H)=5 points;
1, 2 (HE)=10 points;
1, 2, 3 (HEA)=15 points;
1, 2, 3, 4 (HEAR)=20 points;

1, 2, 3, 4, 5 (HEART)=25 points;
1, 2, 3, 4, 5, 6 (HEARTS)=35 points.
If a double (two dice of the same spot value) or a treble appears
in the throw, only one of the letters or numbers counts. But if
three 1s (or Hs) appear, the player's whole score is wiped out
and he has to start again.

Centennial: scoring

CENTENNIAL
Also known as Martinetti or Ohio, this is a game for two to
eight players.
Equipment:
1) three dice;
2) a long board or piece of paper marked with a row of boxes
numbered 1 to 12;
3) a distinctive counter or other object for each player.
Objective Each player tries to be the first to move his counter,
in accordance with throws of the dice, from 1 to 12 and back.
Play begins after a preliminary round has determined who will
take the first turn. Each player on a turn throws all three dice at
once. Turns pass clockwise around the table.
In order to place his counter in the first box, a player must
throw a 1. He can try then for a 2, a 3, and so on, box by box up
to 12 and back again. He can make any number with one or
more dice. For example, a 3 can be scored with one 3, a 1 and a
2, or with three 1s. It is possible to move through more than
one box on a single throw. For example, a throw of 1, 2, 3
would not only take him through the first three boxes, but on
through the fourth (1+3=4), to the fifth (2+3=5) and finally
the sixth (1+2+3=6).
Other players' throws must be watched constantly. If a player
throws a number he needs but overlooks and does not use, that
number may be claimed by any other player. He must do this as
soon as the dice are passed, however, and must be able to use it
at once.

Everest: scoring

EVEREST
This game is like Centennial but has a different layout and
scoring system.
Equipment Each player has a sheet of paper showing two
columns, each divided into 12 boxes. In one column the boxes
are numbered from 1 to 12 in ascending order. In the other they
are numbered from 1 to 12 in descending order.
Objective Each player tries to be the first to score all 24
numbers. The numbers do not have to be scored consecutively
as in Centennial, but as desired and in either column.
Scoring Each die in a throw can be counted only once.

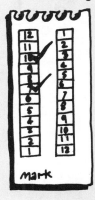

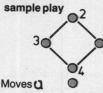

Moves

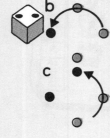

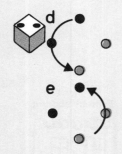

DICE BASEBALL

As a dice game for two players, baseball can be played in several different ways. A popular version using one die is described here.

Equipment:
1) one die;
2) at least three counters for each player to represent his men;
3) a sheet of paper with a simple diagram of a baseball diamond drawn on it;
4) another piece of paper for recording scores.

The objective is to score the highest total number of runs in the nine innings per player that constitute the game. If the two players have equal scores after the usual nine innings, an extra-inning game is played. (Note that in baseball, each player's turn at bat is called a "half-inning.")

Order of play The players throw the die to decide who shall "bat" first (ie shoot the die first). Each player in turn then throws a half-inning. A half-inning is ended when a player has thrown three "outs" (see below).

Making runs At the start of the game, or whenever all bases are empty, a throw of 1, 2 or 3 permits the player to put a man (counter) on whichever of those three bases he has thrown – 1 in the example illustrated (**a**).

If the player throws 1, 2, or 3 again, this permits him to move the man around the diamond by the number of bases thrown, and to place another man on the base that bears the number thrown. For example, if he has a man on 1, and throws a 2, the man advances to base 3 (**b**) and a new man is entered on base 2 (**c**).

Each time a man reaches the home (fourth) base or "home plate," a run is scored. A single throw may give a score of more than one run if it takes more than one man to home base.

For example, if a player with men on bases 2 and 3 throws a 2, both men advance to home base and two runs are scored (**d**). At the same time a new man is entered on base 2 (**e**).

A throw of 4 counts as a home run and advances all men on the bases to home base. The score is thus the home run plus one run for each man brought home.

Outs Throws of 5 or 6 are "outs."

A throw of 5 is as though there had been a hit and a throw-in, so that men on the bases may also be out, as follows:
if the shooter has only one man on the bases, he is out;
if he has men on all bases, the man on base 1 is out;
if he has men on bases 1 and 2, the man on base 2 is out;
if he has men on bases 1 and 3, the man on base 1 is out;
if he has men on bases 2 and 3, both are safe.
Men on the bases who are not out remain where they are.
A throw of 6 is also an out, but it is as if the batter were out

without striking the ball; men on bases are safe, and remain where they are.
Note that three outs end a half-inning. The other player then throws his half-inning to complete the inning.

DICE BASKETBALL
As a dice game, basketball is usually played by two players, but more can take part, each player representing a team. As in the real game, the winner is the team (ie player) making the highest score in the game or series of games.
Equipment Basketball may be played with only two dice or with as many as 10. Many players use eight dice as there are then enough to ensure a rapid game and realistic scores.
Play A game consists of four quarters. In each quarter each player in turn rolls the eight dice once, their total being his score for that quarter.
If the game is played with only two dice, each player rolls the dice four times to determine his score for that quarter.
The player with the highest score for the four quarters wins the game. If the game, or agreed series of games, ends in a tie, this is resolved by playing extra quarters until the outright winner is established.

CHEERIO

This game can be played by any number of players up to a maximum of 12. The greater the number of players, the slower the pace of the game.

Equipment:

1) five dice;
2) a dice cup;
3) a sheet of paper showing the various combinations and with a scoring column for each player.

Objective Each player tries to score the maximum possible for each of the 11 scoring combinations (see below). The player with the highest total score wins the game.

Games are often played as a series, the player who wins the most games in the series being the overall winner.

Alternatively, the scores in each game can be carried forward to the next game until a player has reached a previously agreed cumulative total. If two or more players exceed the total, the player with the highest score wins.

Ties are settled by an extra game.

Play Each player in turn rolls all five dice. Having rolled the dice once, he may pick up all or any of them and roll once more in an attempt to improve his score.

He does not have to try for combinations in any particular order, and he does not have to declare his combination until he has finished rolling. This gives him considerable freedom of choice. For example, if he has rolled 6, 6, 2, 3, 3 he might call sixes (score 12). But if he wanted to keep sixes for a later turn, when he might roll more than two of them, he could call a different combination even if this would give him a lower score or even no score for the throw.

A player is not permitted to call the same combination more than once in a game.

Combinations

Ones Scores one point for each die showing one spot (maximum score five points).

Twos Scores two points for each two-spot die (maximum 10).

Threes Scores three points for each three-spot die (maximum 15).

Fours Scores four points for each four-spot die (maximum 20).

Fives Scores five points for each five-spot die (maximum 25).

Sixes Scores six points for each six-spot die (maximum 30).

Little straight A show of 1, 2, 3, 4, 5 scores 20 points.

Big straight A show of 2, 3, 4, 5, 6 scores 25 points.

Full house Three of a kind plus two of a kind scores according to the numbers shown on the dice (6, 6, 6, 5, 5 scores the maximum 28 points).

Big hand The total spot value of the dice (6, 6, 6, 6, 6 scores the maximum 30 points).

Cheerio Five of a kind in any value, 1 through 6. Always scores 50 points.

Cheerio combinations

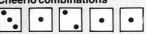

Ones (score 3)

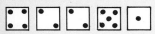

Twos (score 4)

Threes (score 9)

Fours (score 12)

Fives (score 15)

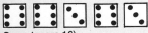

Sixes (score 18)

Little straight (score 20)

Big straight (score 25)

Full house (score 16)

Big hand (score 28)

Cheerio (score 50)

Cheerio score sheet

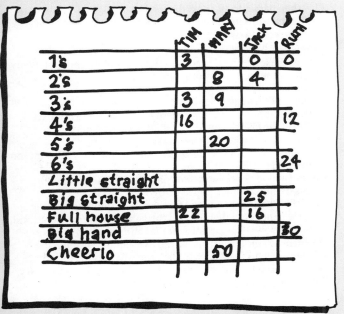

	TIM	MARY	JACK	RUTH
1's	3		0	0
2's		8	4	
3's	3	9		
4's	16			12
5's		20		
6's				24
Little straight				
Big straight			25	
Full house	22		16	
Big hand				30
Cheerio		50		

GENERAL

This game has many similarities with Cheerio (p. 94). It is a major gambling game in Puerto Rico, but can also be played without stakes for amusement only.

Equipment:
1) five dice;
2) a score sheet showing combinations and players' names.

Players Any number may play, either singly or in partnership.

Objective Each player or partnership aims to win by scoring a "big general" (see five of a kind) or by scoring most points for the 10 General combinations. As in Cheerio, each combination may be scored only once in a game.

Order of play is determined by a preliminary round in which each player rolls the dice once. The player with the lowest spot score shoots first, the player with the next lowest score second, and so on.

Play A game normally consists of 10 turns ("frames") per player, but ends immediately if any player rolls a big general. Each player may roll the dice once, twice, or three times during each frame.

If, on his first throw, he fails to make a combination that he wishes to score, he may pick up all or any of the dice for a second roll. But the value of any combination he now rolls is diminished, and a big general now becomes a small general. After his second roll he may again, if he wishes, pick up all or any of the dice for a third roll. After the third roll, he must state which combination he is scoring.

Play then passes to the next player.

If the game runs its full course of ten frames, the player with the highest score wins.

Aces wild "Aces" (1s) may be counted as 2 or as 6 if one or both of these are needed to complete a straight – but not as any other number or for any other purpose.

Combinations

Numbers 1 through 6 Score their spot values.

Straight Either 1, 2, 3, 4, 5 or 2, 3, 4, 5, 6 scores 25 points if made on the first throw, but only 20 points if made on the second or third throw. Only one straight is scored.

Full house Scores 35 points on first throw, but only 30 points on the second or third throw.

Four of a kind Scores 45 points on first throw, but only 40 points on the second or third throw.

Five of a kind If made on the first throw, it ranks as the "big general" and immediately wins the game. Made on the second or third throw it is a "small general" and scores 60 points.

Payment When General is played as a gambling game, the winner receives from each of the other players the difference between his own and that player's point score. The monetary value per point is settled before the game.

DOUBLE CAMEROON
This game is similar to General but has important differences.
It is played with ten dice.
After a player has rolled them for the third time in each turn,
he divides them into two groups of five, and then allots the
score of each group to one of the ten combinations in the game.
So in the course of a game, each player has five turns.
Combinations
Numbers 1 through 6 Score their spot values.
Full house Scores its spot value.
Little Cameroon (1, 2, 3, 4, 5) scores 21 points.
Big Cameroon (2, 3, 4, 5, 6) scores 30 points.
Five of a kind Scores 50 points.
(Unlike in General, a score does not decrease if the
combination is made on a second or third throw.)

©DIAGRAM

Dice games: gambling

These dice games can be played for amusement using counters or matchsticks as stakes, but they are generally better known as private gambling games played for money.

POKER DICE

This game, for two or more players, is usually played for a "pot" (pool) to which each player contributes at the start of each round.

Equipment Five dice are used, and these are normally special poker dice marked with a, k, q, j, 10, 9. The game may also be played with standard dice, with 1 ranking highest, then 6, 5, 4, 3, 2; or alternatively with 6 ranking highest, followed by 5, 4, 3, 2, and with aces wild.

Objective Players aim to make the best possible poker "hand" in not more than two rolls of the dice (or three rolls of the dice in an older form of the game).

Rank of hands is as follows:

1) five of a kind (highest rank);
2) four of kind;
3) straight (an unbroken sequence, either a, k, q, j, 10 or k, q, j, 10, 9);
4) full house (three of a kind and one pair);
5) three of a kind;
6) two pairs;
7) one pair;
8) no pair (the lowest rank – five unmatched values not in sequence).

Hands of the same rank need not tie. They compare as follows.

1) Five of a kind: five aces rank higher than five kings, and so on.
2) Four of a kind: as for five of a kind.
3) Straight: a, k, q, j, 10 beats k, q, j, 10, 9.
4) Full house: the threes decide, with a, a, a, j, j ranking higher than k, k, k, q, q, and so on.
5) Three of a kind: three aces rank higher than three kings, and so on.
6) Two pairs: the highest pair wins.
7) One pair: the higher pair wins.
8) No pair: the highest die wins.

The odd dice in any combination are used by some players as tiebreakers. For example, a, a, q, q, j (two pairs) would rank above a, a, q, q, 9. It is more common, however, for the odd dice to be disregarded, and if two or more players make equal-ranking hands they must roll again.

Order of play is decided by a preliminary round in which each player throws a single die. The highest scorer throws first in the first round. The second highest scorer sits to his left, and so on. Play goes clockwise and each round is commenced by a different player in turn.

Play Each player rolls in turn. He may accept the hand produced by his first throw, or, if he wishes, he may pick up one or more of the dice and roll them again in an attempt to improve his hand. (Some players choose to limit to three the number of dice that may be picked up.) The outcome of his second throw completes his hand and the dice are passed to the next player.

The highest hand in the round wins. If there are only two players, the best two out of three rounds, or the best three out of five, win.

Aces wild Poker dice may be played with aces "wild," ie they may rank normally or count as any other value the player wishes. For example, a throw of q, q, q, q, a could rank as five queens; a throw of a, a, a, a, j could rank as five jacks; or a throw of k, q, j, a, 9 could rank as a straight.

Rank

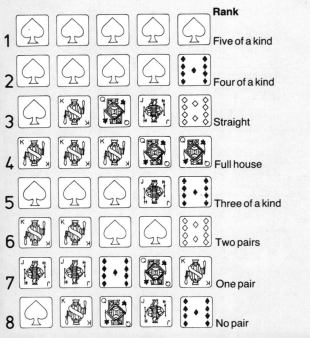

1 Five of a kind
2 Four of a kind
3 Straight
4 Full house
5 Three of a kind
6 Two pairs
7 One pair
8 No pair

INDIAN DICE

Indian dice, a popular game in the USA, is very similar to Poker dice (p. 98). It is played with five ordinary dice, with 6 ranking highest and 1s ("aces") wild. Any number of players may take part.

Objective Players aim to make the highest poker hand. The hands rank as in Poker dice except that straights do not count.

Play begins after a preliminary round to decide the order of play. The highest scorer becomes first shooter, the second highest scorer sits to his left, and so on.

The player who shoots first may have up to three throws to establish his hand. He may "stand" on his first throw, or pick up all or any of the dice for a second throw. He may then stand on that throw or pick up all or any of the dice again for a third and final throw.

No subsequent player in the round or "leg" may make more throws than the first player.

A game usually consists of two legs, with the winners of each leg playing off if stakes are involved.

If there are only two players, the victor is the one who wins two out of three legs.

Rank

Five of a kind

Four of a kind

Full house

Three of a kind

Two pairs

Pair

No pair

101

LIAR DICE

The essence of this game, for three or more players, is deception!

Equipment The game may be played with five ordinary dice, 1s (aces) ranking high, or with poker dice. Each player also needs three betting chips (or counters).

Rank of hands is as in Poker dice (p. 98). Hands of the same rank are also compared as in Poker dice, but in Liar dice the odd dice are always used as tiebreakers if necessary.

Order of play is established by a preliminary round in which each player throws a single die. The highest scorer becomes first shooter. The second highest scorer sits to his left, and so on.

Start of play rotates one player to the left after each game.

Play Each player puts three betting chips in front of him. The first shooter then throws all the dice, keeping them covered so that the other players cannot see them.

He declares his throw in detail, eg "full house, queens on nines" (q, q, q, 9, 9). This call may be true or false and it is for the player to his left to accept or challenge the call. The declaring player may call below the actual value of his throw if he wishes.

If the player to his left thinks the caller is lying and challenges him, all the dice are exposed. If the caller has in fact lied, he must pay one chip into the pot; but if the value of the throw is equal to or higher than the call, it is the challenger who pays into the pot. In either case, it now becomes the challenger's turn to throw.

If the player to the left of the caller accepts the call, he takes over the dice (still unexposed). He may now throw all, any, or none of them, but must say truthfully how many he throws. Keeping the dice covered, he then makes his call, which must be higher than the call he accepted – but it need not be a higher rank of hand; it can be a higher hand of the same rank. His call may be accepted or challenged by the player to his left, and so play continues round the table.

When a player has lost all three of his chips, he is out of the game. Play continues until all but one of the players has been knocked out. The survivor is the winner and collects the pot.

CROWN AND ANCHOR

This is a fast game in which any number of players play against a banker.

Equipment Three special dice are used, each marked with a crown, anchor, heart, spade, diamond, and club.

These symbols also appear on the layout, which is marked on a cloth or board set in front of the banker.

Play Each player puts a wager on one or more of the symbols on the layout. The banker then throws the three dice from a cup and pays out on the result of the throw.

The usual odds are evens on singles, 2 to 1 on pairs, and 3 to 1 on three of a kind. The advantage always lies with the banker.

Crown and anchor

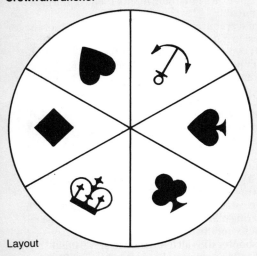

Layout

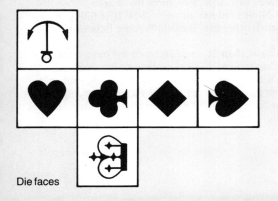

Die faces

©DIAGRAM

TWENTY-ONE

Twenty-one

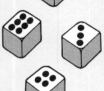

21 points scored

This game is based on the card game Blackjack. Any number of players may take part.

Equipment: one die, and a supply of chips or counters for each player.

Objective Players try to score 21 points.

Play Each player puts one chip into the pool or kitty.

Then each player in turn rolls the dice as many times as he likes in an attempt to make a total of 21 or a number near but below it. If, for example, a player's first four throws are 4, 6, 2, 6 (totaling 18), it would probably be safer to "stick" on this number than risk a fifth throw that might take his total over 21. If his total does exceed 21, he "goes bust" and is eliminated from that round.

Players often agree on a minimum number, eg 16, at which sticking is permissible.

When all the players have thrown, the player with 21, or the number nearest to it, takes the pool, and a new round commences. If two or more players have the same score, the pool may either be shared or decided by a play-off.

Start of play rotates one player to the left with each round.

PAR

Par

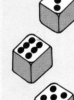

24 points scored

Par can be played with any number of players, but is best played with six or seven.

Equipment:
1) five dice;
2) chips or counters representing the betting unit.

Objective Each player tries to achieve a total score of 24 or more by throwing the dice.

Order of play is established by a preliminary round in which the highest scoring player becomes the first shooter. The second highest scorer throws next, and so on.

Play The first shooter rolls all five dice. He may "stand" on that throw if it makes 24 or more, or he may make up to four more throws in an attempt to improve his score, throwing first four, then three, then two, and then one of the dice.

If he makes 24, he neither gains nor loses. If he fails to make 24, he pays each other player the difference between his score and 24.

If he makes more than 24, the difference between his score and 24 becomes his "point." For example, if he has thrown 26, he has a point of 2. He then throws all five dice again (but once only), and for every 2 that appears he collects two chips from each of the other players. (If 6 was his point, he would collect six chips for every 6 that appeared.)

THIRTY-SIX

This is a game for any number of players, using only one die.
Order of play is determined by a preliminary round in which
each player throws a single die. The lowest scorer becomes first
shooter, the next-lowest second shooter, and so on.
Each player puts an agreed stake in the pot.
Objective Players aim to score a total of 36 points. Any player
scoring more than 36, however, is eliminated from the game.
The winner is the player with the score nearest 36 points and he
takes the pot.
Play Each player in turn rolls the dice once, totaling his score
round by round. As he nears 36 he may choose to stand on his
score in the hope that no other player will score nearer 36.
In the event of a tie, the pot is divided.

Thirty-six

36 points scored

HELP YOUR NEIGHBOR

Help your neighbor, for two to six players, is usually played for
small stakes or just for fun with counters.
Equipment:
1) three dice and a dice cup;
2) betting chips or counters for each player.
Objective Each player tries to be the first to get rid of all his
counters. The winner takes the pot formed during the course
of play.
Order of play is determined by a preliminary round in which
each player throws a single die. This throw also decides which
number(s) each player takes. The highest scoring player in the
preliminary round becomes the first shooter and takes the
number 1. The second-highest scorer becomes the second
shooter and, taking the number 2, sits to the left of player
number 1, and so on.
If there are only two players, the higher scoring player takes
numbers 1, 2, and 3, and the other the remainder. With three
players, the numbers are paired off: 1 and 2, 3 and 4, 5 and 6.
With four players, numbers 5 and 6 are "dead," with five
players, 6 is dead.
Play begins with each player placing ten counters in front of
him, and then proceeds in a clockwise direction from the first
shooter.
Each player in turn throws all three dice once. Any player
whose number comes up in that throw has to put one counter
into the pot for each of his own numbers thrown.
For example, if the first shooter throws 4, 6, 6, the player who
has number 4 puts one counter into the pot; and the player with
number 6 puts two counters into the pot.
When the pot has been taken by the winning player (the first to
lose all his ten counters), the next game is started by the player
to the left of the first shooter in the previous game, and he now
takes the number 1.

BUCK DICE

This is a game for any number of players, using three dice.

Preliminaries Order of play is established by a round in which each player throws a single die. The highest scorer becomes first shooter. The lowest scorer then throws one die to determine a point number for the first game.

Objective Players aim to score a "buck" or "game" (exactly 15 points). On achieving this score the player withdraws from the game, which continues until one player is left: the loser.

Play Each player in turn takes the three dice, and each goes on throwing for as long as he throws the point number on one or more of the dice. As soon as he makes a throw that does not contain the point number, play passes to the next player.

Each player keeps count, aloud, of the number of times he has thrown the point number. Each occasion counts one point.

If, when he is nearing 15 points, a player makes a throw that carries his score beyond 15, the throw does not count and he must roll again.

Some throws rate special values. Three point numbers in one throw ("big buck" or "general") count 15 points. A player making this throw withdraws immediately from the game irrespective of any score he has made previously.

Three of a kind that are not point numbers count as a "little buck" and score five points.

Variation Some players follow the rule that when a player has scored 13 points, he rolls with only two dice; and when 14 is reached, with only one die.

Continuing play Start of play rotates one player to the left after each game. The right to determine the point number also rotates in this way, so that it is always with the player to the starter's right.

HOOLIGAN

Hooligan is played with five dice and a throwing cup. Any number of players may take part. Hooligan is a point-scoring game; the winner is the player making the highest total score.

Preliminaries Aside from a preliminary round to determine the order of play, a scoresheet must be prepared. This sheet should have a column divided into seven sections marked 1, 2, 3, 4, 5, 6, and H (hooligan), against which the score of each player can be recorded.

The game consists of seven rounds, each player throwing in turn. A turn ("frame") consists of three throws.

After his first throw, each player declares which of the numbers on the scoresheet (including H) he is shooting for (ie his point number). He must shoot for H on his final turn, if he has not previously done so. "Hooligan" is a straight, either 1, 2, 3, 4, 5 or 2, 3, 4, 5, 6, and counts 20 points.

If he wishes, a player need not declare a point number after his first throw. In this case he picks up all five dice, shoots again, and then declares his point number; but this counts as his

second throw, so he has only one throw left in this frame.
If he declares his point number after his first throw, he puts
aside all dice bearing that number, then throws a second time
with the remaining dice. Once more, any dice bearing the point
number are put aside. He then makes his third and final throw
with the remaining dice.

Scoring A player's score is determined by mutiplying his point
number by the number of times that he has made that number.
For example, if he were throwing for 4s and made three of
them, his score would be 12.

If a player throws the maximum of five point numbers in his
first or second throw, he counts this score and plays the
remaining throw(s) of the frame with five dice, setting aside
any dice bearing the point number after the first throw if two
throws are involved. The point numbers made on these throws
are added to the five made on the first throw.

A player has only one turn to shoot for each point number. He
must choose a different point number for each frame.

Sometimes games of Hooligan are operated by a banker.
Players play against the bank, and must pay to enter the game.
The odds and rules of such games vary from place to place.

Hooligan score card

Point number	K	J	P	T
1	2	4	1	
2			6	4
3	12	9	3	9
4	12			16
5		10	25	15
6	6	24	18	24
H	20	20		

ACES

This is a game for any number of players. It is usually played for a pot and the winner is the player throwing the last ace (1) with the last die.

Equipment Each player requires five dice and a throwing cup.

Order of play is determined by a preliminary round in which each player tries to throw the highest poker hand (see p. 98). Numbers rank: 1 (high), 6, 5, 4, 3, 2 (low).

The player with the highest ranking hand becomes first shooter. The other players then sit in clockwise order in accordance with the hands they have thrown. Ties are resolved by further throws.

Play The first shooter throws his dice and transfers to the center of the table any 1s that come up. Any 2s in his throw are passed to the player to his left, and any 5s to the player to his right.

He continues throwing until he fails to make any of these numbers on a throw, or until he has disposed of all his dice. Although he may have no dice left, he is still in the game, since he may later receive dice from the players to his left and right. Play continues in a clockwise direction around the table until all the dice except one have been transferred to the center. The winner (or loser) is the player who throws the last ace with that die.

SHIP, CAPTAIN, MATE, AND CREW

This game may be played by any number of people. Five dice are used.

Objective Players try to throw 6 (the ship), 5 (the captain), and 4 (the mate) in that order and within three throws.

Order of play is established by a preliminary round, in which each player throws a single die. The highest scorer becomes first shooter. Play then moves in a clockwise direction around the table.

Start of play rotates one player to the left after each game.

Play The players each put an agreed stake into the pot.

Each player in turn is allowed not more than three throws of the dice.

If he makes a 6 and 5 on his first throw, he can set those dice aside. In his second throw he then rolls the other three dice hoping to make a 4. If, however, he makes a 6 and 4 on his first throw, only the 6 can be set aside, and the remaining four dice must be rolled again for a 5 and a 4. (Similar rules for setting dice aside apply to second-round throws.)

If the player makes 6, 5, and 4 in his three throws, the remaining two dice (the crew) are totaled as his score. But if he makes 6, 5, and 4 in his first or second throw, he may, if he wishes, use the remaining throws to try to improve the total of the crew dice.

The pot goes to the player with the highest score in the round. A tie nullifies all scores and a further round has to be played.

ENGLISH HAZARD

This is a centuries old game played with two dice and a throwing cup. Any number may play.

Play begins when a first shooter, called the "caster," puts his stake in a circle marked on the center of the table. Any other player wishing to wager also puts his stake in the center and the caster accepts his challenge by knocking the table with the throwing cup.

When all betting has finished, the caster throws the dice to establish a "main point," a total of either 5, 6, 7, 8, or 9. If he throws any other total it is "no main" and he must continue throwing until a main point comes up.

Having established a main point, he throws the dice again to establish a "chance point" (a total of either 4, 5, 6, 7, 8, 9, or 10 – but not the same number as the main point number).

When he throws to establish the chance point, the caster immediately loses the bet if he throws an "out." An out is any throw of 2 or 3 (called a "crab"); or a throw of 12 if the main point is 5, 6, 8, or 9.

The caster wins, however, if he throws a "nick." He makes a nick if he throws an 11 when the main point is a 7, or if he throws a 12 when the main point is a 6 or an 8. If he throws the main point itself, this also counts as a nick and he wins immediately.

If he establishes a chance point, he then continues throwing. If he throws the chance point again, he wins the bet. But if he throws the main point again, he loses.

BIDOU

This game can be played by any number of players, but procedures differ according to the number of players. The version for two players is described below. The multihand version is described on p. 112.

Equipment Each player needs three dice and a throwing cup. The game also requires a supply of chips or counters.

Objective Players aim to get rid of their chips by betting on combinations of dice thrown. The last player still holding chips is the loser. If desired, he pays each other player a previously agreed amount.

Bidou combinations There are 22 special combinations, given in ranking order in the table, left. The combination 2,1,1 is sometimes referred to as "bidou" and 2,2,1 as "bidé."

Although 2,1,1 appears first in the table, this combination is beaten by 1,1,1. In all other cases, however, the ranking of 1,1,1 is as given in the table, ie below the other three-of-a-kind combinations.

The remaining 34 possible combinations are ranked according to the spot total, eg 6,3,2(=11) beats 4,3,1(=8). All of these combinations rank below the 22 special combinations.

TWO-HAND BIDOU

Two-hand bidou is played in games made up of three separate rounds. The loser is the player losing at least two of the rounds. (Also see the general rules given above.)

Preliminary round Only nine betting chips are used. They are placed on the table between the two players.

Each player then throws a die once. The player making the higher score becomes "captain" (first shooter) for the first hand.

Play: first round The captain takes his turn first, followed by his opponent. In his turn each player may throw the dice up to three times to achieve the best possible score.

In each throw he must throw all the dice, keeping them concealed beneath his dice cup. He must declare the number of throws he makes.

When both players have thrown, betting on that hand begins.

Opening the betting If both players have made the same number of throws, or if the captain has made fewer throws than his opponent, then the captain bets or passes first.

If the captain has made more throws than his opponent, the latter becomes captain and makes the first bet, or passes.

Betting limits The maximum bet or raise is one chip.

Betting procedure Players use the center chips for betting until these run out. As each player states his bet, he moves the appropriate number of chips away from the center pile and slightly toward him.

When all the center chips have been used up, players may use any chips they have received during the round, moving them slightly toward the center as they use them.

Betting A player need not have a strong hand to make a bet; he may choose to bluff his opponent.

If both players pass, the hand ends. Once one player has bet, the other must call (ie bet an equal amount), raise (ie bet a greater amount), or drop out. If one player raises, the other must call, reraise, or drop out. The betting continues until one player has called or dropped out.

Outcome If one player calls the other, both show their dice. All chips bet are then taken by the loser. The winner becomes the next captain.

If one player drops out, he must take one penalty chip (from the center if possible). All other chips bet are returned to their positions before the hand began. The player who has not dropped out is the next captain.

If both players pass, neither takes any chips, and the captaincy changes for the next hand.

Play: second round Play is exactly as in the first round, except that on any throw a player may put aside any dice whose score he wishes to keep, and throw only the remainder. The dice put aside must remain hidden from the opponent.

Having put aside dice on one throw, a player may still throw all the dice on his third throw of that turn.

Play: third round Play reverts to the rules for the first round.

"Open throw" occurs when one player has eight chips, leaving one chip with his opponent or in the center.

The player with one or no chips is then entitled to not more than three throws of the dice to make the highest possible exposed combination. (Whether he must rethrow all the dice or may select depends on the rules for the round they are playing.)

His opponent then throws in similar fashion and if he loses the throws he takes the single chip and so loses the game. If the single-chip player loses, he takes one chip from his opponent and normal play is resumed.

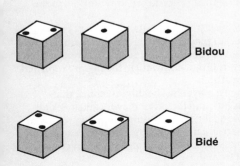

Bidou

Bidé

MULTIHAND BIDOU

When three or more players take part no chips are placed in the center of the table. Instead, each player begins with six chips. (Also see the general rules given on p. 110.)

Captaincy A preliminary round decides who is first captain, as in Two-hand bidou. Play begins with the captain and proceeds in a clockwise direction. The winner of each round becomes captain of the next.

If all players pass, the player to the left of the captain of that round becomes captain of the next.

Play is as in Two-hand bidou. All players must keep their dice hidden from the others until betting has closed.

Opening the betting If all players have made the same number of throws, the same player remains captain. Otherwise, the player making the fewest throws and nearest to the original captain's left becomes captain.

Betting limits The maximum bet is three chips, the maximum raise two chips.

Betting procedure Each player uses his own store of chips, and places his bets in the center of the table to form a common pot.

Betting situations

1) On a showdown between two or more players, the loser collects all chips still in the pot.

2) Players dropping out without betting receive no penalty.

3) For players dropping out after betting at least once, the following rules apply:

the first in a round to do so must take from the pot whichever amount he has put in on that hand, plus the same amount for each player still betting, plus one penalty chip;

each player dropping out thereafter on that round must take one penalty chip.

If the players remaining have bet unequal amounts, whichever number of chips is left in the pot is called or raised by the next player in turn.

4) If all players drop out after a player has raised, any chips left in the pot after penalties have been taken are returned to the raising player.

5) A player who bets his last chips has the right to stay in for the showdown, even if other players take the betting further. If he loses, he receives back his bet and the equivalent amount from each showdown player. Other chips still in the pot are returned to the players who bet them.

6) If there is a tie when a player has bet his last chips, that player takes back his bet, and the other players take back all their chips except one each. The remaining chips are removed from the game. If there is a tie in any other circumstance, each showdown player takes back one chip, and any other chips in the pot are removed from the game.

7) If only one player bets on a round and all the others pass, he can discard one chip even if it is his last.

8) If only two players are left with chips, these two continue until one has lost. Should the two players have more than nine chips between them, each discards one chip whenever he bets and is not called, until the players have a total of nine chips between them. The two then fight out the game as in Two-hand bidou.

9) Any player who passes after betting has begun automatically drops out of that round.

Poor fish is a variation that requires all players to expose their last throws if all have passed. The player with the highest throw is the "poor fish" and receives one chip from each of the other players.

MONTEVIDEO

This game requires three dice, a throwing cup, and chips or counters for each player.

The objective is to win all the chips.

Players Three or more players can take part.

Ante At the start of play each player has six chips. In each round he antes one chip into the pot before throwing the dice.

Betting After the dice have been thrown, betting proceeds as in Bidou.

Play is as in Bidou, with the same combinations, but at showdown, the highest combination wins the pot.

If the game reaches a stage where only two players have any chips, it is speeded up by increasing, round by round, the number of chips each must ante into the pot, to a maximum of six. If there are many players, the same procedure should be followed for the last three players.

Any player may, if he wishes, open the betting by "betting the pot," ie stay in without putting up chips. When this happens, any other player – even if he has already passed – may call the pot. The bet may, of course, be raised in the usual way.

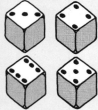

Natural throws

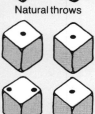

Crap throws

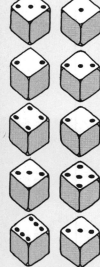

CRAPS

Craps developed in the early nineteenth century, when black Americans adapted the game of English hazard (p. 109). Today, the money wagered at Craps in the United States alone makes it the biggest gambling game in history. Its attractions are its speed of action and large element of participation; yet its essence is that of a mathematical game of numbers and odds. Here we describe the private form of the game, in which players arrange bets among themselves.

Basic equipment is:
1) two matched dice;
2) a playing surface, preferably edged by a wall or backboard;
3) betting chips or cash.

Players: any number over two.

General procedure

a) Any player by common agreement may shoot the dice first; thereafter the dice are passed around in a clockwise direction.

b) A new player may join a game at any stage and sit anywhere in the circle of players – provided that the players raise no objection at the time. He takes his turn in the normal way when the dice reach him.

c) A player may leave a game at any time, regardless of his gains or losses.

Throw of the dice The shooter shakes the dice in his closed hand and throws them onto the playing area. If there is a backboard, it is usually ruled that the dice must rebound from it before they come to rest.

The two numbers face uppermost when the dice come to rest, added together, give the result of the throw.

Basic play The first throw in a shooter's turn is called a "come-out" throw as is the first throw after each time the dice win or lose.

If on a come-out throw, the shooter throws a 7 or 11 he has thrown a "natural": the dice "pass" (ie win) immediately. The shooter may keep the dice for another come-out throw.

If on a come-out throw, the shooter throws a 2, 3, or 12, he has thrown a "craps": the dice "miss out" or "crap out" (ie lose) immediately. The shooter may keep the dice for another come-out throw.

If on a come-out throw, the shooter throws a 4, 5, 6, 8, 9, or 10, he has thrown a "point": for the dice to win he must "make the point," ie throw the same number again before he throws a 7 – no other numbers matter.

If the shooter throws the same number again before he throws a 7, the dice pass (win). The shooter may keep the dice for another come-out throw.

If he throws a 7 before he throws the number again, the dice miss out or "seven out" (lose). The shooter must give the dice to the next player in turn.

Giving up the dice If the shooter sevens out, he must give up the dice.

He may also, if he wishes, pass the dice if:

a) he has not thrown the dice in his turn; or

b) he has not thrown a "decision:" ie a natural, a craps, or a pass on a point.

Change of dice If more than one pair of dice is being used, any player may call for the dice in use to be changed at any time. This is called a "box-up." The change is made immediately before the next come-out throw.

Betting and settlement of bets

Center bet On each come-out throw, the shooter places the amount he wishes to bet in the center of the playing area. He announces the amount, saying "I'll shoot . . ."

Any of the other players then "fade" (accept) whatever part of the total they wish, by placing that amount in the center alongside the shooter's bet.

Unless previously agreed otherwise, the fading of center bets is in no set order and by no fixed amount. Players simply place money in the center until all the shooter's bet has been faded, or until no one wishes to place any further amount. (It is sometimes agreed that any player who faded the entire center bet on the preceding come-out, and lost, can claim the right to fade the entire present bet.)

If the center bet is not entirely faded by the players, the shooter may either:

a) withdraw the part not faded; or

b) call off all bets, by saying "No bet."

Players may not fade more than the shooter's center bet; but if the players show eagerness to bet more, the shooter can decide to increase the amount of his bet.

Settlement of center bet If the dice miss out (lose), the players who faded the center bet each receive back their money together with the equivalent amount of the center bet.

If the dice pass (win), all the money in the center is collected by the shooter.

The center bet is therefore an even money (1 to 1) bet. Since the probability of the dice passing is in fact 970 occasions in 1980, the shooter has 1.414% disadvantage on the center bet.

Other bets are known as side bets. Like the center bet, they must be arranged before the dice are thrown, not while they are rolling. Note that the shooter himself may make any of the side bets he wishes, in addition to the center bet.

Right and wrong bettors All these bets require agreement between two players. One is the "wrong" bettor: he "lays" odds that the dice will not pass or will not make the number(s) bet on.

The other is the "right" bettor: he "takes" odds that the dice will pass or will make the number(s) bet on.

The bet and odds may be proposed by either the right or the wrong bettor; in practice, however, more experienced players tend to be "wrong" bettors and propose odds that the less experienced player will "take."

Flat bet This is a normal bet on whether a shooter's come-out throw will pass, and is made as a side bet between two players (of which one may be the shooter). Flat bets occur especially if one player has faded the entire bet.

Point bet If the shooter throws a point on his come-out throw, players may bet on whether he will "make the point." (The center and flat bets still remain to be settled in the same way.)

Come bet This is a bet on whether the dice will pass – but treating the next throw of the dice, after the bet, as the bet's come-out throw (when in fact the shooter is throwing for a point).

For a "come bet," one player lays odds that the dice will not come, while another player takes odds that they will.

The first throw of the dice after the bet is the "come-out" throw for the come bet. If the shooter rolls a 7, he sevens out on his point – but for the come bet the dice "come," because a 7 on a come-out throw is a natural.

Similarly, 11 is a natural for the come bet, and 2, 3, or 12 is craps – the dice "don't come." (But all these leave the center bet undecided, because they are neither the point number nor a 7.)

If the shooter rolls a point number on the come-out throw for the come bet, this number becomes the point for the come bet. The outcome then depends, in the usual way, on whether the point or a 7 appears first.

If the shooter makes the point on his center bet without making the come bet point, the players making the come bet can agree to withdraw the bet or to continue the number sequence into the shooter's next turn.

Hardway bet (or gag bet) This is a bet on whether the shooter will throw a certain number "the hard way" – ie as the sum of a double. Hardway bets can be placed on 4 (2+2), 6 (3+3), 8 (4+4), or 10 (5+5).

The right bettor loses if a 7 is thrown, or if the number bet on is thrown any other way before being thrown as a double.

Off-number bet Two players agree to bet on any number they choose. The right bettor wins if the shooter throws the number before he throws a 7. Bettors may call off this bet before a "decision" is reached.

Proposition bet refers to any other kind of side bet agreed upon – limited only by players' imaginations! Such bets are always offered at odds designed to give the proposing player an advantage. There are two main categories:

a) bets on whether the specified number(s) will appear within a certain number of rolls after the bet: "one-roll bets," two-roll bets," "three-roll bets;" or

b) bets on whether the specified number(s) will appear before other specified number(s) or before a 7.

In each case, the specified number(s) bet on may be:

a) a certain number to be thrown in any way;

b) a certain number to be thrown in a specified way;

c) any one of a group of numbers (eg a group of specified numbers, odd numbers, numbers below 7, etc).

©DIAGRAM

Table 1: True odds for bets on or between single numbers

Number on dice	Ways of making (a)	Single roll (b)	Before a 7 (c)
12	1	35-1	6-1
11	2	17-1	3-1
10	3	11-1	2-1
9	4	8-1	3-2
8	5	31-5	6-5
7	6	5-1	—
6	5	31-5	6-5
5	4	8-1	3-2
4	3	11-1	2-1
3	2	17-1	3-1
2	1	35-1	6-1

Table 2: Hardway bets

Bet	Ways of making (a)	Other ways of making (b)	Ways of making a 7 (c)
4	1 (2+2)	2	6
6	1 (3+3)	4	6
8	1 (4+4)	4	6
10	1 (5+5)	2	6

True odds Table 1 gives the true odds for various bets on or between single numbers, while table 2 gives the true odds for hardway bets.

True odds for other common one-roll bets are:

a) against any specified pair (eg 3+3): 35-1;

b) against any specified combination of two different numbers (eg 6+5): 17-1;

c) against any craps (2, 3, or 12): 8-1.

Notes on table 1

a) Number of different combinations of two die faces that will give the number. Total of all possible combinations is 36.

b) Odds against making a number on a single roll – calculated by comparing the number of ways of making the number (x) with the number of ways of making another number ($36-x$).

c) Odds against throwing the number before throwing a 7.

d) Odds against making the higher number before the lower number (eg 12 before 4: 3-1). Reverse the odds to give odds against making the lower number before the higher (eg 4 before 12: 1-3).

Notes on table 2

a) Number of ways of making the specified number "the hard way."

b) Number of other ways of making the same total number as the hardway number bet on.

Comparative odds (d)									
12									
2-1	**11**								
3-1	3-2	**10**							
4-1	2-1	4-3	**9**						
5-1	5-2	5-3	5-4	**8**					
6-1	3-1	2-1	3-2	6-5	**7**				
5-1	5-2	5-3	5-4	1-1	5-6	**6**			
4-1	2-1	4-3	1-1	4-5	2-3	4-5	**5**		
3-1	3-2	1-1	3-4	3-5	1-2	3-5	3-4	**4**	
2-1	1-1	2-3	1-2	2-5	1-3	2-5	1-2	2-3	**3**
1-1	1-2	1-3	1-4	1-5	1-6	1-5	1-4	1-3	1-2	**2**

Total ways of losing (d)	Odds against hardway bet
8	8-1
10	10-1
10	10-1
8	8-1

c) Number of ways of making a 7.

d) Total number of ways of losing (**b**+**c**).

Irregularities at private craps include the following. (The shooter must throw again after a void throw.)

1) If the playing area has been specified at the start of the game, the throw is void if either die rolls out of the area.

2) If either die comes to rest under any object on the playing area or tilted on an obstruction, so that it is not clear which of its faces is uppermost, any agreed neutral player or bystander is nominated to decide the question. If he cannot decide, the throw is void.

3) When there is a backboard and neither die hits it, the roll is void. If only one die hits the board the roll counts, but the shooter must be reprimanded. If it occurs again, the other players may designate a player to complete the shooter's turn for him. They may also bar the shooter from shooting for the rest of the game.

4) If either die hits any object or person after hitting the backboard, the roll is counted.

5) A player may not knock either or both dice aside on the roll and call "No dice." If he does this once, the throw counts as it finally shows; if he repeats it, he may be barred from shooting for the rest of the game.

Dominoes

Games with dominoes are played in many countries all over the world. They are now particularly popular in Latin America. It is thought that dominoes may have been brought from China to Europe in the fourteenth century. Certainly domino games were played in Italy in the eighteenth century. In most Western games players add matching dominoes to a pattern or "layout" formed in the center of the table.

Players Some domino games are for two players only. Others are for two or more players, playing singly or as partners. Partnerships may be decided:
a) by mutual agreement;
b) by draw – in which case each player draws one domino and the two players with the heaviest dominoes form one pair. Partners sit opposite each other at the table.
Playing area Dominoes can be played on a table or any other flat surface.
The dominoes are rectangular tiles made of wood, ivory, bone, stone, or plastic. They are sometimes called "bones," "stones," or "pieces." A typical size is 1in by 1⅞in by ⅜in. Each domino's face is divided by a central line and each half is either blank or marked with indented spots (sometimes called "pips"). Dominoes with the same number of spots on either side of the central line are called "doubles" or "doublets." A domino is said to be "heavier" than another if it has more spots, or "lighter" if it has fewer spots. So a double 6 is heavier than 6:5.
The standard Western domino set has 28 tiles (with double 6 the heaviest domino). Larger sets have 55 dominoes (double 9 the heaviest) or 91 dominoes (double 12 the heaviest).
Suits Dominoes belong to different suits according to the number of spots on each of their halves. There is a suit for each number, a blank suit, and a doubles suit.
"Mixed number" dominoes belong to two number suits or to a number suit and the blank suit. Doubles belong to one number suit and to the doubles suit.

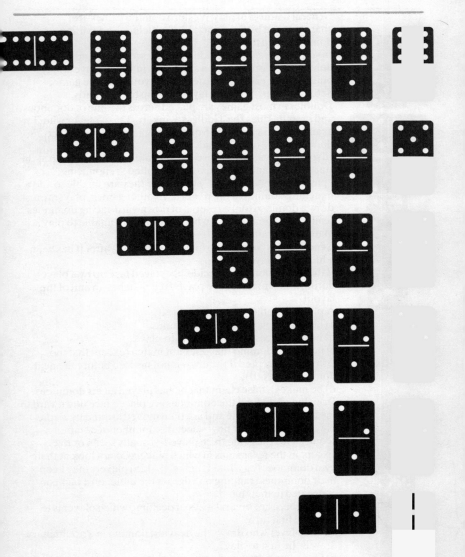

General features of play Western domino games are characterized by the principle of matching and joining dominoes end to end.

In some games, players add dominoes to either end of a line of dominoes. More common are games in which players may build on four ends of a pattern or "layout." In one game, Sebastopol (p. 127), the layout has up to eight ends.

Doubles in most games are placed across the line of dominoes, and in some rules (eg Tiddle-a-wink, p. 125) a player who, for example, plays a double 6 may immediately play another domino with a 6 at one end.

In some games, players use only the dominoes picked up at the start of play, and must miss a turn (called "renouncing," "passing," or "knocking") whenever they are unable to add a matching domino to the pattern. In other games, players must draw a domino from a reserve of downward-facing dominoes (called the "boneyard") whenever they are unable to play a matching domino.

General rules No domino may be withdrawn after it has been added to the layout.

If the wrong domino is accidently placed face up by a player during his turn, it must be played if it matches an end of the layout.

A player is liable to lose the game if:

a) he fails to play within two minutes;

b) he renounces when he is able to play;

c) he plays a domino that does not match (except that the domino is accepted if the error is not noticed before the next domino is played);

d) he makes a false claim that he has played all his dominoes.

Drawing a hand All the dominoes are placed face downward in the center of the table and are then moved around by all the players. Each player now selects the number of dominoes required for the game to be played – usually seven or five.

Except in the few games in which players do not look at their own dominoes (eg Blind Hughie, p. 125) players may keep their dominoes standing on edge on the table, on a rack, or concealed in their hand.

Turns There are several ways of deciding which player is to have the first turn.

a) The player who draws the heaviest domino in a preliminary draw is the first to play.

b) One player draws a domino and his opponent guesses whether its spots add up to an odd or even number.

c) Each player draws his dominoes for the game and the first turn goes to the player with the heaviest double or, if there are no doubles, to the player with the heaviest domino.

In most countries, turns then pass clockwise around the table; in Latin America, the direction of play is counterclockwise.

End of play Games end:

a) when one player has played all his dominoes – after which he calls "domino!" or makes some other recognized signal;

b) when no player can add a matching domino in games with no drawing from the boneyard;

c) in drawing games when no player can add a matching domino and only two dominoes remain in the boneyard.

Result Most games are played to a set number of points.
In some games, the player who first plays all his dominoes claims one point for each spot on his opponents' unplayed dominoes.

If all play is blocked, the player with fewest spots on his unplayed dominoes claims the difference between the number of spots on his own and his opponents' unplayed dominoes. The hand is replayed if opponents' dominoes have an equal number of spots.

In other games (eg Bergen, p. 130), players score points for adding a domino that makes the two ends of the layout match.

©DIAGRAM

BLOCK DOMINOES

The basic Block dominoes game is usually played by two, three, or four players using a standard set of 28 dominoes. (More players can play with larger sets.) Two players usually play with seven dominoes each, and three or four players with five dominoes each.

The first player begins by laying any of his dominoes face up in the center. Turns then pass around the table – with players adding matching dominoes to either end of the line or missing a turn if none of their dominoes matches.

Spots are counted and points scored after one player has played all his dominoes or the game is blocked so that no one can play (see result, p. 123).

The winner of one hand plays first in the next hand. A game is usually played to 100 or 200 points.

PARTNERSHIP BLOCK DOMINOES

The partnership form of Block dominoes is played by four players with a standard set of 28 dominoes.

Play is the same as for basic Block dominoes except that:

a) players sitting opposite each other form a pair;

b) each player draws seven dominoes at the start of the game;

c) the player with the double 6 starts the first hand by laying it on the table;

d) subsequent hands are started by the winner of the previous hand and this player may play any of his dominoes to start;

e) pairs score jointly – as soon as one player has played all his dominoes, he and his partner score the sum of the spots on each of their opponents' unplayed dominoes.

f) in blocked games, the pair with the lowest total of spots on their unplayed dominoes score the difference between their own and their opponents' total of spots on their unplayed dominoes.

LATIN AMERICAN MATCH DOMINOES

This Latin American form of dominoes is played in the same way as Partnership block dominoes except that:

a) the player with the double 6 always starts;

b) each hand won counts as one game;

c) a match ends when one pair has won 10 hands;

d) a match is scored only if the other pair failed to win five hands – otherwise the match is tied.

DOMINO POOL

The rules of standard Block dominoes apply to Domino pool except that, before each hand, players place equal bets in a pool or pot. The winner of the hand takes all; or if players tie they share the pool between them.

TIDDLE-A-WINK

This is a form of Block dominoes particularly suited to larger groups of people. It is often played with sets of 55 or 91 dominoes.

At the start of each hand the dominoes are shared out equally between the players; any remaining dominoes are left face downward on the table. Play proceeds as for the basic block game except that:

a) the player with the highest double always starts:

b) any player who plays a double may add another domino if he is able;

c) a player who has played all his dominoes calls "tiddle-a-wink."

(Another version of the game is played by six to nine players with three dominoes each from a set of 28 dominoes. In this version, dominoes are added to only one side of the starting double and bets are made as in Domino pool.)

BLIND HUGHIE

Blind Hughie is a Block dominoes game of chance.

If four or five players are playing with 28 dominoes, each draws five dominoes without looking at them; two or three players each draw seven dominoes. Each player lays his dominoes in a line face downward in front of him.

The first player starts play by taking the domino at the left of his line and laying it face up in the center of the table.

Turns then pass around the table. At his turn each player takes the domino at the left of his line and:

a) if it matches an end of the layout, he plays it;

b) if it doesn't match, he lays it face downward at the right of his line.

Play continues until one player finishes his dominoes or until the game is obviously blocked.

DRAW DOMINOES

Draw dominoes is characterized by the drawing of dominoes from the boneyard after the start of play.

Players usually start with seven or five dominoes each. Play is as for basic Block dominoes except that:

a) a player who is unable or unwilling to add a domino to the layout must draw dominoes from the boneyard until he draws one that he is able or willing to play, or until only two dominoes remain in the boneyard;

b) when only two dominoes remain in the boneyard, a player who cannot play a domino must end or miss a turn;

c) a player who draws or looks at an extra domino, or who turns a domino up so that other players see it, must keep that domino.

DOUBLES

This game, also called Maltese cross, is played in the same way as basic Draw dominoes except that:

a) the player with the heaviest double leads;

b) play is on four ends from the starting double;

c) a player may add a mixed number domino only if the double of the number he is matching has already been played (eg in the hand illustrated, a player could add 2:3 to the double 2 but could not play the same domino as 3:2 on the 5:3).

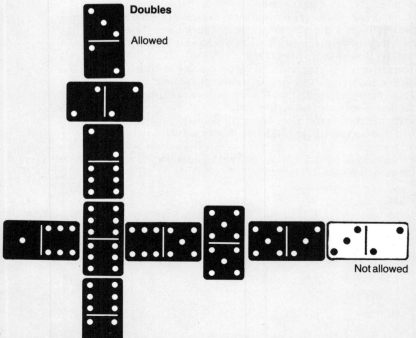

Doubles

Allowed

Not allowed

126

FORTRESS, SEBASTOPOL, CYPRUS

These are names for two closely related games.

a) The first game, usually called Fortress but sometimes called Sebastopol, is a Block dominoes game for four people with 28 dominoes. Each player draws seven dominoes and the player with the double 6 starts.

Play is on four ends from the double 6, and a domino must be added to each of these ends before play proceeds as for Standard block dominoes.

b) The second game, more usually called Sebastopol but sometimes called Cyprus, is a Draw dominoes game played with a set of 55 dominoes. Four or five players start with nine dominoes each; more players start with seven or five.

Double 9 always starts and if no player has this domino, players should draw one domino in turn until someone draws it. Play is on eight ends from the double 9, and all ends must be opened before a second domino may be added to any end.

Players draw one domino from the boneyard whenever they are unable to add a domino to the layout.

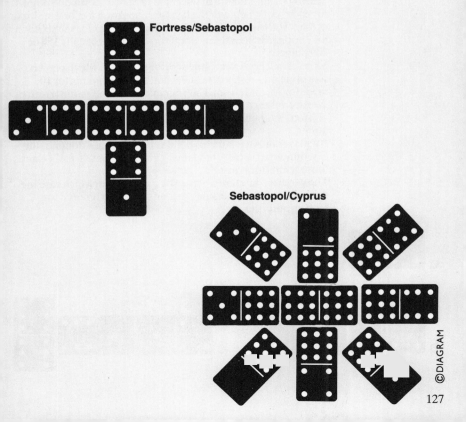

Fortress/Sebastopol

Sebastopol/Cyprus

©DIAGRAM

127

ALL FIVES

This game, also called Muggins and Fives up, is a form of Draw dominoes that is particularly popular in the United States. It is an interesting game characterized by its scoring system based on multiples of five.

Using a 28-domino set, two, three, or four players start with five dominoes each. The first player may lead with any domino – and scores if its ends add up to five (**a**) or 10. The next player scores if the ends of the layout still add up to five or a multiple of five after he has played (**b**). If he is unable to score, he may play another domino (eg the 1:3, which would make the ends of the layout add up to seven), or may draw one domino from the boneyard.

The first double of the game (**c**) opens up a third end (in this case there would be no score since 6+6+4=16).

The next domino (**d**) opens up the fourth and final end of the layout (and in this case it scores since 6+6+4+4=20). Play continues on four ends of the layout until one player finishes all his dominoes or until the game is blocked.

Scoring In one version of the game, a player scores one point for each spot whenever the layout's ends total five or a multiple of five. The winner of a hand also scores points for the spots on his opponents' remaining dominoes. Game is usually 150 or 200 points.

More usual, however, is the scoring system in which players score one point when the ends total five, two points for 10, three for 15, and so on. The winner of the hand scores a fifth of the face value of his opponents' remaining dominoes. In this version, the game is won by the first player to score exactly 61 points.

If a player fails to claim his points after playing a domino, the first opponent to call "muggins" (or sometimes "fives") claims those points for himself.

The game is sometimes played by partners – in which case the dominoes left in the losing partner's hand are ignored for scoring purposes.

All fives

a

b

c

ALL THREES

All threes, or Threes up, is played in the same way as All fives but scoring is based on multiples of three.

FIVES AND THREES

This is played in the same way as All fives, but scoring is based on multiples of both five and three. A player scores one point for each spot whenever the ends of the layout total five or a multiple of five, or three or a multiple of three. If a number is a multiple of both five and three, the player scores two points for each spot. The winner also scores for each spot on an opponent's remaining dominoes.

d

MATADOR

In this unusual draw game, dominoes are played when they make a specified total with a domino on an end of the layout. There are also wild dominoes called "matadors" that can be played at any turn. These are versions of the game for different sizes of domino sets.

When a 28-domino set is used, added dominoes must make a total of seven and the matadors are the 6:1, 5:2, 4:3 (ie those with ends totaling seven), and the 0:0.

For a 55 set the required total is 10 and the matadors are the 9:1, 8:2, 7:3, 6:4, 5:5, and 0:0. (In the game illustrated, play opened with the double 9. This was followed by the 7:3, a matador, and then by three dominoes making totals of 10.)

For a 91 set the total is 13 and the matadors are the 12:1, 11:2, 10:3, 9:4, 8:5, 7:6, and 0:0.

Players usually start with seven or five dominoes each, depending on the number of players and the size of set. The player with the heaviest double starts. In this game doubles are not placed crossways and the layout has only two ends.

If a player is unable or unwilling to add a domino, he must draw one domino from the boneyard. When only two dominoes remain in the boneyard, he must play a domino if he is able. A hand is won by the player who finishes his dominoes or who holds dominoes with the fewest spots if the game is blocked. Points are scored for the spots on an opponent's remaining dominoes, and game is an agreed number of points.

BERGEN

Bergen is a Draw dominoes game in which players score points when there are matching dominoes at the ends of the layout. Using a set of 28 dominoes, two or three players start with six dominoes each and four players with five dominoes each. The player with the highest double starts. Subsequent play is on two ends only, and a player who is unable or unwilling to add a domino to the layout must draw one domino from the boneyard.

A player scores two points whenever two ends of the layout match (a "double heading") – as, for example the 6:2 and the 3:2 in the illustration (ie before the addition of the double 2). A player scores three points for a "triple heading" – ie when there is a double at one end and a matching domino at the other, as after the addition of the double 2 in the example illustrated.

A player scores two points for winning a hand. If no player finishes his dominoes and the game is blocked, the hand is won by the player holding no doubles, the player with fewest doubles, or the player with fewest spots on his dominoes. Game is usually 10 or 15 points.

Matador

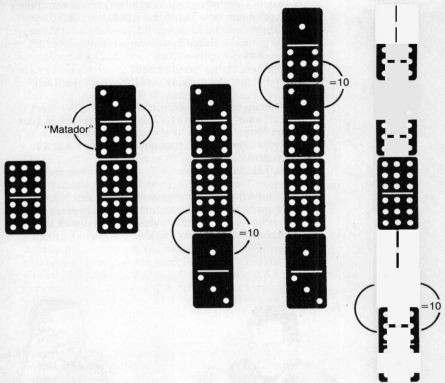

"Matador"

=10

=10

=10

Bergen

Five-spot dominoes

5 points

5 points

5 points

Ten-spot dominoes

10 points

10 points

FORTY-TWO

Forty-two, or Domino rounce, is an adaptation of a card game for play with dominoes. The object is to score points by winning tricks.

The game is usually played by four players with a set of 28 dominoes. Play is usually with partners. Each player draws seven dominoes at the start of a hand.

Bidding is the first stage of play, and tricks are valued as follows:

a) one point for each trick taken;

b) five additional points for a trick containing the 5:0, 4:1, or 3:2 (ie the dominoes with a total of five spots each);

c) 10 additional points for a trick containing the 5:5 or 6:4 (ie ten spots each).

The total tricks value is 42 points (and hence the name of the game).

The player holding the 1:0 domino makes the first bid, and the other players bid in turn. Players may make only one bid and no bid may be for less than 30 points or be lower than a preceding bid. A player may pass if he does not wish to bid.

Taking tricks The player or pair with the highest bid then
attempts to take tricks worth the value of their bid (or more).
There are eight suits – blanks, the numbers 1 through 6, and
doubles. Except when a trump is led, the highest number on a
domino determines the suit. The highest bidder plays the first
domino and this establishes the trump suit for the hand. If he
leads a "mixed number" domino he calls out which number is
the trump suit. The other players then play one domino in
turn.

Except when a trump or a double is played, a trick goes to the
player who played the heaviest domino of the correct suit. A
double is the strongest domino of its suit, and can be taken only
by a trump. As in card games a higher number in the trump suit
takes a lower one.

The player who takes a trick always leads for the next trick.
In the examples illustrated:
a) double 3 takes the trick – and scores five extra points
because the 3:2 is taken;
b) if 2s are trumps, the 2:1 takes the trick – and scores 10 extra
points because the 6:4 is taken.

Scoring If the bidder and his partner take tricks worth as many
or more points than the bid, they score the full value of their
tricks plus the number of points bid.

If the bidder and his partner fail in their objective, their
opponents score the number of points bid plus the value of the
tricks that they have taken.

Taking tricks

a 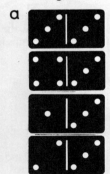   b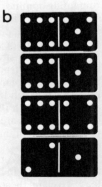

133

DOMINO BINGO

This is another game in which dominoes are used like playing cards and players score points for taking tricks.

It is a game for two players with a set of 28 dominoes. Players make a preliminary draw to determine who will lead for the first trick.

At the start of play, each player draws seven dominoes from the boneyard. The leader then establishes trumps for the hand by turning over a domino in the boneyard. This domino is left exposed and its highest number becomes the trump suit for the hand.

The leader for the first trick then plays one domino and his opponent follows him. There is no need for a player to follow suit, except when the game is "closed" or the boneyard is empty.

Taking a trick The double blank, called "bingo," takes any other domino

If two trumps are played, the higher trump takes the trick.

If one trump is played, the trump takes the trick.

If no trumps are played, the heaviest domino wins the trick.

If no trumps are played and both dominoes have the same total of spots, the leader's domino takes the trick.

As long as any dominoes remain in the boneyard, each player draws a domino after each trick. The winner of a trick always draws first and then leads for the next trick.

When only two dominoes remain in the boneyard, the winner of the preceding trick may take the trump domino or the domino that is face down, and the losing player takes the remaining domino.

Value of tricks There is no score just for taking a trick. The value of a trick depends on the dominoes it contains. Only the following dominoes have any points value (with 2s as trumps in the examples illustrated):

a) the double of trumps is worth 28 points;

b) except when blanks are trumps, "bingo" is worth 14 points;

c) the 6:4 is worth 10 points;

d) the 3:0 is worth 10 points;

e) other doubles are worth their total number of spots;

f) trumps other than the double are worth their total number of spots.

Value of doubles A player can also claim points for having more than one double in his hand at any time when it is his turn to lead. To claim these points he should play one double and expose the others.

For two doubles in his hand he calls "double" and claims 20 points;

for three doubles he calls "triple" and claims 40 points;

for four doubles he calls "double doublet" and claims 50 points;

for five doubles he calls "king" and claims 60 points;

for six doubles he calls "emperor" and claims 70 points;

Value of tricks
(2s trumps)

a

28 points

b

14 points

c

10 points

d

10 points

Value of tricks
(2s trumps)

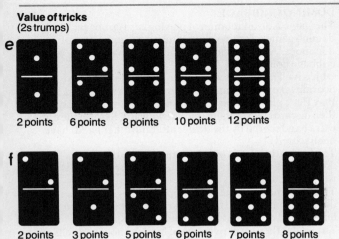

e

2 points 6 points 8 points 10 points 12 points

f

2 points 3 points 5 points 6 points 7 points 8 points

for all seven doubles he calls "invincible" and claims
210 points;
if "bingo" is among his doubles he claims an extra 10 points.
A player is not entitled to these points if he fails to claim them
when laying down a double; nor do they count if he fails to take
the trick.

Closing If a player with the lead believes that he can bring his
score from tricks and doubles to at least 70 points without
drawing any further dominoes, he can "close" the game by
turning over the trump domino.
After the game is closed neither player may draw any further
dominoes and rules for following suit come into force.

Following suit After the game is closed or the boneyard is
empty, a player is obliged when possible to follow suit.
If a trump is led, he must play another trump.
If a domino that is not a trump is led, he must try and follow its
higher number or, failing that, its lowest number. If he can
follow neither of these, he may play a trump. Only if he has
none of these is he permitted to discard.

Scoring A game is won by the first player to score seven sets or
game points.
Sets are scored as follows:
a) one set for every 70 points from tricks or doubles;
b) one set for being the first player to reach 70 points if the
other player has at least 30 points;
c) two sets for reaching 70 points after the other player has won
a trick but has not scored 30 points;
d) three sets for reaching 70 points before the other player wins
a trick;
e) one set for taking the double of trumps with "bingo."

135

DOMINO CRIBBAGE

This game is an adaptation of playing card cribbage. The basic domino game is for two players, using a standard set of 28 dominoes. As in the card game, the score is usually kept on a cribbage board.

Objective The game is won by the first player to score 61 points. Scoring takes place during play and also at the end of a hand.

Play Each player draws six dominoes at the start of play. He then discards two of them, face downward, to form the crib (an extra hand scored by the dealer after the other hands have been scored).

The leader then turns over a domino in the boneyard. This domino is the "starter." It is not used during play but is scored with all hands after play.

Turns alternate. The leader's opponent begins by placing any domino from his hand face upward on the table in front of himself and calling out its total number of spots.

The leader then turns over one of his dominoes and calls out the sum total of spots on both dominoes played so far.

Play proceeds in this way, with each player calling the sum total of spots played, until the "go" rule comes into play. If, at his turn, a player is unable to play a domino that will bring the count to 31 or below, he must call "go." The other player must then play as many tiles as he can until he reaches 31 or is unable to play.

Once a count of 31 has been reached, or if no one can play, a new count from 0 is begun. (Pairs etc cannot be carried over into the next count.)

After both players have played all their dominoes, the leader's opponent scores the points in his hand. The leader then scores the points in his hand and then the points in the crib. The lead then passes to the other player and another hand is started.

Scoring during play For turning up a double for starter, one point.

For reaching a count of exactly 15, two points.

For a "pair" (playing a domino with the same total spot count as the last played domino), two points.

For a "triplet" (a third domino with the same total spot count) six points.

For a fourth domino with the same spot count, 12 points.

For a run of three or more dominoes, not necessarily in order (eg dominoes totaling 7, 8, 9), one point for each tile of the run.

For reaching exactly 31, two points.

For being nearest to 31, one point.

For the last tile of the hand, one point.

For reaching 15 with the last tile, three points.

Scoring after play For a combination totaling 15, two points.
For a double run of three (a three-tile run with a pair to one of them), eight points.
For a double run of four (a run of four with one pair), 10 points.
For a triple run (a triplet with two other dominoes in sequence), 15 points.
For a quadruple run (two pairs and a domino in sequence with both), 16 points.

Scoring during play

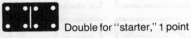 Double for "starter," 1 point

 15, 2 points

 Pair, 2 points

 Run, 3 points

137

PICTURE DOMINOES

Dominoes with pictures are very popular with young children and can be easily bought or made. A typical set contains 28 brightly colored dominoes with combinations of seven different pictures. They are usually made of wood or heavy card.

All the dominoes are shared out among the players, who should keep the pictures hidden from the other players.

One player starts by placing one domino face upward on the table. Players then take turns at adding a matching domino. If a player doesn't have a matching domino he misses his turn. The winner is the first player to add all his dominoes to the row on the table.

Picture dominoes

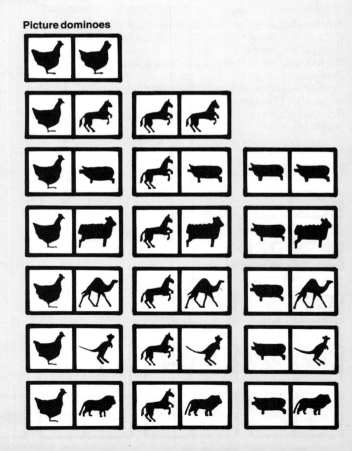

Sample play

©DIAGRAM

139

Dominoes: Chinese

Most Chinese domino games are characterized by the collecting of matching pairs. They are played with sets of 32 dominoes divided into two series – the civil and the military. Players can make their own "Chinese set" from two sets of Western dominoes.

The dominoes Chinese dominoes are longer and narrower than Western dominoes – typically 3in by ⅞in by ⅜in.
Spots on Chinese dominoes are colored red or white:
all 4s or 1s are red;
double 6 is red and white;
other dominoes have white spots.
There are no blank dominoes in a Chinese set.
The civil series comprises 22 dominoes, forming 11 identical pairs: all the doubles plus the 6:5, 6:4, 6:1, 5:1, and 3:1.
The military series comprises 10 dominoes. These form five mixed pairs:
the 4:2 and 2:1 (known as the "supreme pair");
the 6:3 and 5:4 (mixed 9s);
the 6:2 and 5:3 (mixed 8s);
the 5:2 and 4:3 (mixed 7s);
the 4:1 and 3:2 (mixed 5s).
The woodpile The dominoes are stacked in a row – called the "woodpile" – at the start of most Chinese domino games.
The banker for the first hand of a game is usually decided by throwing three dice. The total number thrown is counted around the table and the banker is the player sitting where the count stops.
Turns pass around the table in a counterclockwise direction.

Woodpile

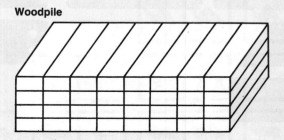

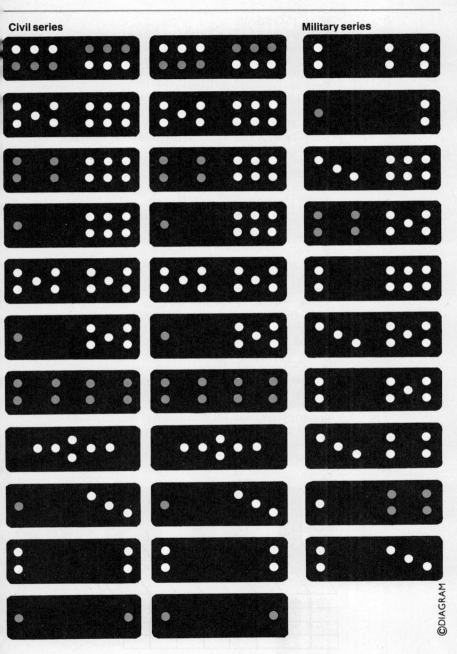

Civil series

Military series

K'AP T'AI SHAP

K'ap t'ai shap (Collecting tens) was a forerunner of Mah jongg (p. 186), and is popular in Chinese gambling houses in the United States.

Objective The game is won by the first player to complete his hand. A complete hand consists of:

a) four pairs, each with a total spot count of 10 or a multiple of 10; and

b) any identical pair.

Start of play A long woodpile five dominoes high is built down the center of the table, using several sets.

Players join the game by placing equal stakes, and dice are thrown to decide who will have the first turn.

The woodpile is then prepared for play by removing the top domino from the third stack from one end and placing it face down at the other end of the woodpile. The top domino is then taken from each alternate stack up to one less than the number of players, and these are also added in order to the far end of the woodpile.

The first player then takes the end two stacks (with 10 dominoes) and the other players in turn each take two stacks (with nine dominoes).

Turns If the first player does not have a winning hand, he starts play by discarding one domino and placing it face up on the table.

Then each player in his turn:

1) may take any discarded domino to complete his hand or to exchange it for one of his own dominoes; and

2) draws one domino from the end of the woodpile, which he may immediately discard or keep in place of another domino from his hand.

Result The game ends when one player completes his hand. This entitles him to the total staked, less the gambling house commission.

Objective

a

b

TIU U

Tiu u, or Fishing, is a game for two or three players with two sets of Chinese dominoes. Players win points for matching dominoes in their hand with dominoes lying face up in the center of the table.

Pairs The 4:2 and 2:1 (the supreme pair) count as one pair. Other pairs are formed whenever two dominoes have the same total number of spots (regardless of whether they are civil or military dominoes).

Start of play At the start of a hand the dominoes are thoroughly mixed and placed face down in a woodpile four dominoes high. Four stacks (16 dominoes) are then taken from one end of the woodpile and placed face up on the table.

Each player then draws his own dominoes. If there are three players, each draws two stacks (eight dominoes); if there are only two players, each draws three stacks (12 dominoes).

Turns In his turn, each player first attempts to match a domino in his hand with a domino exposed on the table. If he succeeds, he places the pair face up in front of him.

Whether he finds a pair or not, he then draws the top domino from the end of the woodpile where the players first drew their hands. If the drawn domino matches a domino exposed in the center of the table, he takes the pair and places it face up in front of him. If it doesn't match, he adds the drawn domino to the dominoes exposed in the center of the table.

Scoring When the woodpile is empty, players score points as follows:

a) the total score for dominoes with less than eight spots (small fish) is obtained by counting one point for each red spot and then rounding up the total to 10 or a multiple of 10.

b) dominoes with eight or more spots (big fish) score two points for every spot – red or white.

The player with the highest score then receives from each opponent the number of points by which their scores differ.

Pairs

Supreme pair

Examples of other pairs

143

TIEN KOW

Tien kow is a game for four players with one set of Chinese dominoes. The object of the game is to score points by winning tricks made up of single dominoes or pairs.

Start of play The dominoes are thoroughly mixed and stacked in a woodpile. The first banker (selected by dice) then deals each player eight dominoes from the woodpile.

Turns The banker plays the first domino for the first trick and the other players follow in turn. After the first trick, the lead goes to the winner of the preceding trick.

At his lead, a player may play either one domino or one or two pairs.

If he leads one domino, the other players must follow with one domino from the same series (discarding if they have no domino from that series).

If he leads one or two pairs, the other players must do likewise.

Taking tricks If one domino is led, the trick goes to the player who plays the heaviest domino from the correct series.

If one pair is led, the trick is taken by the highest ranking pair.

If two pairs are led, the trick goes to the player who plays the highest pair of all – regardless of what pair is played with it.

Ranking of pairs is as follows:

1) the 4:2 and 2:1 (supreme);
2) double 6s (heaven);
3) double 1s (earth);
4) double 4s (man);
5) pair of 3:1s;
6) double 5s;
7) double 3s;
8) double 2s;
9) pair of 6:5s;
10) pair of 6:4s;
11) pair of 6:1s;
12) pair of 5:1s;
13) 6:3 and 5:4 (mixed 9s);
14) 6:2 and 5:3 (mixed 8s);
15) 5:2 and 4:3 (mixed 7s);
16) 4:1 and 3:2 (mixed 5s);
17) double 6 and either of the mixed 9s;
18) double 1 and a mixed 8;
19) double 4 and a mixed 7;
20) 3:1 and a mixed 5.

Scoring Players settle their scores after each hand. Scoring is as follows:

a) a player with no tricks pays four points to the winner of the last trick (except when the banker for one hand wins the last trick and retains the bank – in which case he pays eight points the first time, 12 points the second, 16 the third, and so on until the bank changes);

b) a player with one, two, or three tricks deducts his number of tricks from four and pays the difference to the winner of the last trick;

c) a player with more than four tricks deducts four from his total and claims the difference from the winner of the last trick;

d) if the banker leads the supreme pair, he claims four points from each player;

e) if a player leads the supreme pair, he claims four points from the banker and two points from each other player;

f) the banker claims eight points from each player if he leads two of the following pairs: the double 6 and a mixed 9; the double 1 and a mixed 8; the double 4 and a mixed 7; the 3:1 and a mixed 5;

g) a player claims eight points from the banker and four points from each other player if he makes the leads given under (f).

Ranking of pairs

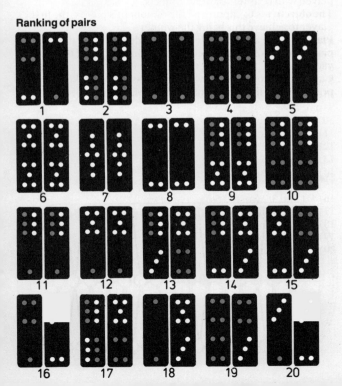

145

Fighting serpents

Fighting serpents is a board game of North American Indian origin. Although similar in some ways to Fox and geese (p. 154), Fighting serpents is a contest between two forces of equal strength. The player who succeeds in capturing all his opponent's pieces is the winner.

The board has a playing area of three parallel lines, intersected by short lines forming a diamond pattern as shown.
The length of the playing area may vary (the one illustrated here with 49 intersections is of average size) and the ends may be either rounded or straight.
Pieces are placed on all the intersections except three along the middle parallel: the two outermost intersections and the one at the center. Each player has pieces of a different color, positioned at the start of the game as shown. Traditionally, small black and white stones are used, but the game can also be played with counters or other objects.
The objective is to capture all the opponent's pieces, the first player to achieve this being the winner.
Play After the starting order has been determined, the first player moves one of his pieces along a line to any of the three vacant points. Thereafter, turns alternate between players. Capturing is compulsory whenever possible and takes precedence if there is a choice of moves.

Start of play

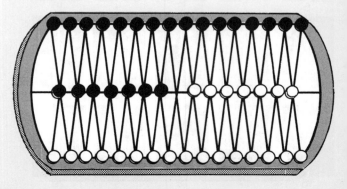

A piece is captured by jumping over it to an empty point beyond (**a**). A taking move is not permitted if it entails a change of direction.

Double or multiple captures in one move are permitted; direction may be changed after each enemy piece has been jumped (**b**).

Whenever a piece is captured it is removed from the board.

In a non-taking move, players may move one of their pieces one intersection along a line in any direction (**c**).

The game ends as soon as one player has lost all his pieces.

Moving

a   b   c

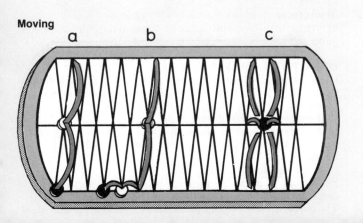

©DIAGRAM

Fivestones

Fivestones, like Jacks (p. 178), is derived from Knucklebones, an ancient form of Dice played with sheep's knucklebones. Today, Fivestones is played in many countries. Players crouch to throw small objects in the air and catch them in various ways in a usually increasingly difficult series of throws.

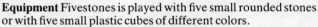

Equipment Fivestones is played with five small rounded stones or with five small plastic cubes of different colors.

The objective is to complete a series of throws in an agreed sequence.

Players The game can be enjoyed by a player on his own – or two or more players may attempt to be first to complete an agreed sequence of throws.

Turns If there are two or more players, the usual practice is to play in turn. First turn may be decided by a preliminary throw, by the toss of a coin, or by agreement.

A player's turn ends when he fails to accomplish any part of a particular throw, and his next turn begins with another attempt at the failed throw.

Throws There are many hundreds of variations of the game, but those given here are among the most widely known.

BASIC THROW

For the basic Fivestones throw, sometimes called the "jockey," the player must:

a) put the five stones in the open palm of one hand;

b) toss the stones up in the air;

c) while the stones are in the air, turn his hand over and catch the stones on the back of his hand;

d) toss the stones from the back of his hand;

e) turn his hand over and catch the stones in the palm of his hand.

ONES, TWOS, THREES, FOURS

Ones The player attempts the basic throw. If he catches all the stones, he goes on to twos. If he fails to catch any stones his turn ends.

If he catches one or more stones, he must:

leave any stones on the ground where they lie;

transfer to his other hand all but one of he stones he has caught;

throw the single stone in the air;

pick up one stone from the ground with his throwing hand;

catch the thrown stone with the same hand.

The player must repeat the procedure for picking up individual stones until all have been retrieved.

Twos The player scatters the stones on the ground, taking care that they do not land too far apart.

He then selects one stone, throws it up in the air, and must pick up two other stones from the ground with his throwing hand before catching the thrown stone with that same hand.

When he has done this, he transfers the two stones to his other hand, tosses up the third stone, and must pick up the remaining two stones from the ground.

Threes is like twos, except that the player must pick up one stone followed by three, or three stones followed by one.

Fours In fours, all four stones are picked up at one time.

Basic throw

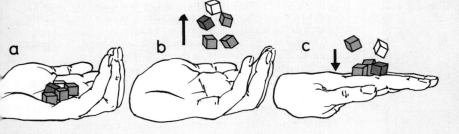

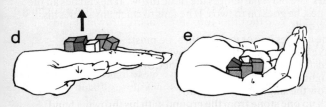

PECKS, BUSHELS, CLAWS

Pecks The player attempts the basic throw. If he succeeds in catching all five stones, he goes on to Bushels. If he fails to catch any stones his turn ends.

If he catches one or more stones, he must:

keep the caught stones in his throwing hand;

push one stone out between his forefinger and thumb and then:

toss the pushed out stone into the air (**1**);

pick up one stone from the ground with his throwing hand (**2**);

catch the thrown stone with his throwing hand (**3**);

repeat this procedure until all stones are picked up.

Bushels The player attempts the basic throw. If he is successful, he goes on to Claws. If he fails to catch any stones his turn ends.

If he catches one or more stones, he must:

throw all the caught stones in the air;

pick up one stone from the ground with his throwing hand;

catch the thrown stones;

repeat this until all stones on the ground are picked up.

Claws The fivestones are tossed from the palm onto the back of the hand – as in the basic throw. If all five are caught, the player attempts to complete the basic throw and if successful may go on to the next throw in the sequence. If none is caught on the back of the hand, the player's turn ends.

If one or more are caught on the back of the hand, the player:

leaves the caught stones on the back of his hand;

picks up the stones on the ground between the outstretched fingers of his throwing hand, with only one stone between any two fingers or between finger and thumb;

tosses the stones from the back of his hand and catches them in his palm;

maneuvers the stones from between his fingers into his palm.

OVER THE LINE

The non-throwing hand is placed with the palm on the ground, and four stones are scattered on the ground to its outer side. The player then throws the fifth stone in the air, and before catching it must transfer one of the other stones to the other side of his non-throwing hand.

This is repeated until all four stones on the ground have been transferred. (It is advisable to place the transferred stones as close together as possible.)

The player then throws up the fifth stone and before catching it must pick up the other four stones in his throwing hand.

OVER THE JUMP

This variation is similar to Over the line, except that the non-throwing hand is placed on edge to make a jump or wall – so making the transference of stones more difficult.

THREADING THE NEEDLE
This also resembles Over the line, but the stones have to be dropped one at a time through a circle formed by the thumb and forefinger of the non-throwing hand held about 8in above the ground.

UNDER THE ARCH
Ones under the arch The player first scatters the stones on the ground and makes an arch near them with the thumb and forefinger of his non-throwing hand.

He then selects one stone and throws it up in the air (**a**). While the stone is in the air, he knocks the other stones through the arch (**b**), and then catches the thrown stone (**c**).

When all four stones have been knocked through the arch, the player throws the fifth stone in the air and before catching it must pick up the other four stones.

Twos under the arch is similar to ones under the arch, except that the stones must be knocked through the arch in two pairs.

Threes under the arch is similar except that the stones are knocked through as a three and a one or a one and a three.

Fours under the arch requires all four stones to be knocked through together.

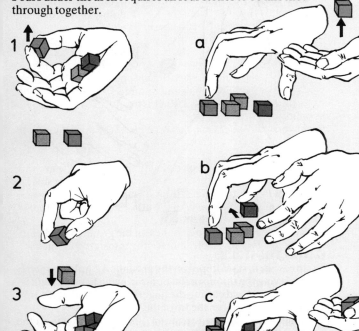

Pecks

Under the arch

151

©DIAGRAM

HORSE IN THE STABLE

The stones are scattered on the ground and the non-throwing hand is placed near them, with the fingers and thumb spread out, the fingertips touching the ground, and the palm raised. The gaps between the fingers and thumb are the "stables." One stone is then thrown into the air (**a**), and before catching it the player must knock a stone into or toward one of the stables (**b**). No more than one stone may be knocked into any one stable.

The player continues throwing, knocking, and catching in this way until all four stables are filled. He then moves his non-throwing hand away from the four stones, tosses the throwing stone and before catching it must pick up the four stones from the ground.

Horse in the stable

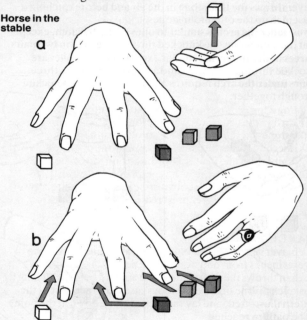

TOAD IN THE HOLE

The stones are first scattered on the ground. A "hole" is then made by laying the thumb of the non-throwing hand straight along the ground and curling the fingers around so that the tip of the forefinger touches the tip of the thumb.

One stone is then thrown into the air, and before catching it the player must pick up one of the other stones, a "toad," and drop it into the hole.

This is repeated until four toads are in the hole. The player then moves his non-throwing hand, tosses up the single stone and before catching it must pick up all four toads.

BACKWARD ONES, TWOS, THREES, FOURS

Backward ones After first scattering four stones on the ground, the player throws the fifth stone in the air and catches it on the back of his throwing hand.

He then tosses the fifth stone into the air from the back of his hand and before catching it in the normal way must pick up one stone from the ground.

The player then throws the two held stones in the same manner and picks up a third stone. The three held stones are used for the next throw, and four stones for the throw to pick up the fifth stone.

Backward twos is similar to Backward ones, except that the player must pick up two stones at his first throw and then the remaining two.

Backward threes is similar except that three and then one or one and then three stones must be picked up.

Backward fours requires the player to pick up all four stones at one time.

TOWERS

These variations can only be played with fivestones that are cubes.

Building a tower. The player first scatters four of his stones. He then throws the other stone and before catching it moves one of the stones on the ground away from the others.

At his second throw he places a second stone on top of the first, at his third throw he places a third stone on top of the other two, and at his fourth throw he completes the tower.

Demolishing a tower is the obvious sequel to Building a tower. At each throw, the player must remove a single stone from the tower.

SNAKE IN THE GRASS

The player sets out four stones in a straight line, with a gap of several inches from one stone to the next.

He then throws the fifth stone in the air, and before catching it, must pick up one of the end stones, use it to trace part of the pattern illustrated, and lay the picked stone down at the point of the pattern reached.

A player is allowed any number of throws to complete his tracing, but his turn ends if he drops the throwing stone, fails to touch the stone he is using for tracing, or touches any other stone.

Building a tower

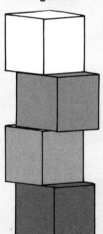

Snake in the grass

©DIAGRAM

Fox and geese

European Fox and geese games originated in Scandinavia in the Middle Ages. Similar games are played in many other parts of the world. In all of them, two unevenly matched forces compete against each other. The smaller force usually comprises one or two pieces and has considerable freedom of movement; the larger force is made up of numerous pieces but has only restricted maneuverability.

Pieces Any suitable pieces such as checkers, counters, or stones may be used (or marbles or pegs if played on a solitaire board). One of the pieces, representing the fox, must be distinguishable in color from the 15 (or sometimes 17) pieces representing the geese.

Board Fox and geese can be played on several different layouts. The layout in these illustrations probably gives the players the most even chance of winning.

Start of play The two players decide which of them is to play the fox and which the geese; they change over after each game. The pieces are put into position on the board – with the geese at

Start of play

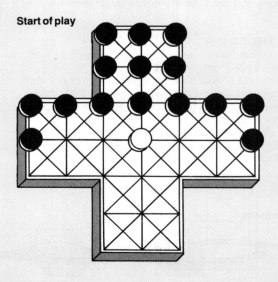

the top of the board (as shown) and the fox usually at the center (although it may be placed on any vacant point that the player chooses).

Moves Players take alternate turns, with the fox starting first.
The fox may move in any direction along connecting lines, moving one point at each turn (**a**).

It may also "kill" a goose by jumping over it to an adjacent vacant point; the goose is then removed from the board. The fox may make two or more jumps in one move (killing each goose that it jumps over), provided there is an empty point for it to land on next to each goose that it kills (**b**).

The fox is obliged to jump if there is no alternative move, even if it puts itself in a vulnerable position by doing so.

Geese may move along connecting lines in any direction except toward the top of the board (**c**). One goose moves one point in a turn. Geese may not jump over and capture the fox; their aim is to surround the fox so that it cannot move.

Result The fox wins if it:
a) kills so many geese that those remaining are not sufficient in number to trap it; or
b) manages to evade the geese so as to give it a clear path to the top of the board (where the geese cannot chase it).

The geese win if they can immobilize the fox by surrounding it or crowding it into a corner.

Moving

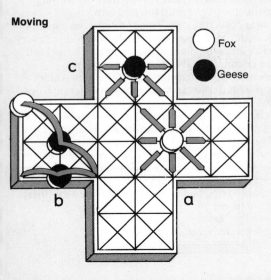

Fox

Geese

Game of goose

Reputedly invented in sixteenth-century Italy, the Game of goose was a favorite in Europe until the end of the nineteenth century. It was the forerunner of many race board games in which the participants' progress may be either hindered or advanced by landing on certain specially marked squares.

Boards of many different designs were used, but the main feature of all of them was a spiral route divided into 63 numbered spaces – starting at the outside and finishing at the center. The boards were often illustrated by, for example, scenes from history or mythology.

In addition, certain spaces on the route were marked with symbols and printed instructions – sometimes these instructions were shown at the center of the board. One of these symbols, appearing on about every fifth space, was a goose. By landing on a marked space, the player was instructed to either:

have another throw;

forfeit a turn;

advance a certain number of spaces; or

retreat a certain number of spaces.

Sometimes the instructions would be linked with the theme of the illustrations. For example, on a board with a military theme, the instruction might state that because of an injury received in battle, the player must forfeit a turn.

For contemporary play, the circuit may be drawn on paper or other suitable material. Geese should be drawn on about every fifth space, and other symbols or instructions may be marked at random on the circuit. (See also the section on play.)

Other equipment To mark his position on the circuit, each player needs a colored counter or other object different from his opponents'. One die is used.

The objective is to travel around the circuit as quickly as possible, the first player to land on the finish with an exact throw being the winner.

Play Throwing the die in turn, players move their counters the thrown number of spaces. If a player's counter lands on a goose space, the player may throw again. By landing on another of the specially marked spaces, the player is instructed to either:

miss one or more turns;

advance a prescribed number of spaces; or

move back a prescribed number of spaces.

End of play The finish can only be reached by an exact throw.
Thus a player throwing more than the number required to
reach the finish must go back the number of spaces by which he
has exceeded the finish. For example, if his counter is on 62 and
the player throws a 3, he must move his counter one space
forward to the finish, and then back two spaces to space 61.

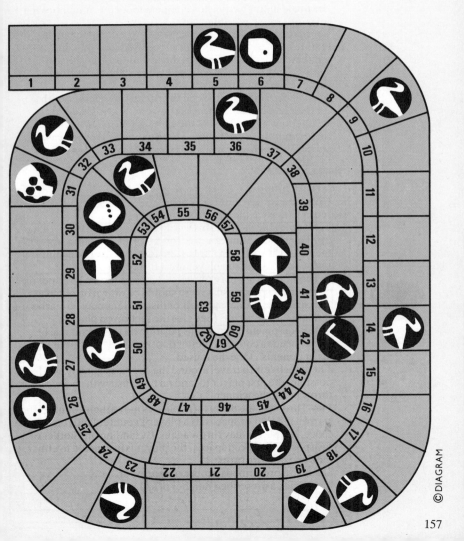

157

Go

Go is thought to be one of the oldest games in existence. It originated in China over 3000 years ago (its Chinese name is Wei-ch'i) and was later adopted by Japan and other oriental countries. It is considered one of the greatest games of strategic skill. Two players compete to secure as much of the playing area as possible.

Board and notation

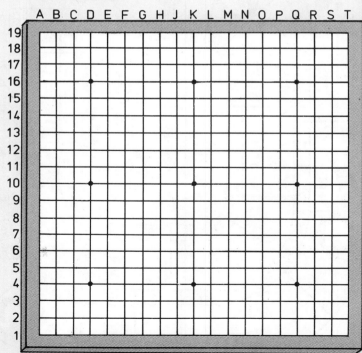

Board The traditional Japanese go table *(go-ban)* is made of wood and is stained yellow. It is about 17½in long, 16in wide, and 4–5in thick, and has four legs roughly 3in high.

The playing area (about 16½ by 15in) is marked out in black lacquer in a grid pattern of 19 parallel lines and 19 lines at right angles to these, forming a total of 361 intersections or points. The intersections of the fourth, tenth, and sixteenth lines in each direction are marked by dots and are known as handicap points.

The two players kneel opposite each other, at the shorter sides of the table.

Pieces There are two sets of stones: a set of 181 black stones and a set of 180 white stones (361 in all). Each player has one set.

The stones are disk shaped, about ⅞in in diameter, and ⅛–½in thick. The stones may be kept in a lacquered box *(go-tsubo)* or other container.

Stones

©DIAGRAM

159

Objective By the positioning of his stones on the board, each player aims to surround more unoccupied territory and enemy stones than his opponent.

Order of play Players take alternate turns. The opening move is usually made by the player with the black stones. (Players take it in turn to play black unless there is a known disparity of playing skill – see handicapping section, below.)

A turn consists of placing a stone on an unoccupied point. Except in the "*ko* situation" (see p. 161), a stone may be placed on any vacant point.

Once in position the stone is not moved again during the game unless it is captured, in which case it is removed from the board.

Playing procedure At the beginning of the game the board is empty except for any handicap stones.

Stones must be placed on the points (line intersections) and not on the squares formed by the lines.

Each player places his stones to form connected groups or chains in such a way as to surround as many vacant points and opponent's stones as possible.

Should all the points adjacent to one or more stones be occupied by stones of the other color, the former stone or group of stones is captured and removed from the board. (Adjacent points are those that are linked directly to a point by a line, and not diagonally.) It is possible to win a game without capturing any stones, since the objective is territorial gain.

Handicapping The player taking the first turn is at an advantage. Black (the opening turn) normally alternates between players. If there is a known disparity of playing skill or if one player wins three consecutive games, the weaker player may be allowed to keep the black stones.

If further handicapping is necessary, the weaker player may place two or more of his stones on the dotted handicap points before the game starts (see the table below), and the opening move then goes to the player with the white stones.

Should the stronger player continue to win, the number of handicap stones may be increased.

Table showing positions for handicap stones

Handicap	Positions
2 stones	D4, Q16
3 stones	D4, Q4, Q16
4 stones	D4, D16, Q4, Q16
5 stones	D4, D16, K10, Q4, Q16
6 stones	D4, D10, D16, Q4, Q10, Q16
7 stones	D4, D10, D16, K10, Q4, Q10, Q16
8 stones	D4, D10, D16, K4, K16, Q4, Q10, Q16
9 stones	D4, D10, D16, K4, K10, K16, Q4, Q10, Q16

Ko situations A *ko* (threat) situation is one that can be repeated indefinitely. In *ko* situations the second player may not recapture until he has made at least one move elsewhere on the board. (Forcing play at other parts of the board is therefore important.)

A single *ko* situation may involve many stones. If there are three *ko* situations on a board at any one time, the game is declared drawn.

Seki situations A *seki* (deadlock) situation exists on any part of the board where opposing groups are so placed that neither player can occupy an uncontrolled point without losing his own pieces. *Seki* situations are left untouched until the end of the game, and all free points in them are disregarded in scoring.

Dame points are vacant points between territories that cannot be played onto with benefit by either side. *Dame* points are left untouched until the end of the game, and then disregarded in scoring.

Prohibitions No move may be made that causes repetition of a position formed earlier in the game.

A stone must not remain on the board if it is entirely surrounded by enemy stones. A stone must not be played onto a point that is completely surrounded by stones of another color, unless the move causes the immediate capture of enemy stones.

©DIAGRAM

Explanation of diagrams

1) Capture of single stones.

2) Capture of groups of stones: a white stone played onto the dotted position would capture the black group attacked.

3a, 4a) Black cannot play onto the point marked with a cross, as the stone would be immediately captured (the arrowed point is vacant – white is not completely surrounded).

3b, 4b) Black can play onto the dotted point because the play puts the white stones out of contact with any empty point. The white stones are captured and removed. All black stones remain.

5a, 5b) A *ko* situation. In (**5a**) a black stone placed on the crossed point captures the white stone; in (**5b**) a white stone replaced on the captured point would recapture the black stone.

5c) A *seki* situation. Neither player can place his stone on the point marked with the cross without losing his formation.

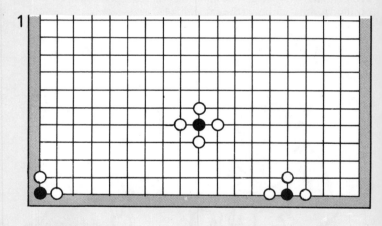

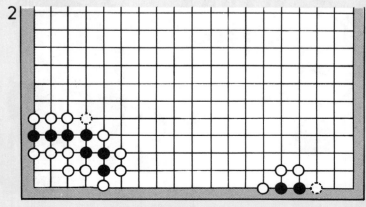

162

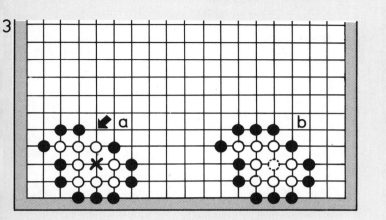

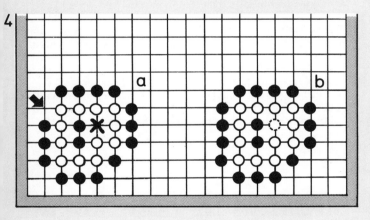

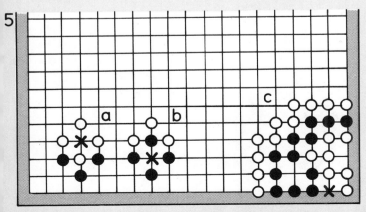

163

End of play The game ends when both players agree that there are no further advantages to be gained by either side.

If only one player considers the game to be over, his opponent may continue to make moves until he too is satisfied that no points or stones remain to be secured. (The first player may continue play, if he wishes, until both players agree that the game is over. But he may not resume play once he has actually missed a turn.)

Scoring An imaginary board, nine lines by nine lines, has been used to illustrate the basic scoring process. (It should be thought of as a simplified complete board, not as a section of a board.)

1) At the end of play all stones left in enemy territory are ruled captured.

2) These captured stones are removed from the board and added to each player's collection of captured enemy stones.

3) Any vacant points in neutral and *seki* situations have stones placed on them to discount them in the scoring. Either player may use his unused stones for this purpose.

4) In order to facilitate counting, black places all the white stones he has captured on vacant points in white's territory and white places all the captured black stones on vacant points in black's territory.

5) The number of vacant points left in each territory is counted.

Result The winner is the player with the larger number of vacant points left in his territory. He scores the difference between his own and his opponent's count. The game is tied if both players have an equal number of points.

Scoring

(Diagrams show
an imaginary
simplified board)

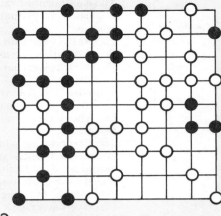

1

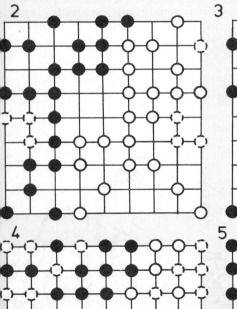

2

3

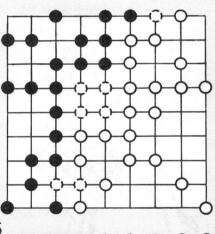

4

5

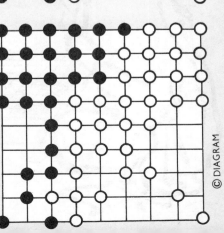

© DIAGRAM

GO-MOKU

This is a straightforward game played on a Go board. It originated in Japan and is sometimes called Go-bang or Spoil five.

Players It is a game for two players.

Board A Go board is used.

Pieces Each player has a set of 100 stones: one set black and the other white.

Objective Players aim to position five stones so that they form a straight line (horizontally, vertically, or diagonally).

Play The board is empty at the start of the game, and black has the opening move.

The players take it in turns to place a stone on any point (line intersection). Once a stone has been placed it may not be moved again until the end of the game.

If all the stones are used up before either player has succeeded in forming a "five," the game may either be declared drawn, or the players may take it in turns to move one stone one point in a horizontal or vertical direction until a "five" is formed.

HASAMI SHOGI

Hasami shogi is an interesting Japanese game that can be played on a Go board.

Players It is a game for two players.

The board is nine squares by nine. A quarter of a Go board may be used – but note that play is on the squares not the points.

Pieces Each player has a set of 18 stones: one uses black stones and the other white.

The objective is to capture all the opposing stones.

Start of play Each player places his stones on his two home rows.

Play Players take alternate turns. A player may move only one stone in a turn.

Moving All moves must be forward, backward, or to the side. No moves may be diagonal. A stone may:

a) move into an adjacent square;

b) jump over a stone, of either set, into a vacant square beyond it.

Jumped stones are not removed from the board. Double jumps are not permitted.

Capture A stone is captured if an opponent's move traps it between two opposing stones. A stone is not captured if it is flanked diagonally by opposing stones.

A stone is not captured if it moves into a vacant square between two enemy stones.

A stone is captured if an enemy move traps it in a corner of the board.

Hasami shogi
Start

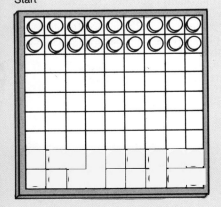

Moving

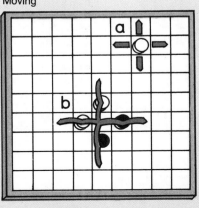

Halma

Halma, which takes its name from a Greek word for jump, was invented in England toward the end of the last century. It is a Checkers type of game for two, three, or four players. There are also Halma solitaire problems to provide an interesting diversion for one player.

Board Halma is played on a board with 256 small squares, 16 along each side.
Heavy lines mark off "yards" in the board's corners. Each corner has a yard with 13 squares, and two diagonally opposite corners have an additional heavy line marking off a yard with 19 squares.

Pieces There are four sets of pieces – each of a different color. Two sets have 19 pieces and the other two only 13.
The pieces may be:
a) small checkers or counters;
b) wooden or plastic cones;
c) wooden or plastic men resembling small chess pawns.

Forms of play The game may be played:
a) by two players;
b) by three or four players, each playing separately;
c) by four players, in partnerships of two.

Partnership halma can be played in two ways:
a) pairs are formed by players with pieces in adjacent yards;
b) pairs are formed by players with pieces in yards that are diagonally opposite.
(The second form provides more scope for partners to help each other.)

Objective Each player attempts to move his pieces from his own yard into the yard diagonally opposite. The game is won by the first player or pair to achieve this objective.

Start of play Starting positions vary with the forms of play:
a) when there are two players, each one takes a set of 19 pieces and positions them in the yards with 19 squares;
b) when there are three or four players, each one takes a set of 13 pieces and positions them in the yards with 13 squares.

Start: two players

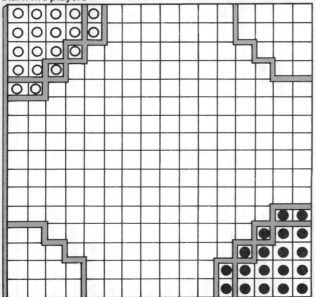

Start: three players

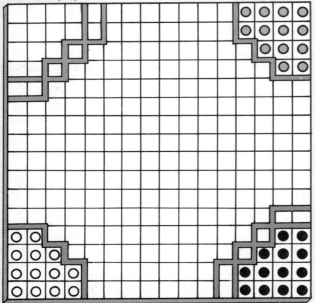

169

Moving

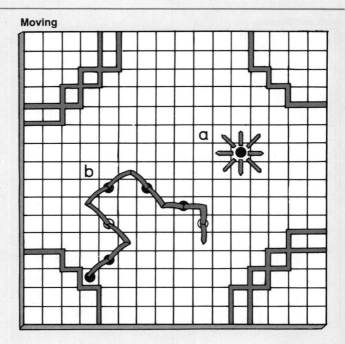

Turns pass clockwise around the table if there are more than
two players. A player may move only one piece in a turn.
Moving Pieces may be moved in any direction – straight or
diagonally, forward or backward, to one side or the other.
Two types of move are permitted:
a) a "step" – by which a player moves a piece into an adjoining
square;
b) a "hop" – by which a player moves a piece over a piece in an
adjoining square into a vacant square directly behind it.
A player may hop over his own or another player's pieces, and
all hopped pieces are left on the board.
A player may make several hops in one move, but may not
combine steps and hops in a move. There is no compulsion to
make any hop.

HALMA SOLITAIRE
An interesting halma solitaire problem requires the player to
place 19 pieces in one of the yards and then in 19 moves
position them in a symmetrical figure across the board's
diagonal.
This problem can be solved in several hundred ways, and the
interest therefore derives from the variety of solutions. A fairly
skillful player should be able to find 50 different solutions
without too much difficulty.

Halma solitaire: start

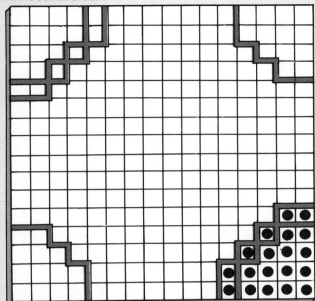

Halma solitaire: objective

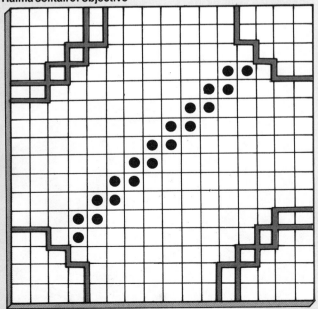

Hex

Hex is a game for two players invented by a Dane, Piet Hein. Hex sets are available in some places, but the game can also be played with improvised equipment. Each player tries to form an unbroken line of pieces between his two sides of the board.

The board has a diamond-shaped playing area made up of adjoining hexagons. Two opposite sides of the board belong to black; the other two to white.

The pieces are all identical in shape, and are in two sets of equal number, one colored black and one white. The highest number of pieces that a player can require for a game is 61; usually he will need far fewer.

Objective The game is won by the first player to place his pieces so that they form a line joining his two sides of the board. The line does not have to be straight, but it must be unbroken. Corner hexagons belong to both players, and either player may use them as hexagons touching his sides of the board.

Play Each player takes one set of pieces. The first player places one of his pieces on the board, on any hexagon he chooses.

Turns then alternate, with each player placing one of his pieces on any unoccupied hexagon.

Pieces may not be moved once they have been placed on the board.

Board

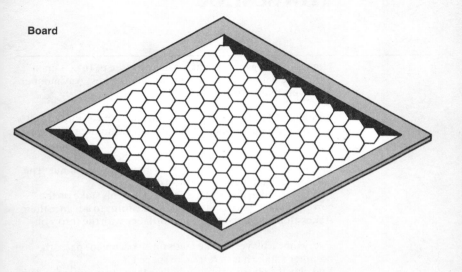

Winning position

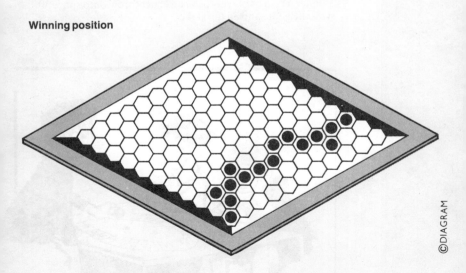

©DIAGRAM

173

Horseshoe

Horseshoe is a game very like Alleyway (see p. 16), its main difference being that it is played for small stakes. Any number of players may take part.

Equipment The layout is drawn onto paper or cardboard and is in the shape of a horseshoe, divided into 30 numbered spaces as shown.

Instead of using counters, players mark their progress along the horseshoe with a stake – such as a candy, coin, or nut. The only other equipment needed is a die.

Play Each player throws the die and places his stake on the corresponding space. Players then take turns to advance their stakes along the horseshoe in accordance with the throw of the die.

Every time a player's stake lands on an occupied space, the occupier's stake has to retreat to space 1.

End play If a player's throw is higher than the number needed for his stake to reach space 30, he must move his stake around the horseshoe past space 30 and on to space 1 or beyond. For example, if his stake is on space 28 and the player throws a 5, he must move his stake five spaces to space 3. He must then continue round the course from that space.

Winner The first player to get an exact throw onto space 30 wins the game and all the stakes.

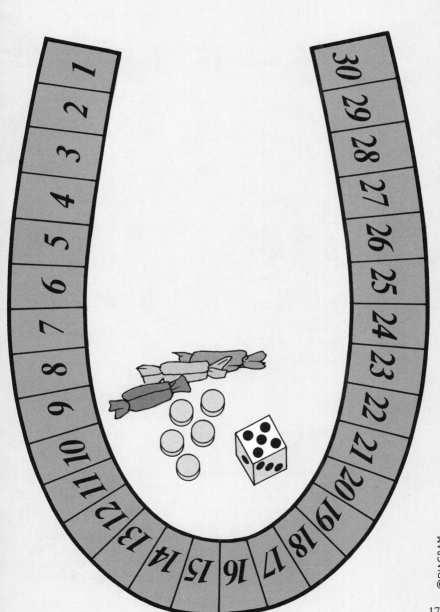

©DIAGRAM

Hyena chase

Hyena chase is a race game from North Africa that provides an amusing alternative to some of the better-known board games.

Board

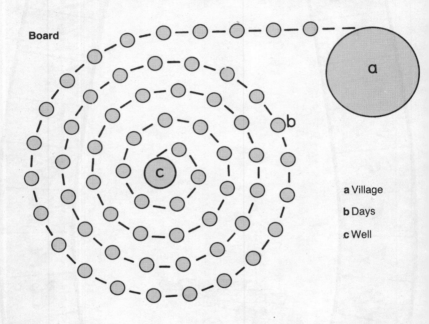

a Village
b Days
c Well

Board Traditionally, the playing area is marked out on the ground, but it may be drawn on paper or other suitable material.

A spiral circle is marked with a random number of small circles along its length, each circle representing a day's journey.

Two large circles are drawn:

one (the "village") next to the start of the spiral;

the other (the "well") at the center of the spiral.

Pieces Each player has one counter or other suitable object, different in color or shape from those of his opponents – this counter represents the player's "mother." One other counter is used to represent the hyena; this counter must also be easily distinguishable.

All the counters are placed in the "village" circle before the start of play.

Dice In the traditional game players use pieces of stick, but one ordinary die may be substituted.

Players Two or more can play this game.

Objective Each player tries to be the first to get his mother from the village to the well and back again – entitling him to let loose the hyena on the remaining mothers!

Play Moves are made by each player in turn in accordance with the throw of a die.

Players must throw a 6 to get their mothers from the village onto the first circle.

Whenever a player throws a 6, he is allowed another throw; if he throws two 6s in succession he is permitted a third throw.

It is permissible for the mothers of two or more players to occupy the same "day."

The well can only be reached by a direct throw. If, for example, a mother is three days' journey from the well, the player cannot move her if he throws more than a 3 – he must await his next turn.

Return journey Once at the well, the mother "washes her clothes" until the player throws a 6 – allowing her to start on her return journey to the village.

End play The first player to get his mother back to the village (he does not need a direct throw) wins the "hyena" counter. He must throw a 6 to get the hyena from the village onto the first circle; once there the hyena travels along the route to the well at twice the speed of the mothers – moving double the score on the die (ie if the player throws a 5, the hyena moves forward 10 days).

Once at the well (only reached by a direct throw) the player must again throw a 6 before the hyena can return to the village. Any mothers that the hyena passes on its way back to the village are "eaten" and removed from the board.

The winning player is, of course, the player who wins the hyena. But the satisfaction of winning is enhanced by the number of mothers that he can eat during the animal's rampage!

Pieces

Mothers

Hyena

Die

Jacks

Jacks, like Fivestones (p. 148), is a descendant of ancient games played with the knucklebones of sheep. It is a game for one or more players. On these pages we describe only the most basic version of Jacks; for greater variety it is possible to adapt most of the Fivestones games described on pp. 149–153.

Equipment Play is with:
a) Five to 12 small, usually six-legged, metal or plastic objects known as jacks;
b) a small rubber ball.

Objective The aim is to complete an agreed series of throws; only after succeeding with one throw may a player go onto the next throw in the series. If there are two or more players, the winner is the first player to complete the series.

Play In games for two or more, the players may decide to play simultaneously or to take turns.

Turns First turn may be decided by a preliminary throw, by the toss of a coin, or by mutual agreement.

A player's turn ends when he fails to accomplish any part of a particular throw. On his next turn he must begin with another attempt at the failed throw.

Basic game The player scatters the jacks on the ground. He throws the ball in the air, picks up one of the jacks with his throwing hand, and catches the ball with the same hand after it has bounced once on the ground. He transfers the jack he has picked up to his other hand. The player then repeats the procedure for picking up individual jacks until they have all been retrieved.

If the player successfully retrieves all the jacks singly, he scatters them again and picks them up in twos. If he successfully picks up all the jacks in twos, he goes on to retrieve them by threes, fours, etc., up to the maximum number of jacks available. Any jacks remaining after the correct groupings have been retrieved are themselves picked up as a group (eg when playing with 12 jacks and retrieving five at a time, the last two jacks are picked up together).

The player may use any throw to adjust the position of the jacks on the ground without losing his turn, providing that he uses his throwing hand to move the jacks, and catches the ball with the same hand after its first bounce.

Variations A player who successfully completes all the stages of the basic game goes on to more difficult variations. He begins each variation by retrieving the jacks singly, then continues through twos, three, etc., to the maximum number available. The many possible variations include:

retrieving the jacks as they fall, ie the player may not use any throw to adjust the position of the jacks on the ground;

throwing the ball in the air, picking up the appropriate number of jacks with the throwing hand, and catching the ball with the same hand before it has bounced on the ground;

throwing the ball against a wall, picking up the appropriate number of jacks with the throwing hand, and catching the ball with the same hand before (or after) it has bounced on the ground.

Jacks

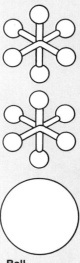

Ball

Lasca

This is an interesting game in the Checkers family. It is characterized by its unusual method of taking, and by the consequent building up of "columns" of pieces.

The board has 49 squares, seven along each side. The squares are alternately light and dark, and play is only on the light squares. (A standard checker board can be used if the squares along two sides are covered, leaving a light square at each corner.)

Pieces Each player has a set of 11 pieces; one set is usually white and the other black or red. Each piece is marked on one side – with a sticker, paint, pen, or pencil.

Objective The game is won when one player makes it impossible for his opponent to make any move.

Start of play Each player positions his pieces, with their unmarked sides face up, on the white squares in the three rows of the board nearest him.

Turns alternate; each player makes only one move in a turn.

Start of play

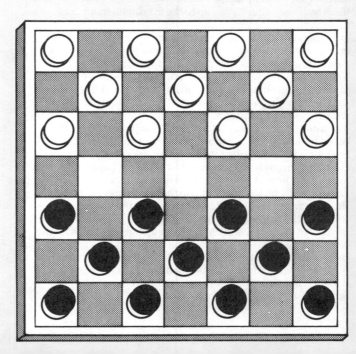

© DIAGRAM

181

Soldier

Officer

A "**soldier**" is a piece with the unmarked side face up. All pieces are soldiers at the start of play. A soldier moves diagonally forward like a man in British or American checkers. An "**officer**" is a piece with the marked side face up. A soldier becomes an officer after it has crossed to the farthest row of the board (like "crowning" in British or American checkers). A player's turn ends whenever a soldier becomes an officer. An officer moves diagonally backward or forward like a king in British or American checkers.

A "**column**" may be a single piece or a pile of pieces.

A "**guide**" is the top piece of a column. The color of the guide shows to which player that column belongs, and its rank (soldier or officer) determines how the column may be moved.

Taking In Lasca, unlike other Checkers games, a piece is not removed from the board when it is taken. Instead, it is added to the bottom of the column that takes it. If a column contains several pieces, only the guide is taken when another column jumps over it.

In the example illustrated:

1) the black column takes the white guide from the white column;

2) the black column (led by an officer) takes the other white piece and black's turn ends;

3) the other white column (led by a soldier) takes the black guide and white's turn ends (**4**).

If a taken guide was an officer it retains this rank in the other column.

As in British or American checkers a player must take a piece whenever possible, but if he has a choice of captures, he need not take the larger number of pieces.

Taking

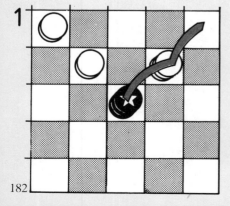

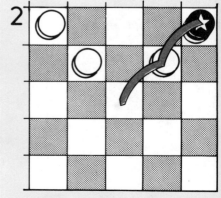

©DIAGRAM

Ludo

Ludo is a popular Western version of the ancient game of Pachisi (see p. 216). It is a game for two, three, or four players.

The board is a square-shaped piece of cardboard, marked out as shown.

The player's "home bases" and starting squares, the central columns of the cross leading to the finish, and the sections of the finish itself are all colored for easy identification – usually red, green, yellow, and blue.

When not traveling around the circuit, the counters are placed on a player's own "home base." There are no resting squares, but once a counter has reached its own colored column leading to the finish, it cannot be followed or taken.

Other equipment Each player has four plastic or cardboard counters – of one of the board's four colors. One die is used; it may be thrown from the hand or from a small plastic dice cup.

Objective Players race each other in trying to be the first to get all four of their counters to the finish.

Board

a Home bases
b Starting squares
c Finish

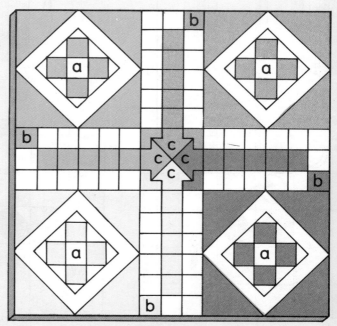

Play Each player chooses a set of counters.

The die is thrown to determine the order of play, the person throwing the highest number starting first.

Players take it in turns to throw the die for a 6 – the number needed to get a counter from its home base onto its starting square.

Whenever a player gets a 6 he is allowed another throw, moving one counter the number of squares indicated by the die.

Counters are moved around the circuit in a clockwise direction, as in Pachisi.

If a player has more than one counter on the circuit and he has a double throw (a 6 followed by another throw), he may move a different counter for each part of the throw.

Should a player throw two 6s in succession, he is allowed a third throw.

Taking If a counter lands on a square already occupied by an opponent's counter, the opponent's counter must be returned to its home base and can only re-enter the circuit on a throw of 6.

End play The finish can only be reached by a direct throw. For example, if a counter is four squares away from the finish and the player throws more than a 4, he must either await his next throw or move one of his other pieces.

The winner is the first player to get all four of his counters to the finish.

Other equipment

Mah jongg

Mah jongg is a tile game of Chinese origin that reached the West in the 1920s. Its name means "the sparrows." Each of four (or three) players plays for himself. Players collect sets of tiles with the object of completing their hands in a prescribed manner. Scores are settled after each hand, and the winner is the player with the most points when play ends.

The tiles Mah jongg tiles are made of bone, ivory, bamboo, wood, or plastic. Tile designs vary. Sets sold in the West usually have Arabic numerals in one corner of the suit tiles, and letters denoting the four winds.
A standard set has 144 tiles – 136 playing tiles and eight flower or season tiles.

Suit tiles

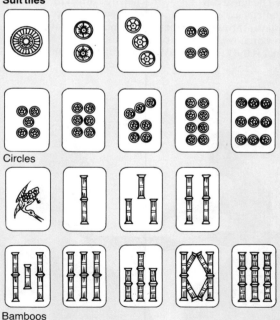

Circles

Bamboos

Suit tiles There are three different suits: circles (or dots), bamboos (or bams), and characters (or craks). Each suit comprises tiles numbered 1 through 9, and there are four of each type of tile. The 1 bamboo usually shows a symbolic bird. All other tiles have symbols for the suits.

Dragon tiles There are three different dragons: white, red, and green (left to right in the illustration). As with the suit tiles, there are four of each type of tile.

Wind tiles East, south, west, and north winds are represented. Again there are four of each type of tile.

Flower and season tiles These are eight individually marked tiles.

Racks Each player is provided with a rack to hold his tiles. The player who is east wind takes the differently colored rack.

Other equipment includes:
a) two dice;
b) scoring counters (small sticks) or a scoring pad;
c) optional wind indicators – either rotating indicators or separate disks.

Characters

Dragon tiles

Wind tiles

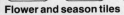

Flower and season tiles

Players Mah jongg is best played by four players, but can be played by three. Each player plays for himself.

Deciding the winds Each player is designated the name of a wind – east, south, west, and north.

Winds for the first hand are decided after the players are seated, when each player takes a turn to throw two dice. The player with the highest total throw becomes east. The other players' winds are determined by their position at the table relative to east: west sits opposite east, south sits to east's right, and north to east's left (not like a compass).

If the player who is east wind does not win the first hand, the winds pass counterclockwise around the table. Thus east becomes north, south becomes east, west becomes south, and north becomes west. If the player who is east wind wins a hand, the players retain the same winds for the next hand.

Duration A complete game consists of four rounds, but the game is in no way spoiled if players choose to stop earlier. Each round bears the name of a wind: the first is east, the second south, the third west, and the fourth north. As well as indicating the stage of the game, the "wind of the round" has an effect on scoring.

A round consists of however many hands are taken before the fourth player has lost a hand as east wind.

Building the wall All the tiles are placed face down on the table, and are thoroughly shuffled by the players.

Then, without looking at the tiles' faces, each player builds a wall that is 18 tiles long and two tiles high (with the long sides of the tiles touching and the faces down).

Each player then pushes his wall toward the center of the table until the four walls meet to form a hollow square representing a city wall.

Breaching the wall takes place once the wall is built. There are two stages.

1) East throws two dice to determine which side of the wall is to be breached. If he throws two 1s, he must throw again. Otherwise, he takes the total thrown and, starting with the length of his own wall as one, counts out the total counterclockwise around the table. The breach is to be made in the side of the wall where his count ends.

2) The player whose wall is to be breached now throws the two dice and adds his total to the total previously thrown by east. The new total is used to determine exactly where the breach will be made. The player counts clockwise along the top of his tiles, beginning at the right-hand corner. If the total is more than 18 he continues along the next wall. When the count ends, the player takes the two tiles from that stack and places them as shown. These moved tiles are called "loose tiles."

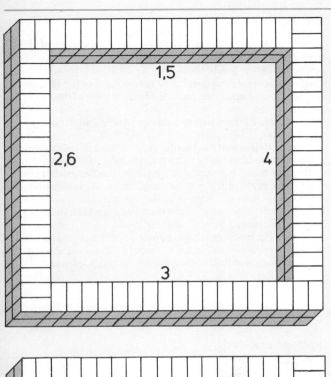

Stage 1 (6 thrown)

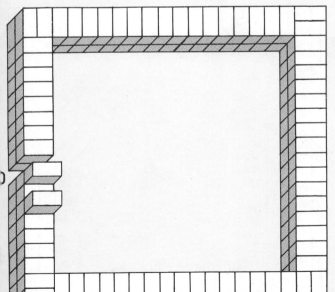

Stage 2 (4 thrown)

©DIAGRAM

189

Drawing the hands After the wall is breached east takes the two stacks (four tiles) from the opposite side of the breach to the loose tiles. South then takes the next two stacks, west the next two, and north the next two. The draw continues in this way until each player has 12 tiles.

East, south, west, and north then take one more tile in turn, and finally east takes one extra tile from the top of the next stack.

At the end of the initial draw east has 14 tiles and the other players have 13 tiles each.

Replacing flower and season tiles Any of these tiles drawn in the initial hand or later in the game must be placed face up in front of the player and replaced by a loose tile. Replacement at the start of the game must be in rotation, with east playing first.

For scoring purposes, each wind has its own season and flower. This is usually shown by numbers on Western Mah jongg sets – with east 1, south 2, west 3, and north 4.

Objective Each player aims to complete his hand and go "mah jongg" (sometimes called going "woo"). A complete hand usually consists of four *chows, pungs,* or *kongs*, plus an identical pair.

Drawing the hands

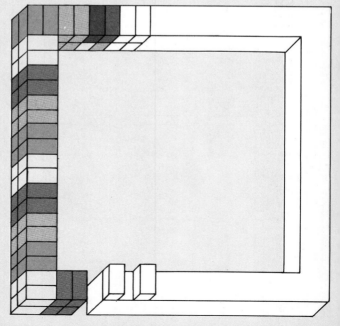

A *chow* is a run of three tiles of the same suit, eg 3, 4, 5 dots (**a**), or 7, 8, 9 craks. Mixed winds or mixed dragons do not count as *chows*.

A *pung* is a set of three identical tiles, eg three green dragons (**b**), three 8 bams, or three south winds.

A *kong* is a set of four identical tiles (**c**).

A pair may be any two identical tiles (**d**).

Special mah jongg hands that do not follow the conventional pattern are accepted by some players as alternative ways of going mah jongg. These special or "limit" hands normally score the maximum permitted for any one hand (see p. 199).

Most commonly accepted of these limit hands are:

1) hand of the thirteen odd majors (a 1 and a 9 of each suit, one of each dragon, one of each wind, and a pair to any of these tiles); and

2) calling nine tiles hand (tiles from the same suit – three 1s, three 9s, one each of tiles 2 through 8, and any one other tile of the same suit).

Parts of a hand

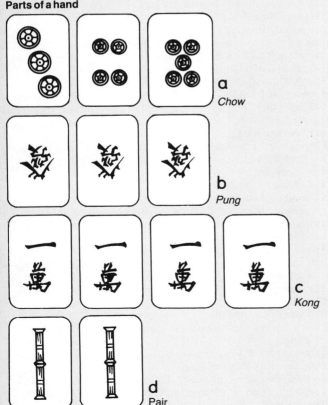

a Chow

b Pung

c Kong

d Pair

©DIAGRAM

Starting play East starts play by discarding any one of his 14 tiles.

Discarding tiles When a player discards a tile he must always call out its name, eg red dragon, east wind, 6 bams.

Discarded tiles are placed in the center of the table – usually face up in Western countries but face down in China and elsewhere in the East.

Playing order Play passes counterclockwise around the table except when a player interrupts the order to claim a discarded tile.

If more than one player claims a discarded tile, the order of precedence is:

1) a player claiming the tile to go mah jongg;
2) a player claiming the tile to make a *pung* or *kong*;
3) a player claiming the tile to make a *chow*.

If the playing order is interrupted for a claim, intervening players lose their right to any turn they may have missed. Thus if player 1 discards a tile and player 4 claims it, players 2 and 3 lose their turns and player 1 has the next turn unless player 4's discard is claimed by another player.

Playing a turn If no player claims the tile that was last discarded, the player to the right of the last player to discard now takes a tile from the wall. The new tile is taken from the end of the wall without the loose tiles. The player may conceal the tile's face from his opponents.

If he wishes to keep the new tile, he does so and discards another tile from his rack. Otherwise he discards the new tile.

Claiming tiles Only the tile that was last discarded may be claimed. It may be claimed to complete a *chow, pung,* or *kong,* or to go mah jongg.

Claims may be made even after the next player has taken a new tile from the wall – in which case the tile drawn from the wall must be replaced. Claims are not permitted if the next player has already made his discard.

Claiming a chow Only the player sitting to the right of the player who discarded is permitted to claim for a *chow*. The claiming player must already hold in his rack the other two tiles needed for the *chow*.

To claim the discard the player must call *"chow,"* pick up the tile, and then "expose" the complete *chow* by laying it face up in front of him.

The player then ends his turn by discarding a tile from his rack.

Claiming a pung Any player may claim the last discarded tile for a *pung* provided that:

a) he holds in his rack two tiles identical with the tile he is claiming;

b) he has played an intervening turn if he failed to *pung* that same tile on an earlier discard.

To claim the discard he must call *"pung,"* pick up the tile, and "expose" the *pung*. He then ends his turn by discarding a tile from his rack.

Concealed chows or pungs A player who has a *chow* or *pung* in his original hand, or who completes a *chow* or *pung* with a tile drawn from the wall, may keep these tiles "concealed" on his rack. This gives him greater maneuverability, conceals the state of his hand from his opponents, and doubles the value of a *pung*.

©DIAGRAM

Claiming a kong Any player may claim the last discarded tile for a *kong* if he holds in his rack three tiles identical with the tile he is claiming. To claim the discard he must call *"kong,"* pick up the tile, and "expose" the complete *kong*.

The player then draws a loose tile before discarding in the usual way. (A loose tile is always drawn after a *kong* because a complete hand has one extra tile for each *kong* it contains.)

Converting an exposed pung into a kong A player may convert an exposed *pung* into a *kong* if he draws the fourth similar piece from the wall. (This is the only time that an exposed set of tiles may be interfered with.)

Players are not permitted to claim discards to convert exposed *pungs* into *kongs*.

After a player has converted an exposed *pung* into a *kong*, he ends his turn by drawing a loose tile and then discarding in the usual way.

A concealed kong A kong is "concealed" if:
a) all four tiles are in a player's original hand; or
b) a player with a "concealed" *pung* in his hand draws the fourth similar tile from the wall.

A player with a concealed *kong* may lay it on the table at any time when it is his turn to play.

A concealed *kong* laid on the table is worth double points and is distinguished from an exposed *kong* by turning over the end two tiles. If another player goes mah jongg while a player has a concealed *kong* on his rack, he scores only for a concealed *pung*.

Only after a player has laid a concealed *kong* on the table may he draw the loose tile needed to bring his hand up to the number of tiles required to go mah jongg.

Drawing loose tiles Loose tiles are used to make a player's hand up to the correct number of tiles – after a flower or season tile has been drawn or after a *kong*.

The tile farthest from the breach is used first and then the other loose tile. After both loose tiles have been used they are replaced by the two tiles at that end of the wall – the top tile going farthest from the breach.

Wrong number of tiles A player with the wrong number of tiles in his hand (on his rack and laid out on the table) cannot go mah jongg.

Excluding extra tiles in *kongs,* each player should always have 14 tiles after drawing or 13 tiles after discarding. A player with the wrong number of tiles must draw and discard tiles normally until another player goes mah jongg.

If the player in error had too many tiles, he pays the other players their scores without deducting any score for his own hand. If he had too few tiles, he deducts the score for his own hand before making payment.

Wrong tile drawn If the wall is breached in the wrong place or if tiles are drawn in the wrong order, the tiles should be reshuffled and the wall rebuilt.

Incorrect combinations If a player exposes an incorrect combination of tiles as a *chow, pung,* or *kong,* he must rectify the error before the next player discards or his hand is declared "dead." A player with a dead hand must pay the other players their scores with no allowance for his own hand.

Last 14 tiles A hand is declared "dead" if no player goes mah jongg before play reaches the last 14 tiles in the wall (including the loose tiles). There is no scoring and a new hand is played with the same player as east wind.

Calling A player is "calling" (or "fishing") when he requires only one tile to complete his hand. If two players are calling and both claim the same tile, precedence goes to the player whose turn would have come first.

A standing hand East wind may declare a "standing hand" if he is calling after making his first discard. Any player may declare a standing hand if he is calling after drawing and discarding for the first time in a hand.

A player who has declared a standing hand must not change any of the 13 tiles then in his hand. At each turn, he draws a tile from the wall in the usual way and then discards it if it is not the tile required to go mah jongg.

A player who completes a standing hand receives a bonus of 100 points.

Snatching a kong A player who is calling may complete his hand by "snatching a *kong*" – ie claiming a tile drawn from the wall by another player who uses it to convert an exposed *pung* into a *kong*.

Going mah jongg As soon as a player completes his hand, he stops play by calling "mah jongg." All players then expose their hands for scoring, turning over the middle tile of any *pungs* that were concealed in their hands.

Incorrect mah jongg If a player who has called "mah jongg" completely exposes his hand and then finds he has made an error, he must pay double the points limit to each of the other players. If his hand is only partially exposed when the error is discovered, he may cancel his call and put the tiles back on his rack.

Settling the scores After calculating the value of their individual hands, the players settle with each other in the following way.

If east wind goes mah jongg, he receives double the total value of his score from each of the other players.

If another player goes mah jongg, he receives double the value of his score from east wind, and the value of his score from each of the other players.

Each loser also settles with each of the other losers. When two losers settle (except when one of them is east wind), the player with the lower score pays the difference between his score and the other player's score.

When east wind is a loser, he pays or receives double the difference when settling with another loser.

Scoring Point values vary in different scoring systems, but the system given here shows the typical characteristics. With the exception of certain limit hands (described on p.199), the points value of each player's hand is calculated from the tables.

Using table A: points are scored by all players for *pungs* and *kongs* and for each flower and season tile (no points are scored for *chows*);

the player going mah jongg also scores for some pairs.

Using table B: the player going mah jongg adds any bonus points.

Using table C: players double their points as indicated, and again there are additional doubles for the player going mah jongg.

Table A   Tile values

All players	Exposed	Concealed
Any *chow*	0	0
Pung of tiles 2 through 8 of any suit	2	4
Pung of 1 or 9 of any suit	4	8
Pung of winds or dragons	4	8
Kong of tiles 2 through 8 of any suit	8	16
Kong of 1 or 9 of any suit	16	32
Kong of winds or dragons	16	32
Any season or flower	4	
Player going mah jongg		
Pair of any dragon	2	
Pair of player's own wind	2	
Pair of wind of the round	2	

Table B   Bonus scores

Player going mah jongg	
For going mah jongg	20
Winning tile drawn from the wall	2
Winning with only possible tile (ie with all other similar tiles exposed)	2
Winning with the last piece from the wall	10
Winning with a loose tile	10
For having no *chows*	10
For having no scoring value except flowers or seasons	10
Completing a standing hand	100

Table C   Doubling

	Number of times doubled
All players	
Pung or *kong* of any dragon	1
Pung or *kong* of player's own wind	1
Pung or *kong* of the wind of the round	1
Player's own season or flower	1
Four seasons or four flowers	3
Player going mah jongg	
Hand with no *chows*	1
Hand with no scoring tiles except flowers and seasons	1
Hand all one suit except for winds and/or dragons	1
Hand all 1s and 9s except for winds and/or dragons	1
Snatching a *kong* to go mah jongg	1
Hand all one suit	3
Hand all winds and dragons	3
Original hand (east wind's 14 tiles when play begins)	3

©DIAGRAM

197

Limit hands Most scoring systems have specified "limit hands," designed to prevent the scoring of an excessive number of points with a single hand.

Limit hands score a fixed number of points – usually 500 – regardless of their actual face value. East wind pays or receives double the limit.

Most limit hands may be obtained only by the player going mah jongg. Typical examples are:

a) hand of all winds and dragons;
b) hand of all 1s and 9s;
c) hand of concealed *pungs* and *kongs*;
d) hand of the thirteen odd majors ;
e) calling nine tiles hand;
f) an original hand (east wind's hand when play begins);
g) hand completed with east's first discard;
h) east wind's thirteenth consecutive mah jongg.

Other hands score the limit whether or not completed. If the player with these hands fails to go mah jongg, he scores the limit from the other losers. Examples are:

i) hand with *pungs* or *kongs* of at least three dragons;
j) hand with *pungs* or *kongs* of three winds and a pair of the other wind.

Hand of all winds and dragons

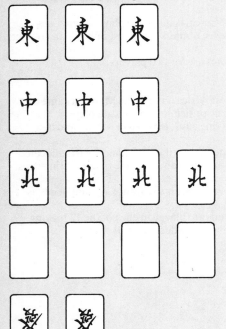

Mancala games

Mancala is the generic name for a group of ancient African and Asian games, in which seeds are moved from cup to cup around a board in an attempt to capture opposing seeds. Names, boards, and rules differ from region to region but the basic principles of play are generally the same. Traditionally played by primitive tribesmen, the strategy of these games is highly complex and demands a fine mathematical calculation of possible moves and their results.

Mancala boards Mancala games are sometimes played in hollows scooped in the ground. They may equally well be played on a layout drawn on paper.
Traditionally, however, play is on a carved wooden board. The finest boards are like pieces of sculpture, intricately carved with patterns of symbolic significance.
Boards can be divided into two basic types according to the number and pattern of their cups. Commonest are two-rank boards. Four-rank boards are largely confined to parts of Southern and East Africa.
Seeds Traditionally Mancala games are played with seeds, beans, or small stones. Counters, marbles, or any small objects may be substituted.
Players Mancala games are for two players.

OWARI
Owari, played in West Africa, is a typical Mancala game and demonstrates the basic principles of Mancala play.
The board has 12 playing cups, in two rows of six, and two scoring cups.
Players face each other across the board and each is allocated the row of cups nearer to him and also one of the scoring cups.
Seeds 48 seeds are required.
Objective Each player attempts to capture as many seeds as possible.
Start of play Four seeds are placed in each of the 12 playing cups. Order of play is usually decided by lot.

Start of play

Sowing seeds

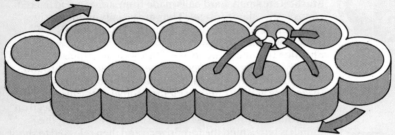

Play Turns alternate. In his turn each player takes all the seeds from a cup on his side of the board and "sows" them one by one in the cups around the board in a clockwise direction – thus if there are four seeds in his cup he sows one of them in each of the next four playing cups.

If there are 12 or more seeds in a cup, then the movement of the seeds from that cup will be more than one circuit of the board. In this case the emptied cup is missed out when sowing. If all his opponent's cups are empty a player must, if possible, move a seed into his opponent's half of the board.

Capturing A player makes a capture if he sows a seed into one of his opponent's cups so that this cup then contains two or three seeds. This entitles the sower to take all the seeds from this cup and to place them in his scoring cup.

After making any capture, a player is also entitled to capture the seeds in adjacent cups containing two or three seeds.

A player is not, however, allowed to capture all the seeds in his opponent's cups (as this would prevent his opponent moving in his next turn). Instead he must leave intact any one cup that he chooses.

End of game Play ends when a player is unable to make a move or when none of the seeds remaining on the board can be captured.

Result The game is won by the player who captures most seeds.

Marbles

Games with marbles have been popular for thousands of years and are played in countries all over the world. The names and rules of marbles games vary tremendously from place to place, but the basic objective of any marbles game is to test how accurately a player can aim his marbles.

Marbles are small, hard balls made from stone, wood, baked clay, plastic, glass, or steel. They are usually about ½in in diameter. A marble actually being used by a player is sometimes called a "taw."

Shooting In some games players throw or drop their marbles. Usually, however, marbles must be rolled along the ground. Maximum accuracy and distance can be obtained by shooting the marble as illustrated – a method sometimes called "knuckling down." The knuckle of the forefinger is placed on the ground, the marble is balanced on the forefinger, the thumb is put behind the forefinger – and then released to shoot the marble.

Claiming marbles is a feature of many marbles games. In some games a player may keep an opponent's marble if his own marble hits it.

Other games are played for points – with the difference in players' scores at the end of the game being settled by the payment of an agreed number of marbles for an agreed number of points.

Shooting

CAPTURE

This is a simple marbles game for two players. Player A shoots his marble and then player B attempts to hit it with his marble. If player B hits A's marble, he may keep it.

If player B's marble misses A's marble, B's marble stays where it is and A attempts to hit it with a shot from where his marble lay after his first shot. If A hits B's marble he keeps it, otherwise turns alternate until one player takes the other's marble.

Spanning

SPANNERS

Spanners, or Hit and span, is a variation of Capture. As in Capture, a player who hits his opponent's marble may keep it. But in this game, a player may choose to attempt a "span" if his marble is near enough to his opponent's. He does so by placing his thumb on his own marble and a finger on his opponent's marble, and then flicking them together.

In one version of the game a successful span entitles him to take his opponent's marble as if he had hit it with his shot, but an unsuccessful span means that he loses his own marble.

In another version a player gains one point for a successful span – after which both players pick up their marbles and the player who did not win the point shoots first in the next play. (An unsuccessful span is ignored in this version.)

WALL MARBLES

In this variation of Capture several players shoot or throw their marbles against a wall. The first player sends a marble against the wall and leaves it where it stops.

Each of the other players then follows in turn, and:
a) leaves his marble where it stops if it fails to hit another marble as it rebounds from the wall; or
b) claims all the marbles on the ground if his rebounding marble hits any other.

If no player has hit another marble when all the players have had a turn, play continues in the same way but with each player delivering his marble from where it stopped in the first round.

RING TAW

Ring taw is a game for any small number of players.

Two circles are drawn on the ground – an inner circle about 1 ft in diameter and an outer circle about 7 ft in diameter. At the start of the game each player puts one or two marbles in the inner circle.

Each player then shoots in turn from any point outside the outer circle.

If a player knocks one or more marbles from the inner circle, he wins them and is entitled to another shot. This shot is taken from where his "taw" (the marble he last shot with) came to rest.

If a player fails to knock any marble from the inner circle, his turn ends and he must leave his taw where it stopped.

Succeeding players may shoot at any marble within either of the circles – taws as well as the marbles originally placed in the inner circle.

Whenever a taw is hit its owner must pay one marble to the player who hit it.

After his first turn, each player shoots his taw from where it came to rest at the end of his previous turn.

The game ends when all marbles have been cleared from the inner circle.

INCREASE POUND

In this variation of Ring taw the inner circle is known as the "pound" and the outer ring as the "bar." Play is exactly the same as for Ring taw except that:

a) there is no extra shot for hitting a marble out of the pound;

b) a player whose taw stops in the pound must lift his taw and pay a marble into the pound;

c) a player whose taw is struck by the taw of another player must pay that player one marble plus all the marbles that he has won up to this stage of the game.

FORTIFICATIONS

This is another variation of Ring taw, for which players draw four circles one inside the other.

At the start of the game each player places three marbles in the innermost circle or "fort" (**a**); two marbles in the next ring out (**b**); and one in the next (**c**). The outer ring (**d**) is left empty.

Each player plays in turn. With his first shot, made from any point outside the outer circle, each player attempts to knock a target marble from ring (**c**). If he succeeds, he keeps the target marble and leaves his taw in the target marble's place. If he fails, he pays one marble into ring (**c**) and leaves the game.

If a player's taw hits an opponent's taw at any stage of the game, the opponent's taw remains in its new position until its owner uses it for his next turn. When requested, a taw may be temporarily lifted to allow a clear shot at a target marble.

For all turns after the first, each player still in the game plays his taw from where it lies or from any point on the outside circle. As in his first turn, he claims any target marble that he hits and, unless he is entitled to an extra shot, leaves his taw in the target marble's place.

As long as any target marbles remain in ring (c), players must attack that ring and are allowed only one shot in a turn. A miss at this stage of the game, however, does not compel players to drop out.

Once ring (c) is cleared of target marbles, players must attack ring (b). Play then proceeds exactly as for ring (c), except that a player who hits one target marble in ring (b) is allowed a second shot.

Once ring (b) is cleared of target marbles, players may attack ring (a). This time the only difference in procedure is that a player is entitled to a third shot if his first two shots both claim a target marble.

Ring taw

Start (three players)

Fortifications

Start (three players)

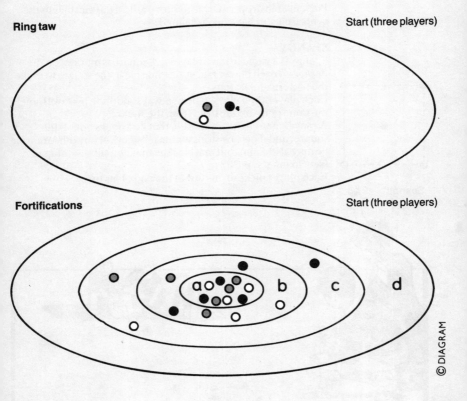

© DIAGRAM

205

DIE SHOT

In Die shot, or Die marble, players shoot their marbles at a target comprising a die balanced on a marble that has been filed down to make it more stable.

Each player becomes "die-keeper" for one round, while the other players make one shot in each turn. Before making a shot, each player must pay the die-keeper one marble.

If a player knocks the die off the marble, the die-keeper must pay him the number of marbles shown on the uppermost face of the die.

BOUNCE EYE

In this game for two or more players, each player places one or more marbles in a central cluster in a circle about 1 ft in diameter.

The first player then stands over the ring and drops a marble onto the cluster. He may claim any marbles that roll out of the circle, but if no marbles roll out of the circle he must add one marble to the cluster.

Players then drop a marble in turn until all the marbles in the central cluster have been claimed.

SPANGY

Spangy is a game for five players. A square is marked on the floor, and each player places one marble in the square to make the pattern illustrated.

Each player then plays in turn, always shooting his taw from the same point about 10 yd from the square.

A player may claim any marble that he knocks out of the square, and if his taw stops within a "span" of any other marble he may also claim that marble if he makes a successful span (see Spanners, p.203).

Each player picks up his taw at the end of his turn.

Spangy

HUNDREDS

This game for two players is usually played outdoors but can easily be adapted to indoor play. Outdoors, players shoot marbles into a shallow hole; indoors, a drawn circle can be used.

At the start of the game each player shoots one marble toward the ring. If both players' marbles stop in the ring, both players shoot again.

When only one player's marble stops in the ring, he scores 10 points and then continues shooting and scoring until he misses or scores 100 points. If he misses, his opponent shoots and scores until he misses.

The game is won by the first player to reach 100 points.

THREE HOLES

This game can also be played indoors with drawn rings instead of holes. Three rings, about 3in in diameter and 5 ft apart, are marked on the floor.

The game is won by the player who "kills" (puts out) all his opponents or is first to shoot a marble into each ring in the correct order.

Each player plays in turn, and gains an extra shot if his marble stops in the correct ring or hits another player's marble. At the end of his turn a player must leave his marble where it lies. Only after a player has scored the first ring can he "kill" another player by hitting his marble; he is, however, permitted to hit and move an opponent's marble before this stage.

When a player is "killed" he must pay his hitter the marble that was hit plus any marbles won in the game.

Hundreds

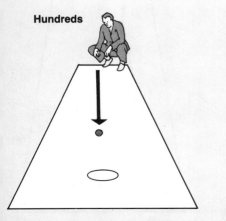

Three holes

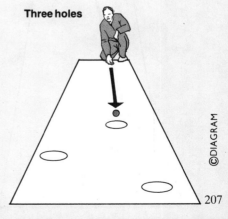

©DIAGRAM

ARCHBOARD

In Archboard, or Bridge board, players attempt to shoot their marbles through arches cut out of a piece of card or board.

Each player is keeper of the arches for one round of the game, while the other players shoot one marble in each turn. Before making a shot, each player pays the keeper one marble.

When his marble passes completely through an arch a player receives from the keeper the number of marbles shown above that arch. (Usually numbers are higher toward the outside of the bridge.)

If a player's marble misses the bridge completely, he must pay another marble to the keeper.

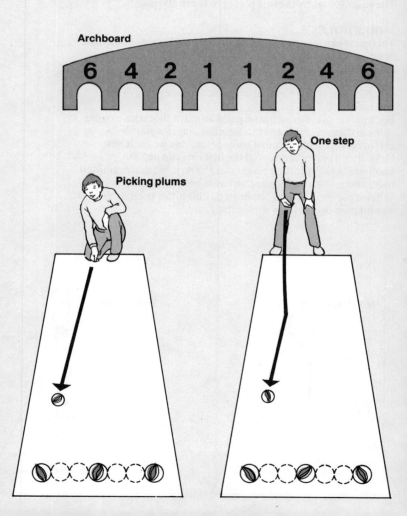

Archboard

Picking plums

One step

PICKING PLUMS

Picking plums is a game for any small number of players. Each player places one or two marbles in a row – with room for two marbles to pass through the gaps.

Each player then shoots in turn and may keep any "plums" knocked from the line. A player is entitled to an extra shot whenever he picks a plum; all shots are made from the original position and not from where the marble lies after the previous shot.

DOBBLERS

This game is played in the same way as Picking plums except that:

a player's taw stays where it lies at the end of a turn;

subsequent turns are played from where the taw lies;

a player whose taw is hit by another player's taw must add one marble to the row.

ONE STEP

One step is another game in which the target is a row of marbles made up by the players. It is played in the same way as Dobblers except that:

a player's first shot is made by taking one step and then throwing his taw from an upright position;

subsequent shots are made from an upright position but with no step forward;

a successful shot entitles a player to an extra shot from where his taw lies.

©DIAGRAM

Nine men's morris

Nine men's morris, also called Mill, Morelles, or Merels, is one of the oldest games played in Europe and was particularly popular during the Middle Ages. It is a game of strategy for two people in which each player attempts to capture or block his opponent's pieces.

Board The game is played on a specially marked-out board, with three squares one inside the other and with points in the centers of the squares' sides connected by ruled lines. Bought boards are now usually made of wood. In the past, boards have been carved out of stone or, often, cut out of turf. A perfectly satisfactory board can be drawn on paper.

Pieces At the start of a game each player has nine "men" (counters, stones, or other appropriate pieces) distinguishable in color from those of his opponent.

Objective By the placing and maneuvering of men on the board, each player attempts to capture all but two of his opponent's pieces or to make it impossible for his opponent to move any piece at his turn.

Board and pieces

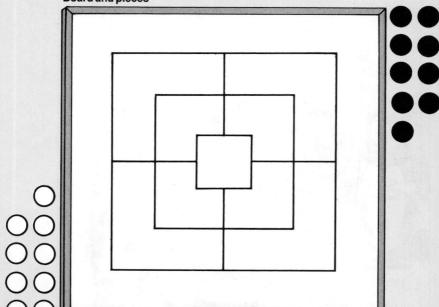

Play There are usually three stages of play:
1) placing the men on the board;
2) moving the pieces around;
3) "hopping" them.
(The third stage is sometimes disallowed, as it gives one player a distinct advantage over his opponent.)

Placing the pieces The players decide which of them is to start. Each one, in turn, then places one man of his own color on the board at any point of intersection not already occupied by another piece.

Players aim to get three of their own men into a straight line along one of the lines of the board, so forming a "mill."

Pounding Once a player has formed a mill he is entitled to "pound" his opponent by removing one enemy piece from the board. A player may not, however, remove an opponent's man that is part of a mill, unless there is no other man available. Once removed from the board, a piece is dead for the rest of the game.

Players continue their turns (nine turns each) until each of their men has been placed onto the board.

Placing the pieces

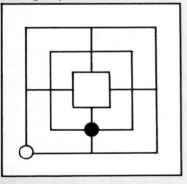

A mill

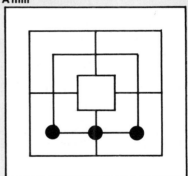

Pounding

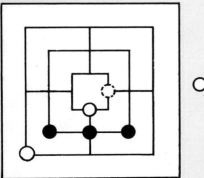

©DIAGRAM

Moving the pieces Still taking alternate turns, players now move their men to try to form new mills and so pound their opponent.

A move consists of moving a man from his existing position on the board to any adjoining vacant point of intersection.

(According to some rules players may take pieces by passing over an enemy piece to a vacant spot beyond it, as in Checkers, see p. 36.)

Players may form new mills by opening existing mills. This is achieved by moving a man one place from his position in a mill, and then returning him at the next move to his original position. Mills may be broken and re-made any number of times, and each new mill formation entitles the player to pound his opponent.

Play continues until one of the players is reduced by successive poundings to having only two men on the board; or until one player's pieces have been so blocked by his opponent's men that he is unable to make any move.

Should a player's only remaining pieces form a mill and it is his turn to move, he must do so even if this results in his losing a piece and the game at his opponent's next move.

Hopping is an optional stage of play, and begins when either player has only three men remaining.

The player is now no longer restricted to moving his men along a line to an adjacent point of intersection, but may "hop" to any vacant spot on the board. This freedom of movement gives him a certain advantage over his opponent, and so restores his chance of winning.

Results A player is defeated when either:

he is reduced to having only two pieces; or

his pieces are blocked by enemy men in such a way as to prevent further moves.

(If hopping has been allowed the game ends when one player has only two pieces remaining.)

Moving

Hopping

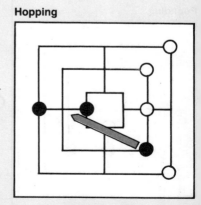

THREE MEN'S MORRIS

Three men's morris is a game for two players, each player
having four counters of his own color.
The board is marked out as shown. Players take turns to put
one man on a point of intersection, in an attempt to form a mill
along one of the lines marked on the board. The first player to
achieve this is the winner.

Three men's morris: start

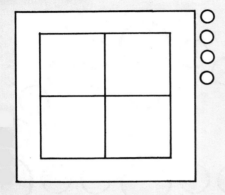

SIX MEN'S MORRIS

This game is played in much the same way as Nine men's
morris. Players each have six counters and take it turn to place
them, one at a time, on the board (which is marked out as
shown).
The objective is to form a mill along one of the sides of either of
the squares. If a player succeeds in doing this, he may pound
his opponent. As in Nine men's morris, once all the men have
been played onto the board, the game continues with players
moving their men to form new mills. When one player has only
two men left, he loses the game.

Six men's morris: start

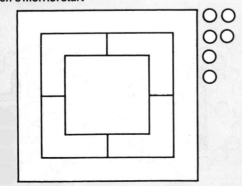

Nyout

Nyout is a Korean race game that was probably played over a thousand years ago. It has retained its popularity over the centuries, now being played chiefly for money.

Board

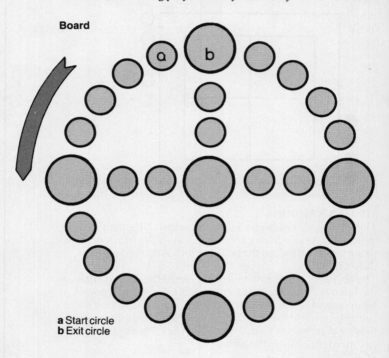

a Start circle
b Exit circle

Alternative routes

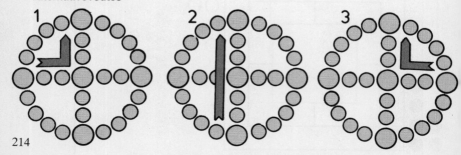

The board is marked out with colored circles; 20 circles form a ring and enclose a cross of nine other circles, as shown. The central circle and the four circles at the cardinal points are larger than the others. (Traditional boards have marks or symbols in place of circles.)

Horses

The pieces are traditionally carved from wood or ivory and are known as "horses." Any other counters or pieces may be used, provided that each player's pieces are easily distinguishable from those of his opponents. Each player has an agreed number of horses – usually two, three, or four.

Dice Koreans play with small flat strips of wood that score a maximum of 5, but a standard die may be used – rethrowing if a 6 shows.

Die

Players Any number of players may take part, although the usual number is four – two players sometimes playing in partnership against the other two.

Objective Players race each other to be the first to get their horses around the board.

Play Players throw the die to determine their starting order, the player throwing the highest number starting first.

Each player in turn throws the die, advancing one of his horses the appropriate number of circles, and counting the start circle as 1.

Players may have more than one of their horses in the ring at any time. (In partnership play, a player may move either his own or his partner's horses.)

Horses are moved around the board in a counterclockwise direction, leaving the ring at the "exit" circle.

Alternative routes Whenever a horse lands on one of the large circles, it is allowed to take the alternative route along the horizontal and/or vertical arms of the cross. Routes (**1**) and (**2**) provide a short cut; route (**3**) can be a useful means of evading enemy horses on the circles leading to the exit.

Players need not take the alternative routes if, for strategic purposes, they consider it imprudent to do so.

Taking If a horse lands on a circle occupied by an opponent's horse, the opponent's horse is "taken" and returned to the start. The taker is then allowed another throw.

Double pieces If a horse lands on a circle already occupied by one of his own or his partner's horses, the horses may be moved together as a "double piece" in subsequent moves.

Pachisi

Pachisi is thought to have originated several thousand years ago and was the forerunner of many contemporary racing board games. Several older forms of the game are still played in Asia and South America. The game described here is that played in the Indian subcontinent.

Board The traditional Indian board is either woven, or made of cloth with the playing area marked out in embroidery. The playing area is in the shape of a cross and is divided into small squares, 12 of which are distinctively colored to identify them as "resting" squares (where any number of pieces is safe from capture).

Board

a Starting squares

b Resting squares

c Finish

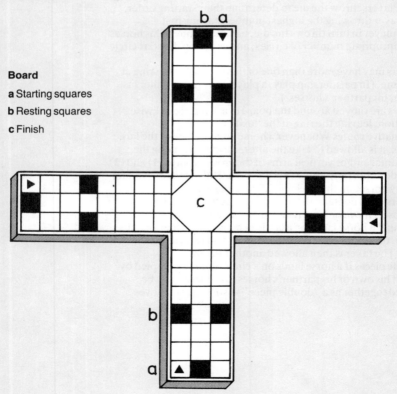

Pieces Each player has four shells, stones, or other objects that must be easily identifiable from those of his opponents.

Dice Traditionally, six cowrie shells are used. They are thrown from the hand and the position they adopt indicates the number of squares a piece must be moved, as follows:
two shells with their openings uppermost, two;
three shells with their openings uppermost, three;
four shells with their openings uppermost, four;
five shells with their openings uppermost, five;
six shells with their openings uppermost, six.
If only one shell falls with its opening uppermost, the player moves forward ten squares.
If all the shells fall with their openings facing down, the player moves forward 25 squares.
If a player throws a 6, 10, or 25 he is allowed another throw.

Players Two, three, or four may play.

Objective In this race game, each player tries to be the first to get all four of his pieces around the board from the starting point to the finish.

Pieces

©DIAGRAM

Play Each player in turn throws the cowrie shells, and moves one of his pieces the number of squares indicated by the shells. Pieces are moved in a clockwise direction around the board (see diagram).

At the start of the game each player's first piece may enter the race with any throw, but subsequent pieces (or the first piece if it has to repeat the route) may only enter the game if a 6, 10, or 25 is thrown.

A player may have one, two, three, or all of his pieces on the board at any one time.

After the players have each had one turn, they may – if they wish – miss a turn or decline to move a piece after making their throw.

Taking If a piece lands on any square other than a "resting" square already occupied by an opponent's piece, the opponent's piece is obliged to return to the start. It may only re-enter the game with a throw of 6, 10, or 25.

The player who took the opponent's piece is allowed another throw.

Once a piece has reached the central column of its own arm, leading to the finish, it cannot be taken.

Double pieces If a piece is moved onto a square occupied by another piece belonging to the same player, both pieces may be moved together as a "double piece" on subsequent moves. A double piece may never be overtaken by other pieces – whether the player's or an opponent's – and can only be taken if an enemy piece of equal strength lands directly on its square.

End of play The finish can only be reached by a direct throw. If, for example, a piece is seven squares away from the finish and the player throws more than a 7, he is obliged to await his next turn, or move one of his other pieces.

As soon as a piece lands on the finish, the piece is removed from the board.

The winner of the game is the first player to get all four of his pieces to the finish, and the game may be continued to determine the finishing order of the other players.

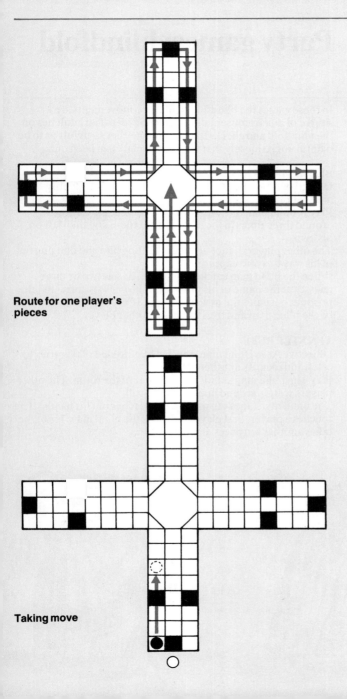

Route for one player's pieces

Taking move

Party games: blindfold

In these games the blindfolded player's movements are a source of much amusement. It is a good idea if an adult ties on the blindfold and checks that it is tied neither so tightly as to be painful nor so loosely that the "blind man" can peep out.

BLIND MAN'S BUFF
Objective A blindfolded player tries to catch and identify another player.
Play A blind man is chosen and blindfolded. He is turned around three times in the center of the room and then left on his own.

The other players dance around, taunting him and dodging out of his way to avoid capture.

When the blind man catches someone, he has two or three guesses at the name of his prisoner. If he guesses correctly, the prisoner becomes the new blind man. If wrong, he continues to be the blind man and tries to catch another player.

TEN STEP BUFF
Objective As in Blind man's buff, a blindfolded player tries to catch and identify another player.
Play The blind man stands in the center of the room. The other players scatter around him and stand still.

The blind man takes ten paces and stretches out his hands. If he touches a player, that player becomes the blind man. If not, he takes another ten paces and tries again.

Blind man's buff

SQUEAK-PIGGY-SQUEAK

Objective A blindfolded player attempts to identify another player by getting him to squeak.

Play One player is blindfolded, given a cushion, and turned around three times in the center of the room. The others sit down around the room.

The blind man must then place his cushion on another player's lap and sit on it. He then calls "squeak-piggy-squeak" and the person he is sitting on squeaks like a pig. If the blind man recognizes the person, he changes places with him.

Once the new person is blindfolded, the players all change seats before he tries to sit on a player's lap.

BLIND MAN'S STICK

Objective A blind man tries to identify a player from the noises he makes.

Play One player is blindfolded and given a stick. The others form a circle and slowly move around him.

If the blind man touches a player with his stick, the player must grasp the stick. The blind man then asks the player to imitate a noise – for example a creaking door.

If the blind man guesses the player's name, that player becomes the new blind man. If he guesses incorrectly, the blind man must touch another player.

BLIND JUDGMENT

Play One player is blindfolded and placed on a "seat of judgment."

Another player then stands quietly in front of him, and the player in the judgment seat gives a brief description of whoever he thinks might be standing in front of him.

If the other players think that the "blind judgment" was reasonably accurate, the player in front of the blindfolded player becomes the new blind man.

If his judgment was inaccurate, the original blindman must pass judgment on another player.

BLIND MAN'S TREASURE HUNT

This game is an excellent way of giving out small presents at a party.

Objective Each player chooses a parcel by touch and tries to identify the contents before opening it.

Preparation Objects of different shape and feel are wrapped up – one parcel per player. The parcels are piled on a table.

Play Each player in turn is blindfolded and led to the table to choose a parcel. He then takes off his blindfold and waits until all the players have chosen a parcel. Each player then guesses what is in his parcel before opening it.

BLIND POSTMAN

Objective A blindfolded player tries to sit in a vacant seat while two players are changing places.

Preparation One person is chosen to be postmaster. All the others choose a town, and the postmaster makes a list of their choices.

Play One player is blindfolded and becomes the first postman. All the other players sit in a circle. The postman stands in the center of the circle, and is turned around several times by the postmaster.

The postmaster then announces that a letter has been sent between two of the towns on his list, for example from Cambridge to Birmingham. The two players whose towns are called then try to change places before the postman sits in one of their empty seats.

If the postman gets a seat, the player without a seat becomes the new postman. More than one letter may be sent at a time.

Mode of travel The postmaster can also say how the letter traveled – and so indicate how the players should move. For example, if the letter went:
a) by air, they hop;
b) by sea, they walk backward;
c) by train, they crawl; and
d) by Pony Express, they bunny hop.

THIEVES

Objective A blindfolded player tries to catch players stealing from him.

Play One player is blindfolded and given a rolled newspaper to hold in his hand.

The blindfolded player sits in the middle of a circle made by the other players, and a pile of treasure – necklaces, brochures, bracelets, etc – is placed in front of him.

Players in the circle quietly take it in turns to steal a piece of treasure. If the blindman hears a thief, he strikes at him with the newspaper and calls "thief, thief."

If he touches a thief, the thief must return empty-handed to his place to await his next turn. The thief who collects most treasure wins the game.

JAILER

This is similar to Thieves except that the blindfolded man is guarding a bunch of keys.

The organizer names a player, who then has to take the keys from the jailer and carry them around the outside of the circle and back to his place.

The jailer listens for the thief and if he hears him points at him. If the jailer locates the thief the thief takes over as jailer.

DONKEY'S TAIL
Objective Blindfolded players try to pin a tail in the correct position on a drawing of a tailless donkey.
Preparation The organizer draws a large picture of a donkey without a tail and fastens it onto a pinboard propped upright. He also makes a donkey's tail out of cardboard or wool and sticks a large pin through the body end.
Play Each player in turn is blindfolded and turned around so that he is in front of and facing the donkey. He is then given the tail and attempts to pin it on the correct part of the donkey. The organizer marks the position of each player's attempt. The player who pins nearest the correct place is the winner.

ELEPHANT'S TAIL
This is similar to Donkey's tail but instead of pinning on a tail players draw one. Each blindfolded player is given a crayon and draws a tail on a picture of an elephant (or any other animal).

MURALS
Preparation The organizer cuts out large pieces of paper for drawing on.
Play Each player in turn is blindfolded, given a crayon, and asked to draw a picture on a piece of paper pinned on the wall. The subject of the picture is chosen by the other players – good examples are a house, a person, or some kind of animal. The artist feels the edges of the paper and has one minute in which to draw the chosen subject. When everyone has had a turn, the drawings can be judged by an adult or by all the players together.

©DIAGRAM

223

SWEET TOOTH

Objective Each player tries to identify foods that he has eaten while blindfolded.

Play Each player sits down and is then provided with a plate of foods such as chocolate, fudge, nuts, liquorice, and pieces of orange.

When all the players have eaten or tasted all their foods, any leftovers are taken away and the blindfolds are removed.

The players then write down what they think they have eaten. If the players are too young to write, they can whisper their answers to an adult.

BLIND MAN'S SORT OUT

Objective Blindfolded players race to sort a collection of objects into categories.

Preparation The organizer collects a selection of buttons, screws, nails, beans, beads, etc.

Play The game is usually organized as an elimination contest – with two players competing at a time.

The objects are divided into two similar piles. The first two players are then blindfolded and each is placed in front of a pile of objects.

When the organizer calls "Go!" each of the blindfolded players starts sorting his objects into groups of buttons, screws, etc. The first player to finish sorting his objects into categories goes forward into the next round of the contest.

All the other players then compete in pairs, and the winners all go into the next round.

Further rounds are held until only two players remain for the final. The winner of the final wins the game.

BLINDFOLD OBSTACLE WALK

Blindfold obstacle walk

Preparation Everyone lays out obstacles – a pile of books, a glass of water, cushions, etc – from one end of the room to the other.

Play Several of the players volunteer to walk the course. They then leave the room to be blindfolded. Meanwhile the others quickly and quietly remove all the obstacles.

Each of the blindfolded volunteers is then brought in one at a time.

The blindfolded player then attempts to walk across the room without hitting the obstacles. To add to the fun all the onlookers utter appropriate gasps and shudders.

When he has completed the "course" the blindfold is removed.

NELSON'S EYE

This game plays on a blindfolded person's heightened imagination.

Play Several volunteers who do not already know the game are asked to leave the room. They are blindfolded and brought back into the room one at a time.

One of the other players begins by asking the blind man to feel "Nelson's good leg" – and the blind man's hands are guided so that he can feel someone's leg.

He is then asked to feel Nelson's bad leg – and his hands are guided to a chair leg.

Next the blind man must feel Nelson's good arm – and feels someone's arm. Then he must feel Nelson's bad arm, which can be a stuffed stocking.

This is followed by Nelson's good eye, which can be a marble. Finally he is asked to feel Nelson's bad eye – and is presented with a squashy pickled onion or a soft flour and water mixture. The blind man usually becomes rather squeamish at this point – much to the amusement of the other players!

MURDER IN THE DARK

Although players are not blindfolded for this game, a "detective" attempts to identify an unseen "murderer." The opening stages of play take place in the dark.

Preparation One small piece of paper per player is folded and placed in a hat. One is marked with a cross, another with a D, and all the others are blank.

Play Each player draws a piece of paper from the hat. The player who gets the paper with the cross is the murderer and the one with the D the detective. The detective first leaves the room and the lights are switched off.

The other players then dance slowly around the room in the dark. The murderer catches a victim and puts his hands on the victim's shoulders. The victim must scream and fall to the ground. The lights are then switched on and the detective is called in.

The detective tries to identify the murderer by questioning everybody except the victim. All the players except the murderer must answer his questions truthfully.

After the questioning the detective accuses his prime suspect of the murder, saying "I charge you (name of suspect) with the murder of (name of victim)." If the accusation is correct, the murderer must admit his guilt.

Party games: contests

In these games players perform various feats of skill. Some of the games are a test of physical strength or ability, others need ingenuity in order to outwit opponents. It is a good idea in case of dispute for someone to act as referee.

Balloon flights

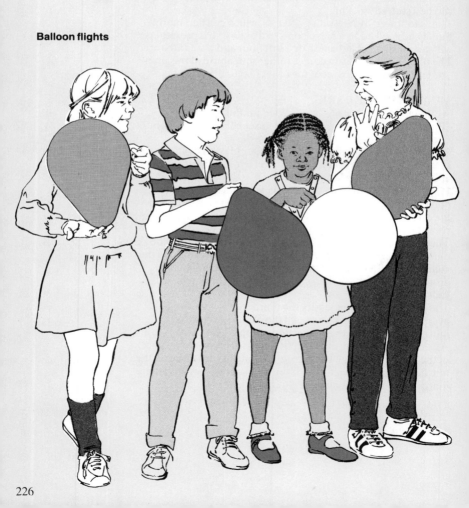

BALLOON FLIGHTS

Objective Each player tries to flick a balloon the farthest distance.

Play Players form a straight line. Each person balances a balloon on the palm of one hand. Balloons should all be a different color, or marked with the players' initials.

The referee counts "One, two, three, go," and each player then flicks his balloon with the first finger and thumb of his other hand. The player whose balloon makes the longest flight is the winner.

STATIC ELECTRICITY

Objective Each player tries to have the most balloons clinging to a wall at the end of a time limit.

Preparation Plenty of balloons are inflated and their necks tied.

Play The balloons are placed in a pile in the center of the room and each player is allocated an area of wall.

On the word "Go," each player takes a balloon, rubs it on his clothing to create static electricity, and then tries to make it cling to the wall.

If he succeeds, he takes another balloon and does the same, and so on with as many balloons as possible. If the balloon falls off the wall any player may use it again.

End At the end of a time limit, the player with the most balloons still clinging to the wall wins.

HOPPIT

Objective Each player tries to hop the farthest while making progressively larger hops.

Play Using strands of yarn, two straight lines are marked on the floor. The lines are about 1ft apart at one end of the room and fan out to about 5ft apart at the other.

Players take turns at hopping back and forth across the two lines. They start at the narrow end and move down the room. The player who gets the farthest down the line before failing to hop right across the two lines, is the winner.

SINGING HIGH JUMP

This is a test of vocal range – each player aims to sing the most widely spaced low and high notes.

Play The referee stands by a "take-off" line ready to score each player's attempt.

In turn, each player runs up to the take-off line, stops, and sings two notes: the first as low as possible, the second as high as possible. The player who makes the highest musical "jump" is the winner.

APPLE ON A STRING

This game is an old favorite for Halloween. Players try, without using their hands, to eat apples suspended from strings.

Play A piece of string is hung across the room, well above head height. One apple (or currant bun) per person is suspended from it, also on a string.

The players try to eat their apples or buns without using their hands. The first player to eat the apple down to its core, or to finish eating the bun, is the winner.

APPLE PARING

Objective Each player tries to peel the longest unbroken paring from an apple.

Play Each player is given an apple, a knife, and a plate. All the apples and all the knives should be of similar quality.

The players then peel their apples. The winner is the one to produce the longest and narrowest paring.

CANDY WRAPPER

This game is similar to apple paring, but instead of fruit the players get a candy to eat.

Objective Each player aims to tear a candy wrapper into a long, thin, spiral strip.

Play Each player is given a candy, which he unwraps. While eating the candy, he tears its wrapping paper, starting at the outer edge and tearing round and round toward the center. The player with the longest unbroken strip of paper wins.

Apple on a string

HAPPY TRAVELERS

Each player tries to be the first to sort the pages of a newspaper into the correct order.

Preparation For each player the pages of a newspaper are put together in the wrong order – some pages may be upside down or back to front – and then folded.

Play Players sit facing each other in two rows. They should sit very close together like passengers on a crowded train.

Each player is given one of the newspapers. At the word "Go!" each player tries to rearrange the pages of his newspaper into the correct order. The first player to succeed wins the game.

PRINTERS' ERRORS

In this game players try to set out jumbled lines of a printed article into their correct order.

Preparation A jumbled article is needed for each player. The organizer makes as many copies of the article as he needs and then jumbles each one by cutting it into pieces after each line.

Play Each player is given his jumbled article. When the organizer gives the signal players start to sort out their articles. The winner is the first player to put his article into the correct order.

CARD AND BUCKET CONTEST

Objective Players try to flick all their cards into a bucket or other large container.

Play Each player is given ten playing cards – preferably old ones – and writes down which ones they are.

The players then form a large circle around a bucket. At a call of "Go!" each player tries to flick his cards into the bucket. When all the players have flicked all their cards, the cards in the bucket are identified.

The winner is the player who gets most cards into the bucket. Several rounds may be played.

Card and bucket contest

GRANDMOTHER'S FOOTSTEPS

Objective Each player tries to be the first one to creep up behind the "grandmother" without her seeing him move.

Play One person is chosen as the grandmother and stands, with shut eyes, facing a wall.

The other players line up against the opposite wall. When everyone is ready, the players start to creep up behind the grandmother – but whenever she looks round they must "freeze" into statues.

The grandmother may look round as often as she likes. If she sees anyone moving, she points to him and he has to go back to the start. The grandmother turns round to face the wall, and the players move forward again.

The first player to touch the grandmother's wall wins – and takes the next turn at being grandmother.

LIMBO

Originally a West Indian acrobatic dance, this is a test of suppleness and sustained contortion.

Play Two people gently hold a long stick horizontally and at chest height.

Each player in turn bends backward and edges himself under the stick. He must neither touch the floor with his hands nor touch the stick.

If a player, after two attempts, fails to pass under the stick he is eliminated. After each round the stick is lowered a little. The last person to stay in the game is the winner.

Limbo

TWO-MINUTE WALK

Objective Each player tries to walk from one end of the room to the other in exactly two minutes.

Play Players line up along one wall. On the word "Go," they set off across the room. Without using a watch or a clock, each player tries to reach the other side of the room in exactly two minutes. The organizer times the players' walks.

When all the players have finished, the player whose time was nearest two minutes wins.

Two-minute walk

RUMORS

This is a competitive form of the popular old game of Chinese whispers.

Objective Each player tries to pass on a message that has been whispered to him.

Play Players divide into two equal teams and each team sits down in a circle. Players take it in turns to be team leader. The organizer decides on a message and whispers it to the two leaders.

Each leader then whispers the message to the player to his right. This player then whispers the message as he heard it to the player to his right, and so on around the circle. Whisperers are not allowed to give the message more than once.

The last player of each team tells the leader the message as he heard it. The leader then tells the message as it began. The team that kept the message most intact wins the game.

STORK FIGHTING CONTEST

Play Two players tie their left ankles together with a scarf, and hop on their right feet.

Each player then tries to make his opponent's left foot touch the ground – without putting down his own left foot.

If a player's left foot touches the ground, his opponent scores a point.

The winner is the player with the most points at the end of a time limit.

COCK FIGHTING CONTEST

Play Two players crouch on the floor facing each other.

Each brings his knees together under his chin and clasps his legs with his arms. A walking stick is then passed under his knees and over his arms.

The two players then try to tip each other over.

The first player to succeed in making his opponent fall over is the winner.

Cock fighting

TRIANGULAR TUG-OF-WAR

This is a game for three players.

Play A circle is made from a rope about 3yd long. Three players space themselves around the rope and hold it taut, forming a triangle. A handkerchief is placed at each corner of the triangle, out of reach of the players.

On the word "Go!" each player tries to pick up the handkerchief nearest him without letting go of the rope. The first player to pick up his handkerchief is the winner.

Triangular tug-of-war

ARM WRESTLING

Play Two players sit facing each other at either side of a table. Resting their right elbows on the table and with crooked arms, they clasp each other's right hands. (Both players may use their left arms if they prefer.)

On the signal to begin each player tries to force his opponent's right hand back until it touches the table. Elbows must be kept firmly on the table. The winner is the first to succeed.

Arm wrestling

Party games: goal scoring

Although goal scoring games are often based on energetic outdoor sports, they can safely be played in the home if a balloon, soft ball, or large rag is used. Playing with balloons is particularly enjoyable as they are difficult to control and unlikely to cause damage.

AVENUE GOALS
Players try to score goals by patting a ball or balloon so that it goes beyond their opponents' end of the avenue.
Players The players form two lines about 5ft apart, and sit or kneel facing each other on the floor.
Counting from one end, the odd-numbered players in one line belong to the same team as the even-numbered players in the other line.
Each team is allotted one end of the avenue as its goal.
Play The organizer puts the ball into the center of the avenue. Each team tries to score by patting the ball by hand down the avenue into its opponent's goal. Players are not allowed to hold or throw the ball. The ball is put back into the center of the avenue after each goal. The winning team is the one with most goals at the end of a time limit.

OVERHEAD GOALS
Players try to score goals by patting a balloon over their opponents' heads.
Players The players form two teams in rows about 4ft apart, and sit facing each other on the floor.
Play The organizer tosses the balloon into the center.
Each team tries to score goals by knocking the balloon over the heads of the opposing team and onto the ground behind them. The winning team is the one with most goals at the end of a time limit.

©DIAGRAM

BALLOON VOLLEYBALL

In Balloon volleyball players hit a balloon over a piece of string held taut by two players standing on chairs.

Players The players divide into two teams, one on either side of the string. Players within a team take turns at serving (hitting the balloon into play at the start of play or after a break).

Play Players hit the balloon back and forth over the string with the aim of making a shot that their opponents will not be able to return.

A team scores a point whenever it hits the balloon over the string onto the floor on its opponent's side. If the ball goes under the string, the opposing team serves it.

The winning team is the one with most points at the end of a time limit.

BLOW VOLLEYBALL

This is played in exactly the same way as Balloon volleyball except that the balloon is blown rather than hit, and the string is held lower.

Balloon volleyball

ASTRIDE BALL

This is a goal-scoring game without teams.

Players One player stands in the center of a circle formed by the other players standing with their legs apart.

Play The center player has a ball to be rolled along the ground. If he rolls it between the legs of a player in the circle, he "scores a goal" and changes places with that player.

The players in the circle should keep their hands on their knees except when trying to prevent a goal.

HOCKEY RAG TIME

In this game team members take turns at trying to shoot a goal.

Players The players form two rows about 6ft apart and sit facing each other on the floor. Each team member is given a number, starting with one.

A rag and two walking sticks are laid on the floor between the two rows of players. A chair is placed at each end of the avenue as a goal. Each team is allotted one of the goals.

Play The organizer calls out a number. Each player with that number picks up a walking stick and uses it to maneuver the rag into his opponent's goal. The successful player scores a point for his side.

The rag and walking sticks are replaced and the organizer calls another number.

The winning team is the one with most goals at the end of a time limit.

Astride ball

© DIAGRAM

237

Party games: musical

These are all active games in which players move around to music. When the music stops, the players must immediately stand still or change what they are doing. All the games require someone to organize the music.

MUSICAL CHAIRS
Preparation Chairs are placed around the room in a large circle. There should be one chair fewer than the number of players.
Play The players stand in the circle and, when the music starts, all dance around.
When the music stops, each player tries to sit on a seat. The player left without a seat is eliminated.
One chair is then removed from the circle and the music is restarted. The last person to stay in the game is the winner.

MUSICAL BUMPS
This is like Musical chairs, except that it is played without the chairs. When the music stops, players sit down on the floor. The last person to sit down is out.

OWNERSHIP MUSICAL CHAIRS
In this version of Musical chairs there is one chair per person. Before the music starts each player sits on a chair and marks it as his own.
When the music starts, the players dance around the circle in the same direction.
When the music stops, the players continue moving around the circle. As each player comes to his own chair he sits down. The last player to sit on his chair is out and remains seated.
The organizer may vary the game by calling directions to the players as they move around – eg walk backward, or turn to the right.
The last person to stay in the game is the winner.

MUSICAL BLACKOUT
This is played like Musical chairs except that when the music stops, the lights are switched off for five seconds. When the lights are switched on again, any player who has not found a chair is eliminated.

Captured Lightning

Award-Winning Student Articles
Volume I

Captured Lightning

Award-Winning
Student MagazineArticles

• Volume I •

edited by
Ann deG Marshall and Alison J. Wright

apprentice
house

Baltimore, Maryland
www.apprenticehouse.com

Edited by Ann deG Marshall and Alison J. Wright

Cover and internal design by
Ann deG Marshall and Alison J. Wright

First printing
10 9 8 7 6 5 4 3 2 1

ISBN: 978-1-933051-06-2

apprentice
house

Baltimore, Maryland
www.apprenticehouse.com

"The difference between the right word and the almost right word is the difference between lightning and a lightning bug."
-Mark Twain

Captured Lightning is the first of what we hope to be an annual publication of AEJMC award-winning magazine articles written by college students across the country. Apprentice House, as a student-run organization, is proud and pleased to publish the award-winning works of our peers.

AEJMC, the Association for Education in Journalism and Mass Communication, continues to set the highest standards for student work. Their annual magazine writing contest highlights the outstanding work of journalism students throughout the country – and 2005 was no exception. The students represented in this compilation certainly meet, if not exceed, the AEJMC level of excellence, with topics ranging from drag shows to awareness of AIDS in Africa.

As a non profit, student-staffed publishing house organized by the Communication Department at Loyola College in Maryland, Apprentice House approached this project with enthusiasm. Having worked closely for the past months with professors, advisors and, most significantly, student writers to produce such an outstanding compilation of work, has been a powerful reminder of what can be accomplished with hard work and determination – no matter what one's age or level of experience.

As college seniors, our work on Captured Lightning has been frustrating, fun, challenging and fulfilling – much like our college careers. On that note, we look forward confidently and expectantly to a long tradition of team-work between student writers and student publishers in the continuing pursuit of capturing creative lightning.

Enjoy!

Ann Marshall
Alison Wright

Loyola College in Maryland

contents

consumer magazine article: service & information

consumer magazine article: first person

specialized business press article

Consumer Magazine Article: Places

billy goat gruff goes to washington

Sarah Bailey, Northwestern University

The city of donkeys and elephants is about to have a goat.

It's not just any goat that's coming to Washington, D.C. It's the Goat – as Chicago's Billy Goat Tavern is known on its home turf. In August, the Goat's owner, Sam Sianis, plans to open a new branch of his populist bar in the nation's capital.

With its epithet-hurling Greek servers, red-and-white checked tablecloths, and an eight-item menu topped by a $4.35 double cheeseburger, the Goat has become a Chicago landmark. Its earthy ambiance has attracted enough journalists and celebrities to impress the most shameless Washington name dropper. The Goat has political panache, too: Politicans from President Bush to Hillary Clinton have dropped by in the last 15 years. But it remains to be seen how a place straight out of the movie My Big Fat Greek Wedding will play amid the expense-account swollen watering holes of Capitol Hill.

It was the National Association of Realtors that persuaded Sam Sianis to send a delegate to Washington. The trade group owns the Michigan Avenue building above the place the Goat calls home. When the realtors decided to open a Washington office, they quickly realized they could not leave home without their Goat. So the group proposed that the restaurant come along. Sianis hesitated at first. "The family's had this bar for 70 years now and it's never left Chicago," his eldest son Billy says. "But after we talked for a long time we decided, 'Hey, let's try something new.'"

Cheezeborger! Cheezeborger!

When the Sianises move this summer, they are not sure what type of crowd their new location will attract. There are 878,000 different restaurants nationally, and four out of five new restaurants fail within their first year, according to the National Restaurant Association. In order to compete, each must have a special quality. The Goat's name has cachet. But will the restaurant's mystique as a Chicago place survive in D.C?

After all, the Goat has been a unique windy city institution since it first opened in 1934. Founder Gus Sianis created the place as a hangout where locals could get cheap food and drinks during the Depression. But it was Chicago's writers who made the bar special. Located just a stone's throw from the Chicago Tribune offices, journalists quickly made it into a late-night second home. Then they wrote about it so much it finally became a Chicago icon. When Mike Kilian was a 22-year-old rookie reporter at the Tribune, for example, he would finish up his stories around midnight. Then, ready to relax, he and his cohorts would descend from the snowy white Tribune tower and make their way towards the neon sign of relief peeping out from the looming shadows of the Grand Street Bridge, the sign that signaled the singular comforts of the tavern.

Three groups went to the Goat after deadline: the pressmen, young reporters and the famous Tribune columnist Mike Royko – a group of one, Kilian notes. It was always rowdy late night. Royko made the restaurant the setting for so many of his columns that Chicago readers felt it was their own neighborhood bar. The tavern is devoted to its journalist patrons. Framed pictures and articles by such writers as CBS anchor Walter Cronkite and movie critic Roger Ebert hang on each wall.

But journalists are in short supply around the Goat these days. Some loyalists, such as Tribune columnists Rick Kogan and John Kass, still frequent the bar by day – Kass eats an egg sandwich and reads the newspaper there every morning at 10:00 am. But the restaurant has overflowed with tourists ever since 1977 when John Belushi brought the bar national attention with his "Saturday Night Live" routine – mimicking the Goat's Greek servers yelling, "Cheezeborger! Cheezborger! No fries – chips!" Since then tourists have swarmed the place – at least three bus loads crowd in on Saturdays. As a result fewer journalists and locals think of it as their secret escape.

Goat in the Political Zoo

Tourists may scare off journalists, but they help the Goat financially. In the last two decades the restaurant has begun dishing up its famous burgers in three other Chicago locations. Now the Goat will try Washington, but some wonder how successful a Goat can be in such a political city.

The bar has a forthright quality that may confuse a city immersed in politics. During the 1944 Republican Convention, William "Billy Goat" Sianis put a sign on his door that read: "No Republicans Allowed." The phrase had a magnetic attraction. Soon GOP stalwarts were swarming the bar demanding service. In 1991, then President George H. W. Bush rearranged a day of meetings in Chicago to make a surprise appearance at the Goat. He wanted to meet Royko, then the city's best-known columnist. But Royko – never one to bow to VIPs – responded he would rather watch the William Kennedy Smith rape trial on T.V. Sianis framed Royko's column about that incident and hung it, together with three from other columnists expressing outrage at the Bush visit – on the tavern's left wall.

Though the bar is primarily Democratic, the Goat's regular patrons did not exactly roll out the red carpet for Sen. Hillary Rodham Clinton [D-NY], either. In 2001 the Senator took the unprecedented step of renting the entire place for a night meeting. The Secret Service required the Sianises to lock the doors and plan an escape route in case of an emergency. The Goat's regulars were furious. They threw food at the locked doors and shouted in protest, demanding their regular spots at the bar. Such loyal objections could be expected in a city that hosted the 1968 riots, but the behavior wouldn't be acceptable in an area of conference calls and lobbyists.

D.C. Crossover

Marketing would be a drastic change for an establishment that prides itself on never advertising, so Sam Sianis will avoid promotions. Since friends first started raving about the bar in the 1930s, the place has thrived on reputation alone. "My dad has never advertised," says son Tom Sianis. With reporters writing columns about the bar frequently, the Goat has always had all the free publicity it needed. "He has never once asked someone to write a story, that's why people do it," Tom Sianis adds.

Sianis says the Goat has "tons of friends" – former Chicagoans now living in Washington who will try to help the bar remain ad free. The family has started calling members of this clan to ask them to spread the word that the new Goat is opening. Many former Tribune reporters have moved on to the Washington Post or D.C. bureaus of other papers, bringing die-hard Goat loyalties with them. Chicago politicians love the Goat, too, so the Sianises figure they have a wide base of support.

But Kilian says that touristy restaurants in Washington,

such as Planet Hollywood, have failed recently because big names alone aren't enough to pull in big crowds. "This is a pinstripe and briefcase type of town filled with people who go home to the suburbs at night – not to bars," Kilian says.

Pinstriped politicos would indeed be new for a restaurant used to serving customers in jeans and t-shirts. Anthony Greco, a journalism graduate student in Northwestern University's Washington program, says he thinks it would be hard for the Goat to replace the National Press Club as a hangout for journalists. Greco, 24, represents the twenty-something journalism audience that used to flood the Goat. But Greco said that right now he and his friends never go out during the week. They conduct interviews and cover congressional hearings and political meetings during the day, so by 6:00 pm they are usually exhausted. They usually rent a movie and go home. On Thursday and Friday nights they may stroll half a block to the National Press Club and enjoy student drink specials, but they wouldn't catch a cab over to the Goat. "The Press Club is where most journalism action is in Washington," Greco says. "There's always something going on. I can't really see the Goat replacing that."

Steve Rhodes, editor of Chicago Magazine thinks writers just party less nowadays. "Younger journalists are so lame right now anyway that they're probably going to Starbucks instead of a bar after work," Rhodes says. "Maybe the Goat just needs to make some changes. They don't even have music playing in there right now. What kind-of newspaper bar doesn't have great rock and roll?"

The food selection may fail to attract customers too. In Washington, the Goat will add an open "beer garden" outside where people can drink and eat. But the eight item menu will stay the same, and so will the prices. A triple

5

cheeseburger will still sell for under $5. "The Goat was popular in my day with people looking for cheap eats and drinks," said Kilian, who now works as a Tribune Washington correspondent. "I don't know if you'll find people wanting that in Washington. This is really a salad kind of place."

Greco says that even twenty-somethings don't like burgers in Washington like they do in Chicago. "All of my friends just want to go grab a salad at lunch, myself included," Greco adds. He explains he couldn't "eat burgers as greasy as the Goat's every day and still live very long."

The Sianises will also keep Chicago journalism as the bar's theme. Billy Sianis explains that they plan to still hang framed Chicago newspaper clips as wall decorations. But after the opening they may add some articles from Washington journalists. "We'll see how things go, but if we can get some good Post columns or clips we may start hanging those too." Billy said. "We're not completely sure what direction we're taking this place yet."

Kilian thinks that keeping a strictly Chicago theme will be good for the bar. "I think they need to keep a Chicago flavor because otherwise they're not themselves, and that's not what people want," he said. "People will like having a little bit of a real city here. I don't think Washington is a real city. It's a federal park with some parasitical buildings around it for lawyers and lobbyists. A Chicago bar would attract the large number of people here who came from Chicago and miss it."

The Sianises are also looking for Greeks who can work in the Washington location. Many people flock to the Goat just to hear servers like Tom Sakkos, a Greek man who has worked at the Goat for 14 years, yelling at people when they walk in: "Come in, sit down, get a double burger! No da triple is beder! Get da triple!" He claims nine out of 10 people always order the double, but he keeps pushing for the triple with every person anyway. In order for the new Goat to be successful, the workers need to yell with the same vigor as the current ones. So Sianis is combing the Washington area searching for Greeks with vigorous lungs. "He'll probably start looking around at the local penitentiary," Tom Sianis jokes. "He needs to find tough waiters." Once Sianis finds potential waiters, he will transport some of his current servers to Washington to teach the news ones the tricks of the trade. Greco says the Greeks' yelling style might intimidate some people on the Hill when they first walk into the bar. "I wonder if people will realize that they're kidding around when they yell at you right away," Greco says. "People around here can be kinda stiff. That could scare some of them off."

Also, in order to keep track of the new place, the Sianises have to break down and buy their first computers. "My dad works non-stop right now, going from bar to bar, manually keeping track of sales and everything else," Billy Sianis says. The family does still plan on keeping the Chicago Goat computer free, but Billy Sianis says they may upgrade their cash register; they currently use the same one they've had since the Goat opened its Michigan Avenue location in 1964.

Chicago in a bottle

With long-standing traditions and unchanged technology, it figures that some people are angry that the Sianises are moving a Chicago bulwark. "To me, the move kind-of detracts from the Billy Goat mystique of a special Chicago place," Rhodes says. "It hypes the brand name and gives people a reason to not have overly romantic feelings about the place. You can't bottle bar magic and try to export it."

Killian is also skeptical about whether the Goat will survive in a place that's "not even a real city." He added: "There are few things that were as unique as the BG. It belongs in a tough town. People in Washington are workaholics. Parties are work. You can't bring a bar like the Billy Goat to a place like that."

Rhodes worries about the politicians: "It will attract tourists and politicians, but is that what you really want? Do you want Trent Lott drinking in your bar? No, you want Trent Lott as far away from your bar as possible."

Congressmen may order burgers at the Goat. The skeptics could be right and the Goat will fail. Or perhaps the bar will help add a little night life and relax one of the nation's most uppity cities.

But this summer the Sianises will see if their simple Goat will find friends among a stubborn jackass and a slow-moving elephant and break loose in Washington's political zoo.

notes from underground
Robert Perkins, University of Kansas

The door opens a crack immediately after I knock on it. From inside the house, a figure lurking in the shadows peers out at me.

"Hello?" the figure asks.

"Um, this might sound like a weird question, but is this where the Haunted Kitchen is?" I ask. I know full well that it is, but I don't want to alarm my barely visible host by making any accusations.

"Just a second." The figure leaves the cracked doorway to consult with someone behind the door. It is early in the afternoon on a Wednesday and I'm hoping to talk to the guys responsible for the Haunted Kitchen, one of Lawrence's underground music venues. The Kitchen is run out of the house that I'm standing in front of, whose address the owners have asked me not to publish. The guys in charge have a reputation for being secretive, which has helped them avoid the trouble with the law that other, similar venues face.

From behind the door I hear a barely audible "... wants to know about the Haunted Kitchen," followed by a murmured response. Just as my eyes begin to adjust to the darkness behind the sliver of doorway that I'm peering into, the door swings open and two guys with long hair and black t-shirts invite me inside.

As it turns out, I'm face-to-face with Jeff Milner and Daniel Noakes, the guys who do most of the work for the Haunted Kitchen. When they're not at their day jobs or practicing with their band, the two spend their time booking bands and setting up shows.

They've been friends since they were kids together back

in Oklahoma City, and have been running music venues for
the better part of a decade, yet they're both only 22 now.

When we met later for an interview, I discovered that I
had stumbled upon a world unto itself, a world I hadn't even
imagined existed. I'd stumbled onto DIY. DIY, which stands
for Do It Yourself, is an anti-consumerism counterculture
that exists not only in music but in film, art, and anything
else that people have gotten fed up with buying from corpo-
rations and want to make for themselves. DIY music venues
are pieced together by music lovers who build stages in their
basements, build or buy their own sound equipment and
host their own shows – usually free of charge, as they tend
to exist in areas that aren't zoned for commercial activity. On
Saturday, Feb. 19, I set out to experience the world of DIY
by hitting as many underground shows as I could in one
night, starting with the Haunted Kitchen.

The Haunted Kitchen is really the basement of a
decrepit old house near the student ghetto. The first thing
you notice when you see it – after the flaking yellow paint
– is the porch, which looks precariously like the deck of
a sinking ship. Somehow it manages to support a stained
couch by the front door, where a half dozen people hang
out to smoke while the show's going on. I get there painfully early, so the porch is empty when I arrive. The flier
had said that the show began at 8 p.m., which actually
means 11 as it turns out.

Inside, old couches held down by silent, half-awake
guys wearing black hoodies make up the bulk of the living
room's furniture, along with a hefty stereo system on the
wall blasting a hardcore punk CD when I get there. While
the house's tenants tend to be into punk and metal, they
say that they've booked all kinds of bands, including local
indie rock groups.

The Kitchen's décor matches the musical tastes of its occupants. Posters from a couple of bands and random artwork, some of it Noakes', patchily cover the walls. Beyond the kitchen at the back of the house lies the door to the real Kitchen – the basement. As small as it is, the basement is impressively well laid-out. Milner and Noakes have been doing DIY shows since they were 15, so they full well know how to set up a basement venue. When they first got the house, it already had a short stage built in the corner. They added a merchandise bar in the adjacent corner and a slew of decorations, like a plastic head hanging from the ceiling by a hook. Pillows sit in all of the window cases with foam eggcrate scattered around on the walls to muffle sound to the outside. They say that their neighbors never complain about the noise, and that the only time they had any real trouble with the police was when someone accidentally left the back door open, which they now keep locked shut.

The basement holds about 30 or so people, though when I get there – way too early – there are only a couple of people milling around. Noakes is the first to greet me as I walk inside, offering me a beer and the spot where he'd been sitting on the broken futon against the living room wall. He apologizes for the quality of the beer (Milwalkee's Best) as he presses the warm can into my hand, reminding me for all the world of my parents apologizing to company about the quality of their food whenever guests arrive for a dinner party. He frets a little about the lack of people at first, but he doesn't need to worry – about 40 more people will show up before the show starts. Though the Kitchen relies entirely on word-of-mouth and fliers to advertise, their shows tend to draw enough people to fill the basement.

As the night wears on, I find myself talking to an

orange-haired girl who is a bit tipsy from pre-partying and a diminutive-looking guy who seems to know everyone in the house. The girl is a freshman at the University of Kansas, and both are veterans of Lawrence DIY shows.

"I just have to see the Roustabouts," the girl gushes, talking about the headlining band. She turns to address the other guy, whom she knows from before. "Did you see them last time they came through?" He laughs.

"Uh, sort of. I was on mushrooms at the time, and I kind of freaked out and had to leave." Eventually the two leave me to go have a smoke on the porch, so I join a couple of other guys in helping the Roustabouts to carry in their equipment. The guys in the Roustabouts tell me that though they don't play a lot of DIY shows (they're still in high school, which makes touring difficult), they know Noakes and Milner from the old days when the two used to run DIY venues back in Oklahoma City and have come up specifically to see them. Some bands, however, tour the DIY circuit almost exclusively. Milner and Noakes say they've brought in bands from as far away as the Netherlands, which is amazing considering that the bands don't really get paid.

The money issue is a big one for DIY venues. As it would be illegal for residents of a house to charge money for holding shows in their basements – the houses are in residential, not commercial, zones – the people running DIY venues almost always ask for donations to pay for the band's gas and such. The line between 'donation' and 'entry fee' can be a thin one for police wanting to shut down a continual noise problem or landlords wanting to protect their property from the damage that is associated with running a DIY venue. Meredith Vacek, who graduated from the University last May, used to live at the Pink House and now lives at the Horror House, and says that a misunderstanding about money was one of the things that got her first venue shut down. She and her former roommates at the Pink House used to run shows in their living room until a couple of articles published in the Lawrence Journal-World reported that, among other things, the Pink House was charging admission. Pete Berard, who also used to live there, says that he and his roommates did shows only as a "labor of love," but that the landlord shut the venue down shortly after the articles ran. Berard, who graduated in December, moved out to New York last month to continue his labor of love by working for Domino Records, Franz Ferdinand's label.

The Pink House was just one of the DIY venues to pop up in Lawrence during the past five years. Seniors at the University of Kansas might also remember shows at the Halfway House, the Pirate House, the Horror House and the Kremlin. The residents of these houses formed a network for underground music in Lawrence. They all knew each other; the residents of the Pink House and Halfway House in particular used to hang out together all the time, and they both used the same guy as the Pirate House to book bands sometimes. And almost every member of each house has been involved with KJHK at some point during their time in Lawrence. Yet despite their closeness, the houses booked a wide variety of music. Vacek says that while the Pirate House focused on punk and crust metal, the Halfway House and Pink House pulled in all kinds of bands: punk, pop, screamo, avante garde post punk – you name it. Neil Mulka, Leavenworth senior and former resident of the Kremlin, says that his house would take in whoever was willing to play there. With DIY venues, availability of bands often determines a show's content more than the musical tastes of the house's residents.

At about 11 the opening band, Öroku, goes on.
Öroku is the Haunted Kitchen's house band. All five of the
members live in the house; Milner is the lead singer and
Noakes plays guitar. As soon as they assemble on the stage,
the incandescent lights are replaced with red ones and the
collection of long-haired, black-wearing guys rip into a set
of crust metal songs for an audience of about 20 people.
The environment is as relaxed as the music is loud. Dylan
Desmond, a former resident of the Pirate House, happens
to be in the crowd that night. Desmond, Overland Park,
senior, lived at the Pirate House for a year when it was still
a DIY venue. He says he still tries to hit DIY shows every
now and then. The community was and is tight, which
is why it wasn't surprising to find out that the guys from
1331 Vermont – my next stop for the evening – know all
about the Haunted Kitchen and had even been to a couple
of shows there.

The only thing the Haunted Kitchen and 1331 Vermont have in common, aside from both being DIY venues,
is that they're both yellow houses. While the Kitchen is
the very embodiment of secrecy and organization, 1331
Vermont has an open, haphazard feel to it. It doesn't even
have a name; it's just "1331 Vermont." And while Milner
and Noakes of the Haunted Kitchen have asked me not
to publish their address, the residents of the other yellow
house were more than happy to see their address in the
paper, saying that they hope it will attract more people to
their shows. Despite the lack of an address on the outside
of the house, I have no problem finding it. Loud music
blasts from the door as a swarm of people spill out of it,
covering the porch and the lawn. With a crowd of easily 60
people milling about holding plastic cups, it lookes more

like a house party than anything else, which is roughly what the residents are going for. Patrick Struebing and Kevin Thompson, two of the four people who live at 1331 Vermont, say that the events at their house aren't strictly shows or parties, but more a combination of the two.

In a tiny living room sandwiched between the kitchen, filled with kegs, and the foyer, filled with people looking for kegs, is Ike Turner Overdrive and at least 30 cheering people. I elbow my way around, trying to find a good spot, but eventually give up and resign myself to getting bumped into continuously by the stream of keg traffic. As I stand there, mashed in a crowd of people wearing hipster clothes and thick black-rimmed glasses, the lead singer and guitarist of Ike Turner Overdrive rip their shirts off and decide to deafen me with driving, high-energy rock. Thompson says that he and his roommates don't have a specific musical preference for the bands they book; they usually just ask their friends' bands to play their shows. In this case, at least, they seem to have lucked out and to have been friends with a band that the crowd likes. The audience screams and cheers at the end of every song, completely unlike the relaxed, Zen-like enjoyment of Öroku at the Haunted Kitchen. Near the end of Ike Turner Overdrive's set, the guitarist starts spraying whatever he was drinking over the crowd, nailing us at point-blank range.

Patrick and Kevin say that 1331 Vermont tends to have some crazy party/shows, which can be expensive for them. The night that I went to see them, Kevin got a $70 ticket from the police because of a noise complaint from an unknown neighbor – unknown thanks to the new Lawrence code that allows people to make such complaints anonymously. While the Haunted Kitchen has homemade soundproofing to prevent problems like that, 1331 Vermont has a broken window that does nothing to stop the music from leaking out. They also had a bathroom door kicked down by a member of the band Vibralux, who claimed he thought there was an orgy going on inside. Add that to the lovely pencil mural of random people's outlined faces found on their wall that they'll have to explain to their landlord, and all of the personal belongings that always get stolen from any DIY venue, and you can see that they aren't making any money on this deal. But when I asked if they were going to stop having shows because of the expenses (particularly the ticket), I got a laugh and a "fuck that – no" from Kevin. "We're having a party five days after I have to pay the fine." he says. Patrick says that they keep on hosting events because, after years of going to great parties in Lawrence, he and his roommates want to give something back to the community. That, and they just really like to have huge parties.

The last venue I want to hit is Solidarity, at 1119 Massachusetts. After parking my car, I walk past the Greek-looking crowd outside of It's Brothers and find my way to the radical library. There's no music – the first bad sign. The lights are off; also bad. Finally I see a sign on the door that says the show had been cancelled. Later I was told that the show had been cancelled because the band had broken up – no guarantees in DIY, but then, even mainstream venues are subject to cancellations.

Solidarity does double duty as both a radical library and a music venue. Volunteers Kat Randolph and Katy Andrus say that the venue does about two shows each month, packing people into the deceptively large space. Originally, they were worried that they'd have problems with the police (being right across from the station), but Randolph and Andrus say that It's Brothers and the dance studio next door tend to make much more noise. One of the driving forces behind the music at Solidarity is Dave Strano, who has lived at the Pirate House (well, former Pirate House – now its tenants call it the Joe Hill House) since the days when it was still a music venue.

The main way that the DIY scene actually works is simply word-of-mouth, friend-to-friend communication, says Vacek of the former Pink House. With her punky hair and multiple piercings, Vacek sticks out in the typical Lawrence crowd, and she seems to know everyone. She says that she and her roommates never had trouble finding enough people to fill their house for shows. When it comes to organizing on a national scale, DIY venues and the bands that play at them turn to a higher power: Book Your Own Fuckin' Life. BYOFL began its life as a page in the Maximumrocknroll Magazine 15 years ago. Venues, bands and anyone who had a couch for traveling punk musicians to crash on posted their contact information. The page quickly became an independent book, which came out once each year. The problem with this was the considerable cost of putting out such a publication – sans advertising, which would be counter to the generally anti-consumerism bent of the DIY scene – made it expensive to produce. In addition, the original editors grew frustrated that much of the information would be outdated by the time it made its yearly run. Eventually the book went on the Internet at www.byofl.org. Today it's run by Ernst Schoen-Rene, a self-described "computer guy" who took over after a devastating computer crash that wiped out a lot of information three years ago. It has 17,000 listings for bands, venues, labels, promoters, etc. and gets 15,000 hits every day. Schoen-Rene also runs New Disorder Records and used to play in the punk band Jack Acid, which worked the DIY circuit from '91 to '92. In Lawrence, the Haunted Kitchen is listed on the site, but the guys from 1331 Vermont haven't even heard of it and the volunteers from Solidarity say they should really get around to listing themselves on it one of these days.

Schoen-Rene says that the DIY scene started about 25 years ago, mostly as a result of how small and connected the punk rock community was. People would pass around lists of who to call to find a venue or a couch to crash on. As no one back then got into punk rock to make money – this was before the days when bands like Blink 182 made punk rock into pop – everyone was more or less in it for the love of the music, Schoen-Rene says. During those early years, there were venues a-plenty and tons of donation money. Bands could pay for all of the gas and food and make a little on the side too, Schoen-Rene says. Now, he says, the money's tighter and a lot of the bands are in it with a delusion of making it big. The golden years are over, he says.

The scene is far from dead, however. BYOFL is still going strong and Bruce Haring, founder of the DIY Convention, says it's only continuing to grow. The DIY Convention started in 2000 and drew more than 1,000 people this year. Haring says that with the rise of digital tools like the Internet, DIY has gotten huge – for better or for worse. "You have a ton of people producing out there now, which means you get a lot of really great stuff and a lot of shit," he says. Also, DIY has branched out from punk to other genres, to an extent changing the types of people associated with the scene.

Locally, despite the loss of venues like the Pink House, the Pirate House and the Kremlin, there are still places like the Haunted Kitchen, 1331 Vermont and Solidarity that plan to keep having shows. In addition, ex-Kremlin resident Emily Elmore says she is planning to start a new DIY venue with her friend April Flemming and anyone else they decide to live with. The Springfield, Mo., senior says that she and Flemming are hoping to find a place in the student ghetto – a welcome change for Elmore, who moved to Eudora after leaving the Kremlin – and plan to start having shows as early as this May.

I drive past the Haunted Kitchen on my way home. My route doesn't take me by 1331 Vermont, but if it had I probably would have seen the police handing them their $70 ticket while the party raged on. Instead, I see a quiet crowd smoking on the porch – probably unaware of all of the work that has gone into the evening they're enjoying – just waiting for the next band to go on.

Consumer Magazine Article: People

teeth in the closet: an odyssey of abuse

Christopher Sheppard, Arizona State University

Bob, a 56-year-old unemployed construction worker, fired up his Harley Davidson outside the Iron Horse Saloon in North Phoenix. He was of medium height and build. His thinning brown hair hung in a mop on his head. His blue eyes wandered down the street and lazily scanned for oncoming traffic. He felt good. His buzz gave him courage.

"Let's go get some wings!" he yelled to his friends Tom and Drew.

His friends rolled out of the parking lot ahead of him, their Harleys belching a throaty snarl. His only thought as he roared onto the street was looking cool. He accelerated wildly, laying a rooster tail of sparks as the Harley's tail pipes scraped the asphalt. Bob barely kept the bike under control as he turned and rocketed down the street. His only thought now was getting to Hooters quickly for some wings and more beer.

"Oh, God, I'm sorry about this, Jenny," Pamela said to her friend as she shook her head. Pamela, Bob's wife, was utterly embarrassed. Pamela was also of medium height and build, with dyed red hair and brown eyes. Her weathered face spoke of many hard, stressful years. Also 56, she could only shake her head in disgust that her husband was acting like a 19-year-old in front of her long-time friends.

Pamela got into the car with Jenny and Becky. They had come all the way from Indiana to visit her, only to watch Bob drink himself stupid. As they headed to Hooters, she wished the night would be mercifully short.

Bob consumed three more beers at Hooters. He was overly amorous with Pamela, and she didn't know how to take it. Bob had long ago ceased to show interest in her. The public displays of affection, at Hooters no less, were disconcerting to her.

When the women got back to Bob and Pamela's house, the three men on their hogs were already in the driveway. Pamela hit the garage door opener. Bob saw the garage door opening up and decided to look cool again. He gunned the Harley, and it bolted toward the garage while the door was only two-thirds of the way up. Bob missed hitting his unprotected head by a fraction of an inch.

Bob barreled into the garage and crashed headlong into a stack of souvenirs and gifts Jenny and Becky had bought earlier in the week. Bob killed the bike and looked around. Broken gifts and souvenirs lay all over the garage. He began to stammer broken apologies to Jenny and Becky. The women just looked at each other and decided this was the end of the evening. Jenny and Becky awkwardly wished Pamela a good night, got into the car, and drove to their hotel.

Bob went into the house for another beer.

Pamela sighed. She was tired and embarrassed.

Pamela didn't realize she was about to become a domestic violence statistic. She didn't understand that the night's events would cause her to become a refugee from her own life. Pamela couldn't comprehend that she would endure a year of physical, mental, emotional, and legal suffering.

She closed the garage door and wearily entered the house.

This Doesn't Develop in One Night

Pamela and Bob had been married 20 years earlier. They clicked from the start. They had found a relationship where each could talk to the other about anything. Pamela was more comfortable with Bob than with any man she'd ever met.

About five years ago, their relationship began to erode. Bob slipped from being merely a heavy drinker into alcoholism. So slowly, in fact, that Pamela dismissed each new warning sign as a coincidence or bad luck.

Around 1998, Bob started drinking heavily. He had torn his rotator cuff in a snowmobile accident while drinking. He couldn't work, so he filled his newfound free time with beer.

Bob's best friend, Tom, found Bob a job supervising a roofing crew. Tom also enabled Bob to pursue his beer-drinking hobby on the job. They were very discrete about drinking and roofing.

Tom eventually lost his business because of a construction-related mishap. Bob was unemployed again. Tom managed to work out a deal where both he and Bob would go work for another company. Both men continued to sip beer while working until the company office began receiving calls from customers complaining that they could smell alcohol on their breath. Bob was "laid off" in early 2002. In reality, he was fired because of drinking on the job.

Now collecting unemployment, Bob could devote more time to his drinking hobby. His friends would come over during the day and at night. Bob never got hammered; he just maintained a steady buzz with a coozie-covered beer in his hand.

Bob began mistreating Pamela early in 2002. Since he wasn't working, Pamela assumed responsibility for the family finances. She worked 40 hours a week as a dispatcher for a steel company, but the money wasn't enough to make ends meet. When money became tight, Bob would verbally abuse Pamela. He would become irate, screaming at her and blaming her for the family's financial difficulties.

Bob and Pamela didn't celebrate Christmas in 2002 because their bank account was empty. Even though they couldn't afford to buy presents for Bob's three children (from a previous marriage), he always managed to find money in their joint checking account to keep the refrigerator stocked with beer.

The financial stress and Bob's verbal abuse eventually took their toll on Pamela. Early in January 2003, her body failed her.

In January, Pamela came home from work to find Bob trying to set up an office in one of the spare rooms. He wanted to start a roofing company and said he needed her help to move furniture into the new office.

"Bob, I'm tired and don't want to do this tonight," Pamela said.

Bob looked crestfallen, then angry. He snarled, "You never want to help me get ahead. You don't care if my business succeeds, do you? I can't believe you are so selfish!"

Pamela acquiesced and helped Bob even though she was dog-tired and not feeling well. She figured it was better to do what he wanted than be subjected to a guilt trip all night. After they were done, Pamela went to bed, exhausted.

She woke up in the middle of the night with a strange feeling in her arms, chest, and stomach. There was no pain, just a sensation she had never experienced before. Pamela called 911. The fire department showed up quickly and took her to the hospital.

The doctors told Pamela she had had a mild heart attack. As she lay in the emergency room, the doctors recommended an angioplasty. Scared, she agreed, and the doctors anesthetized her. When she awoke, she was told she had just undergone a double bypass. The doctors had harvested veins for the bypass from her right leg. She looked down to find her breastbone stapled up and stitches down her chest and all over her legs.

Pamela went back to work one month after open-heart surgery. Bob wasn't working, and they were in dire financial straits. Someone had to pay the bills. On February 18, only three days after she returned to work, her leg became infected. The pain was excruciating. She spent another week in the hospital on antibiotics.

Bob didn't go out and get a job. He visited Pamela in the hospital only a couple of times. When he did, he was distant, cold, and buzzed.

Just Left Alone

When Pamela and Bob entered the house, a curtain of silence dropped down between them. Bob went to bed, feeling foolish about running over the souvenirs in the garage. Pamela sat down in the living room, enjoying the silence and solitude. She thought the stress of the evening was over.

Bob came out of the bedroom, sloppily remorseful about making an ass out of himself. He wanted Pamela to come to bed. He wanted to make love to her.

Pamela simply didn't want to. She felt humiliated by his antics. She told him she just wanted to be alone in the living room.

Bob kept pleading for her to come to bed with him. The thought of lying with him repulsed her. She could imagine the alcohol oozing through his pores and making a smelly, sweaty mess on the sheets. Pamela vehemently refused and told Bob to leave her alone.

Bob continued to push the issue. He went to the

refrigerator and cracked open another beer. He entered the dining room and stared vacantly at Pamela in the adjoining living room. He was now pleading with her, telling her how much he loved her and wanted to sleep with her.

Pamela refused for the third time.

Bob became angry and decided to pick a fight.

Warning Signs

In early April 2003, Pamela was still recovering from open-heart surgery. Bob approached her one evening, beer in hand, and told her he wanted to fly his daughter and grandson down to Phoenix from Oregon. Pamela tiredly tried to reason with him by pointing out that they didn't have any money for airline tickets. Pamela couldn't even cover the house payment.

Bob exploded like a Roman candle. His rapid-fire tirade shook her. "You try to ruin everything. You never agree with anything I say. You always try to make me look like the bad guy."

Bob shoved Pamela hard in the shoulder. The staples in her breastbone strained under the force of the thrust. Bob walked off in disgust. When she regained her balance and the pain subsided, she got her purse and the keys to the truck. She had to get away. She thought he needed to cool down. She walked out the door wearing nightclothes and fuzzy slippers.

Pamela got into the pickup truck, drove a couple of blocks, and pulled over. She put her head down on the steering wheel and cried. She thought she needed to find another place to live. She couldn't take this any more.

Bob called her cell phone and told her she needed to find another place to live.

Pamela remembered that she had left her heart medicine at the house. When she returned, she was locked out. She pleaded with Bob through the door until he let her back in.

Pamela lay down on the spare bed. Her chest ached. She cried silently, wondering how her seemingly happy marriage had slowly evaporated. She was done making excuses for Bob. There was no love left in their relationship; they had quit being intimate more than a year before. The situation was getting out of control.

Confrontation in the Kitchen

After Pamela refused to sleep with Bob, he took his nearly full can of beer, sloshed it in her face, and then poured it over her head.

Pamela seethed, "Don't pour your beer on me!"

Bob dropped the half-empty can.

Pamela picked it up and lobbed it at Bob. It bounced off his thigh.

Enraged that she put up a defense, Bob reached down, picked up the can, and hurled it at Pamela. It struck her left hamstring, the very spot where the doctors had harvested the veins for her angioplasty and where infection had set in. Pamela screamed from the throbbing pain and limped into the hallway, trying to get away from Bob.

Bob had thrown the can so hard he fell on an oak icebox and smashed it to pieces. This made him even angrier. He pulled himself back up on his feet.

Pamela turned around in time to see an enraged Bob charging her like a bull, right hand raised and fist clenched. She felt his fist make contact with her lip. Her teeth crunched, and she fell backward.

Becoming a Statistic

According to the Supreme Court of Arizona, one million American women suffer nonfatal violence by an intimate partner each year. While Pamela may not have realized it, she was becoming a statistic. What statistics do not convey is the horror of having a husband turn from being a life partner into an emotional, mental, and physical threat.

AARDVARC (Abuse Rape and Domestic Violence Resource Collection), an online clearinghouse of information about domestic violence, defines four ways Pamela was abused by her husband.

First, Pamela endured emotional and mental abuse when Bob put her down by accusing her of being selfish, calling her ungrateful, and humiliating her in front of mutual friends.

Second, Pamela suffered economic abuse when Bob took her money, called it theirs, and used it for his own purposes.

Third, Bob used privilege when he elevated himself to a position above Pamela by attempting to make all the decisions in the relationship and treating her like a servant.

Finally, Pamela endured physical abuse when Bob pushed her, threw his beer at her, and hit her.

ARRDVARC identifies four traits among men who abuse their partners; all apply to Bob. These men have low self-esteem, are extremely sensitive to mild criticism, blame others for their problems, and use drinking to cope with stress. For Bob, the cycle of unemployment and alcoholism destroyed his self-esteem. Both conditions fed on each other. Because of his low self-esteem, Pamela bore the brunt of the shame and anger generated by Bob's alcoholism and depression. He used his wife as his crutch and enabler, and she ultimately became his victim.

Blood on the Tile

In an instant, Pamela went from watching a fuming, enraged Bob charging her to lying on the dining room floor. Her mouth tasted like salty iron. As her eyes began to focus on the room's white walls, she struggled to her knees. Blood flowed from her mouth. Her lip was split. She could feel with her tongue that teeth were missing.

Pamela managed to stand up and stumble down the hall. Blood stained the taupe tile as she struggled toward the bathroom. She flipped on the cold water in the sink, put her mouth under it, and washed the blood down the drain. Her chest hurt from the impact of hitting the ground. A six-inch bruise was forming where the beer can had hit her leg. Pamela looked in the mirror and cringed at what she saw. Blood oozed from her mouth, which had begun to swell. Her entire body ached – her face, back, and chest – from Bob's slugging her.

Bob, meanwhile, was drunkenly grabbing his clothes in the bedroom. He knew what he had done and was planning a quick exit.

Bob growled at Pamela, half-pleading and half-threatening her. "You better not call the police." He grabbed three armloads of clothes, dumped them into the bed of his pickup truck, and took off.

Pamela cleaned herself up as much as she could. The silence in the house was eerie. Five minutes earlier, it had been a war zone.

Pamela called Tom, Bob's best friend, and he and his girlfriend Jeannie came right over. Jeannie walked into the house and saw the blood trail going down the tile. She looked at Pamela, defeated, scared, and shell-shocked. Jeannie immediately called 911.

Police and Paramedics

Ten minutes later, Officer Angel Gonzalez arrived on the scene to find Pamela, Tom, and Jeannie in the living room. Pamela was nearly catatonic with fright. Officer Gonzalez took down information for his police report. He asked his dispatcher to send a car to look around the neighborhood for Bob's Chevy pickup, but they came up empty.

A first-responder fire truck arrived, and a paramedic treated Pamela. Four upper teeth on the left side of her mouth were missing. Her lip was split halfway to her nose. A purple and yellow bruise was forming over the surgery scars on her leg.

Pamela was in shock and couldn't speak. When Officer Gonzalez asked if she wanted to press charges against Bob, she nodded.

A police photographer took digital photographs of the crime scene – Pamela's split lip and missing teeth, the blood in the hallway and the bathroom. A police officer found Pamela's teeth inside the open closet in the hallway – ten feet away from where she had been hit.

Tom and Jeanie took Pamela to the hospital to get stitched up. Every time she closed her eyes, she cringed, haunted by the image of her enraged husband charging at her with a raised fist.

Reinventing a Ruined Life

Pamela's universe changed drastically after that evening. Bob's violent outburst proved to be the fulcrum of her life – the defining moment. Before Bob hit her, Pamela's life revolved around her marriage. Afterward, her life centered on recovering from Bob. When reflecting back on the process of starting over, Pamela said, "After Bob hit me, I felt like my life was being flushed down the toilet and all of my energy was spent swimming against the current as the bowl drained."

In the year after Bob battered her, Pamela moved seven times. She has struggled with poverty, her health, and her self-esteem. Leaving Bob and her abusive situation was only the beginning of her battle.

Tom and Jeanie took Pamela back to their house at 5:30 a.m. after only a few hours in the hospital. The doctors stitched up her lip, but they couldn't reattach her teeth. The next day, after Tom and Jeanie went to work, she was terrified at being alone in the empty house. Every passing car might be Bob.

Tom was angry with Bob for striking Pamela and wanted to help her get back on her feet. Tom had recently inherited a house from a deceased uncle and offered to let her live there. Instead of paying rent, she would remodel the interior.

Pamela moved in and went to work. She painted most of the interior, wallpapered the kitchen, refurbished the cabinets, and cleaned the carpets – all out of her own pocket. She also packed up the uncle's possessions to pay Tom back for letting her live there rent-free.

About three months after the incident, Tom and Bob began to hang out again. They patched up their differences, and Tom began to sympathize with Bob. When a battered woman like Pamela chooses to leave her abusive situation, her path to emancipation often runs into complications – mutual friends.

Pamela had a hard time paying the utility bills. She made only $1,700 per month as a dispatcher. Between the truck payment, cell phone, health insurance, heart medication, food, and previous medical bills, she had no disposable income. Pamela now felt married to her truck. It was worth less than what she owed on it, but it was her only way to get to work.

Pamela lived in the house for eight months until Tom asked her to move. He gave her a week to find another apartment and move her furniture. He didn't offer to help.

Pamela had to put her household goods into storage and move into Cassie's House, a Christian shelter for abused women in Phoenix. She had to attend church on Sunday and Wednesday. Although not particularly religious, she was grateful to have a place to live.

After a few weeks, Pamela and the other residents were forced to move into a temporary shelter because Cassie's House was approaching its five-year mark of operation and needed to renew its operating license from the state. The temporary shelter, a dilapidated house near the state fairgrounds, was infested with sewer roaches.

Ten days later, Pamela contacted DOVES (Domestic Older Victims Empower and Safety), a Glendale group that helps older victims of domestic violence. Alice Ghareib, the domestic violence program coordinator, helped Pamela find an apartment in an assisted-living home for the physically and mentally disabled and crime victims. The apartment wasn't ready yet, so Pamela had to move into another temporary apartment in the meantime.

Finally, in late April, Pamela moved into her new home.

One year, seven moves.

Bob and the Law

Bob was never punished for what he did to Pamela.

He ran. He grabbed his clothes and ran.

Pamela filed an order of protection on May 12, 2003, the day after Bob struck her. This order prohibited Bob from coming near her, her place of employment, or her home.

Pamela kept pestering the police to investigate her complaint against Bob. Finally, on September 18, 2003, a detective arrested Bob. His brother posted bail. Bob was charged with a felony assault and battery. He pleaded not guilty.

The wheels of justice turned slowly. Finally, on February 5, 2004, the trial started. It lasted six days. Tom spoke for the defense and vouched for Bob. Pamela avoided eye contact with Bob during the trial, which ended in a hung jury. One male juror decided there wasn't enough evidence to prove Bob had hit Pamela, despite the photographs, the testimony of Officer Gonzalez, and Pamela's own testimony.

The judge was furious at the outcome.

In the case of a hung jury, another jury must be selected and the case must be tried over again. While the case was in the process of going to trial again, Bob accepted a plea bargain and pled guilty to one misdemeanor count of assault and battery. He is still awaiting sentencing.

Pamela wants a clean break from Bob financially, legally, and emotionally, but her financial circumstances make a proper divorce impossible. She can't afford a divorce attorney to file for a contested divorce, yet she makes just enough money to disqualify her from free legal assistance from the state.

She has received paralegal assistance from the state of Arizona, but the counselor could only give her guidance, not advice. To be free from Bob's financial debt, Pamela must find a pro bono divorce attorney to take on her case. She's still looking.

In the meantime, Bob lives in their house with his girlfriend.

The Road Ahead

Pamela can't fathom how her life spiraled into her current situation. She is deeply embarrassed about her missing teeth and scarred lip. She is humiliated every time she has to tell her story at one government agency or another, trying to get legal help or basic necessities. She feels like a refugee every time she returns to her assisted-living apartment. She lost her family and her identity. Pamela is a defeated victim from an unjust and undeclared war.

Pamela gets up in the morning and goes to work out of habit. Something inside her keeps her functioning. It's an innate, almost unconscious hope that things will someday get better. She wants a normal, fulfilling life once again. As her tongue feels the empty space where four teeth should be, she wonders, "I'm a good person, aren't I? It has to get better."

roadside respects

Drew Bratcher, University of Missouri

The second week of March has not been good for John Stone — another sub-par week following a sub-par month in which he only picked up 16 deer, nine fewer than his average. Most people don't measure their months in deer, but for Stone each road-killed deer is $40, and nine below average is a $360 hit.

At 42 years old, with short hair, short sideburns and a thin beard and mustache the color of a freshly paved road, Stone is a deer cleanup specialist who couldn't care less about the squirrels, rabbits, skunks, dogs, possums, raccoons, snakes, armadillos, blown-out tires or any other inanimate object that has been known to occupy a Missouri road shoulder. Stone is a deer man in a city where it pays to be one. According to the Department of Conservation, in 2003 Boone County roads were the reported death sites of at least 463 deer, many of which took their last breath on Columbia roads.

Stone won his year-long contract, the only one issued by the Department of Conservation for deer cleanup in Columbia, last summer because he offered the lowest bid — $35 less than the next lowest bidder. But he made up the difference during the next year when on some days he'd load the rack on the back of his gold Chevy truck with up to eight deer carcasses.

However, by the end of the second week of March, Stone begins to accept that maybe the drastic changes in the weather — warm and sunny one hour and chilly and cloudy the next — had kept young bucks from trying their hooves at outrunning headlights. But at 4:30 p.m. Thursday he gets a call. A deer is down off Chapel Hill Road. It isn't much, but it is $40 toward making the week bearable, a modest prize at the end of winter.

When he cruises by on Friday morning, he sees it. Because the deer is small, he decides to pick it up on his way home from the construction site where he's been working as part of a three-man crew remodeling a dilapidated Columbia home. Once the conservation department, which must first receive a call from the public, calls Stone, he has 24 hours to scoop up the deer. If he can find it. Some scavengers, animal and otherwise, have been known to beat Stone to the scene, robbing him of his collection and leaving a bloodstain in its place.

On Friday afternoon, when he and the crew get to a stopping point, Stone throws his tools in the metal box in his truck bed, mounts the truck and steers it into the bumper-car track of rush hour in Columbia. The dust that hovers over tire-whipped gravel roads on early spring days covers Stone's truck like sugar on a donut. The dirty Chevy is more than an extended cab, bed, tires and rack. Stone's truck is his moving connection between carpentry and deer cleanup.

Inside, dirt-matted seats lie beneath root beer-colored windows littered with deer stickers. Above the window of the same door panel that's chalked with sawdust and bleached from sunshine, Stone keeps pictures of his two boys and the deer they killed. The one thing Stone loves more than shooting deer himself is watching his boys shoot them. Fingerprints mark the bent left corner of the picture of his youngest son holding up an eight-pointer. On lunch breaks and while waiting at stop lights, Stone has pulled the picture down and shown it to many passengers.

Stone wears his jacket — the type worn by little league

baseball coaches and copied by renegade kids who spend $1.50 at thrift stores to look retro — for the same reason he wears his ink-blue jeans and striped Adidas shoes: it's functional. He speaks with the sincere and occasional slang and swear of the Midwest that comes out clean no matter how dirty it gets. Most Columbians don't know Stone, but they'd know if he didn't do his job. If he worked in a slaughterhouse, he'd be the guy who keeps the floors clear. As it is, he helps keep Columbia from looking like a slaughterhouse.

But the real work is disposing of the deer once he's racked them up. Stone decides among five options: Dig a hole and bury them; cover them with brush and burn them; put them out as bait for coyote hunting; take them to D-D Farm and feed them to the big cats; or, if the deer are too rotted to be moved in one piece, drag them into a nearby ditch and pour lime on them. Stone often waits until the morning after he picks them up to dispose of carcasses. In the meantime, the deer go anywhere Stone goes: the bank, the grocery store, the gas station.

One day he stopped at Dairy Queen before disposing of a carcass. The deer's legs and head were dangling off the rack and polluting the thought of ice cream for anyone in the parking lot who happened to catch a whiff of the dead animal rising up on the afternoon air. Within moments, a conservation department officer pulled up, handcuffs jingling against the driver-side window.

"What's the deal with this deer on the back of your truck?" the officer asked, ready to take the necessary action. Possession of a road-killed deer requires a disposition form that can be obtained by the Department of Conservation. "I'm the guy who picks them up," Stone said. The officer's eyes dipped down behind his sunglasses and came back,

"Oh, OK. You're John."

"Yessir," Stone said. The officer swore it was the first time he'd met Stone and told him he appreciated his work. Looking him straight in the eyes, he firmly shook Stone's hand, the same hand that gripped a deer carcass minutes earlier.

Most days are not as eventful. On this Friday, he pulls his truck over, cautiously opens the squeaking door to avoid becoming roadkill himself and slaps a yellow strobe light on the roof.

"Yep. It's a button buck, 1-year-old. Would have sprouted antlers next year if he'd made it," says Stone, touching the stubs buried beneath the fur between its ears. If the deer had been older and sprouted antlers that hadn't been thieved before he got there, Stone would have skull-capped it and added the horns to his massive collection. Antlers once graced the walls of his den, when he had one. Now they rest in a box and are spilling onto the floor in the corner of his parent's garage because a recent divorce robbed him of his trophy room. In the box, there is a seven-point rack that Stone cut from a road-killed deer, only three points less than the largest rack that once looked out over his den. Some people would have sold the antlers or ground them into a tincture that happens to be a popular natural aphrodisiac, but for Stone the antlers are simply a nice trophy, a small perk that sometimes comes with the job.

A black stream of blood runs from the yearling's left ear into the dark puddle near its eye. The deer has been dead for several days, and the stench is enough to make the tough-stomached Stone, a man known to plunge his hands into a deer's gut to warm them on cold hunting mornings, cringe.

A memory flashes in his mind. Last summer he'd gone to pick up a doe, and an army of plundering maggots, sensing new flesh, soon turned on him quicker than static hopping across a television screen when the cable cuts out. He almost lost his stomach when the adrenaline he'd exerted from swatting the parasites away wore off.

"Just go ahead and multiply the smell of this one here by three in the summer," he says, pulling his rubber gloves over his hands. A passing truck with a loud muffler lets out a honk. Stone throws up a wave, unsure if the driver knows him or was simply thanking him for his service. For the first time all week, he is happy it is March. Sure it had been a disappointing month, full of deer dashing to safety across car-sparse streets, but at least he doesn't have to resort to the stick-and-a-spoon method, which is the term used to explain the process of shoveling up a sun-melted deer in the summer months, meaning you need a stick and a spoon to do the job. Picking them up is like trying to eat soup with a fork.

He rolls the lifeless beauty over to get a good enough handle to toss it onto the rack like a bag of dog food, and blood erupts like lava out of the buck's ear and onto Stone's shoes. He doesn't flinch. He holds the deer in his arms in a paternal way, aimed at securing some sort of dignity for the animal despite the idiocy and sloppiness of its death. As a man in touch with nature, Stone is a throwback colliding with contemporary Columbia. And in that sense, he's not so unlike the deer he scoops up. He's a deer lover, and deer lovers love deer to the bloodiest end.

It's not until the dead animal is on the rack, where nearly 200 deer have lain before, that Stone finally notices his shoes. He wipes his mustache with the back of his hand, and is assured that in the same way that the jet-propelled wind would shortly blow away the blood-smeared leaves the deer has left behind, the fresh blood on his shoes is nothing a little bleach can't make white again.

a habit that sucks?

Paige Greenfield, Northwestern University

Katie Lowes, a 22-year-old actress, travels across Manhattan from auditions to rehearsals to performances to meetings with agents. Each time she boards the subway, she shuffles into a vacant seat, and as her wavy chestnut hair tumbles in front of her face, she sneaks her left thumb into her mouth until she reaches her next stop. "It's an extremely calming habit," says Lowes, who has sucked since ultrasounds depicted her thumb-in-mouth in utero. "Although it could lead to crooked teeth, it doesn't kill you like smoking cigarettes, or heroin or crack."

Lowes sucks her thumb throughout the day, but mostly at night when she returns home exhausted. She types on the computer using one hand while sucking her other thumb. Before going on stage, Lowes indulges to calm her nerves. Her mother jokes that, when she becomes famous, Jay Leno will taunt her with photographic evidence of her sucking habit. "I wouldn't care," says Lowes. "It's who I am, it's what I do."

Few adults will admit to clinging to their childish habits. But when they fall asleep clutching their tattered teddy or wash-cloth sized security blanket, or sneak into the bathroom during work for a quick thumb-suck, the truth emerges: some have never abandoned their childhood habits. In fact, more than 250,000 U.S. adults suck their thumbs, says Harvey Miller, 53, who runs thumbsucking-adults.com. In a typical week, Miller's website averages 1,200 hits. While all visitors may not be thumb-suckers, the website alone can change people's views about the social stigma attached to adult thumb-sucking.

The habit is becoming increasingly visible in public

spaces, in literature, in movies and especially on the Internet. With the summer 2005 release of the film Thumbsucker, featuring Keanu Reeves, Benjamin Bratt and Vince Vaughn, it will receive national exposure. Thumbsucker, based on the 1999 comedic novel of the same title by former New York Magazine book critic Walter Kirn, is a coming-of-age tale about a teen thumb-sucker who turns to his hippie orthodontist (Reeves) and high school debate coach to conquer his habit.

Miller, a business owner in East Meadow, N.Y., who sucks his thumb, launched thumbsuckingadults.com in Sept. 1998. His inspiration came during a two-week Florida vacation, where he witnessed three different women thumb-sucking in public. He searched the Internet and discovered a site exploring this phenomenon, but the webmaster was shutting it down because his girlfriend was unhappy with his frequent communication with other women. Miller created a new site, and six years later thumbsuckingadults.com is the only resource of its kind.

The website features an extensive Frequently Asked Questions section, ranging from thumb-suckers' inquiries about disclosing their habit to their partners to why they have continued sucking and whether they should quit. There are links devoted to celebrities who publicly admit to sucking their thumbs, including Kyra Sedgwick, Suzanne Sommers and Rosanna Arquette, and even those who have been photographed seductively with thumb-in-mouth, such as Madonna and Courtney Love. Most significantly, thumbsuckingadults.com has evolved into a support group for those who indulge. The members post messages on the website's forum and connect with each other.

Miller jokingly highlights the habit's advantages, pointing out that it is legal, moral and calorie and carbohydrate-free. Thumb-sucking can enable a person to think better, to sleep under a variety of conditions and possesses no ill health effects, he says. Psychologist Dr. Susan Heitler, although critical of the habit, adds that thumb-sucking "can be tempting because it is genuinely physiologically soothing and is probably less detrimental than smoking for being a soothing habit." It affects brain waves, lowers the heart-rate, and releases the same brain chemicals as meditation, says Heitler.

Thumb-suckers across America agree: this is their relaxation method. Lowes, who will star in a July episode of a new FX dramatic-comedy, Rescue Me, and will play Juliet in the New Canaan Shakespeare Festival's production of Romeo and Juliet in Connecticut this summer, says that she always has the ability to calm herself in the palm of her hand. Deon Rodden, a 22-year-old thumb-sucker and computer consultant from Boca Raton, Fla., echoes Lowes' sentiment. "It has a calming effect," he says. "My heart beat slows down, it makes me more relaxed, helps me when I'm extra stressed and makes me fall asleep."

Fifteen years ago, Eric, 47, who requested that his last name be omitted because he worries he will be judged for his habit, rediscovered thumb-sucking after more than a decade-long hiatus. Out of curiosity, he placed his left thumb into his mouth. "It was like a bolt of lightening," he says. "I thought, 'I forgot how nice this can be.'" Eric, an entertainment executive in Los Angeles, Calif., sucks his thumb throughout the day. "It's not like I walk down the street with my thumb in my mouth," he says. But when stressed, he closes his office door or huddles in a bathroom stall to privately indulge.

But the question remains: What makes these adult thumb-suckers different from those who stopped before their age reached a whole hand? Heitler, author of David Decides: No More Thumbsucking, says that most children should and do stop before they are 3 or 4 years old. "Most people are tuned in to what's appropriate," she says. Thumb-sucking as an adult is "age inappropriate" and is probably the result of "excessively permissive parents, which encourages children to stay on and on." Lowes' parents never approved of her thumb-sucking, but, she says, "I think they've given up."

Miller attributes adult thumb-sucking to a cost/benefit ratio in which the calming effects outweigh any negatives, such as dental problems, calluses and embarrassment. Thumb-suckers capable of hiding their habit enjoy the benefits without negative reactions from others. "Still some, the confident ones, have the attitude that they have a right to thumb-suck, especially since they weren't hurting anyone," says Miller. And some continue because their habit is part of their identity. "It's really my thing," says Lowes. "I'm an actress. I'm a thumb-sucker."

Heitler likens thumb-sucking to the rhythmic activity of sitting in a rocking chair. Both actions are mindless and soothing. Susan O'Neill, 27, a first grade teacher at a Chicago elementary school, says the habit comforts her, especially when she's tired or upset. "That's why I never stopped," she says. "It makes me relax, it calms me down." Rodden, who often works during the night and sleeps at erratic hours, says thumb-sucking gives him the flexibility to nod off at different times. "I find it very difficult to sleep without it; it's my procedure," he says.

But thumb-sucking has its disadvantages. Rodden wore braces when he was 17 to correct the overbite that thumb-sucking caused. But he admits that his dental problems, which cost more than $5,000, did not incite a desire to quit. "Braces are worth the cost," he says. When Lowes was 11 years old, thumb-sucking resulted in an infected gland on the inside of her lower lip from her thumb rubbing against her bottom teeth. The gland swelled to a bubble that had to be removed through surgery. She has also worn a retainer and currently wears Invisalign braces, removable clear molds placed over her teeth to correct their crookedness. Lowes' sucking-related dental problems ring up to at least $7,000.

Many adult thumb-suckers attempted to quit when they were younger but determined that trying to quit was not worth the struggle. Lowes tried breaking her habit through numerous methods but each failed. At 10, she tried covering her thumbs with Band-Aids, but instead she sucked right through them. At night she rubbed a bitter-tasting substance, Thumb/Off, onto her thumbs, but discovered that sucking her thumb for five minutes would eliminate the awful taste and then "it would be smooth sailing," says Lowes. Some thumb-suckers go to more extreme lengths to quit. A retainer-like dental appliance called a "fence" can be bonded to the palate, removing the pleasurable, sucking action that thumb-suckers enjoy.

Despite past efforts, most thumb-suckers do not want to stop. Miller says many people visit the website with intentions to quit, but once they look at the material and realize they are not alone, they almost invariably decide to continue. "The only reason they quit is because of outside values placed on them," says Miller.

For many adult thumb-suckers, the social stigma attached to thumb-sucking frustrates them. Eric, who has been married for 20 years, says he wishes thumb-sucking was socially acceptable. "People are so individual," he says. "They have other habits – cigarette smoking, nail-biting

– different characteristics of our personalities that make us predisposed to certain habits." Thumb-suckers, he says, are just like everyone else. Rodden, whose thumb's calming effects help him to relax and fall asleep, sees no end to the habit. "If anyone felt what I feel when I suck my thumb they'd never want to stop," he says.

Thumb-suckers disagree about whether their habit is indicative of a bold or weak character. While Miller contends that public thumb-sucking is a sign of confidence, Natasha Johns, 26, a human resource specialist for the federal government, insists that she is "a weaker person." Some people can stop cold turkey, says Johns, but "I'm just one of those people who's a little weaker, and continues to hold on to thumb-sucking." But Anji Petroski, 35, a stay-at-home mom, sees it differently. "I don't have a baby complex," she says. "I'm a very aggressive female. It's something that I couldn't break and didn't want to break. We're not hurting anybody by doing it, we don't infringe on anyone, it's not a big deal."

For many thumb-suckers, using accessory objects is another component of their habit. Some suck with a beloved security blanket while others rub silk fabrics, like women's nightgowns or bra straps. For ultimate comfort, Rodden sucks his thumb while lounging upon over-stuffed feather down pillows. Fifteen years ago, when taking a cloth diaper out of the dryer, Eric, a father of now an 11 and 18-year-old, noticed that it was too thin and holey to be used anymore. He stuck his left ring finger through one of the holes, lifted his thumb to his mouth and started sucking. "It was a piece of the missing puzzle," says Eric. He cut off a section and used it for about five years until it shredded. Within another five years, Eric went through another piece and figures he has a few months left with the current segment. The more worn the cloth becomes, the more Eric says he loves its softness and the odor that he can only describe as "being very uniquely it." To prolong the cloth's life, he washes it in a net bag designed for delicates, and dreads the prospect of starting a new piece. The three-inch cloth is tattered, frayed and dotted with holes. Eric says that it is the perfect size to bunch into his hand and keeps it in his left pants pocket during the day. The accessory, he explains, is a companion to his habit: "My thumb-sucking doesn't feel as complete without it and it doesn't feel as complete without my thumb-sucking."

To the chagrin of many thumb-suckers, celebrities, such as Madonna and Courtney Love, have used the habit to sell albums. According to a section of Miller's website, "Why it's Sexy," thumb-sucking's sexualization is to be expected since it focuses on the "sensual oral center…and so much of what is human has become sexualized in one way or another." A 56-year-old man, who spoke on the condition of anonymity, says he finds thumb-sucking women "very erotic." When he was in graduate school, he accidentally caught his girlfriend, a CEO of a large company, thumb-sucking during the night. "I have since come to the conclusion that my erotic experience may have been that by her sucking her thumb – so totally out of character from her powerful woman, independent image – she showed a human and a bit vulnerable side that I enjoyed," he says. "But wow, it was an intense feeling."

Thumb-suckers can face a difficult challenge when revealing their habit to their partners. Johns has had the same boyfriend for three years, but never told him that she sucks her thumb. She makes sure that she is alone or waits for him to fall asleep at night before sneaking her left thumb into her mouth. In the past, boyfriends left because of her habit, so she decided to avoid the risk with this relationship. "At first they think it's cute," says Johns. "But once they realize how involved it is they've broken up with me." For Lowes, sucking her thumb in front of others depends on her comfort level. "If I'm comfortable around you, then I'll suck my thumb around you," she says. Lowes has had steady boyfriends since age 15, and has been dating the same man for more than four years. "No one has ever had a problem with it. They find it kind of cute, become used to it and stop noticing," she says. Rodden's fiancée is not as comfortable with his habit. "At first she was OK with it," he says. "Now she seems to be somewhat jealous. I'll be lying next to her sucking my thumb, and she feels she has to compete with it."

When Miller began the website, he corresponded with a 44-year-old woman who never admitted her habit to her spouse. She said that she would rather her husband find out she was having an affair than know that she sucked her thumb. Heitler warns that thumb-sucking can be detrimental to a person's mental health if it is kept a secret. "Those adults who would be embarrassed if the habit was public can hold them back from relationships if a woman doesn't want a man to know she sucks her thumb at night," says Heitler. She adds that thumb-suckers have failed to develop effective ways of dealing with everyday stresses and resort to their habit for relaxation. "Being able to think in a constructive way about what the stresses are, living life in a pace that's calming enough or putting on upbeat or soothing music are more age-appropriate calming methods for adults," says Heitler.

Still, many adult thumb-suckers across America intend to continue their habit and are increasingly taking it out from under the covers. Thumbsuckingadult.com's forum is as active as ever with 835 members posting more than 30 messages each week. Miller is currently processing 2,500 surveys he administered to thumb-suckers over the past five years. The responses, he hopes, will shed light on the characteristics of those who share the habit.

In a country where 23 percent of the adult population smokes despite its deadly consequences, it is curious that smoking continues to be socially acceptable. Perhaps we would all be healthier if we exchanged our Marlboros, Big Macs and Miller for our thumbs.

surviving the guilt
James Carlson, University of Missouri

John Krogh woke from the flashback with a shudder. God, won't these ever stop? His short, cropped white hair glistened with sweat, and his blue eyes peered around the hospital room.

Please God, give me the strength to endure.

That uneasy feeling swept over him again. Guilt. A heavy blanket of guilt weighing him down. Guilt because he is 69 and alive. Guilt because they were younger and are now dead. He wished for the times back home when he'd go to bed dreaming of his next home-improvement project.

His home in Utah sits on a plateau atop a canyon on the outskirts of Wallsburg, which is 56 miles away from Salt Lake City. Outside his back-facing window pine trees dot the snow-capped mountains of the Wasatch Range. Through the windows in his bedroom, the sagebrush valley rolls down to Wallsburg three miles away. Deer and elk trod through the area often.

The house John and his wife, Karen, built was complete in anyone else's eyes. But as John lay down every night for bed, visions of the next task bounced around his head: crown moldings and baseboards, cabinets and maybe a fireplace in the basement. He used to picture it all.

Not anymore.

Lying in a Missouri hospital 1,200 miles from his canyon-side home, he could only picture the horror. Every time he closed his eyes, it was there. The dead woman across his lap. The burning plane. The guilt.

What if ... what if ... what if ...

On Tuesday, Oct. 19, 2004 commuter airplane Flight 5966 crashed into a wooded area near the Kirksville airport. The largest section of the plane that remained intact was burned to only ashes as firefighters fought the flames throughout the evening. Of the 15 on board, only two survived. (Courtesy of Al Maglio/Kirksville Daily Express)

Just a Medical Conference

John gathered his luggage on October 19, 2004 and headed for his front door. He grabbed his wallet, keys and Listerine Cool Mint PocketPaks from a table by the entrance. He was flying to Missouri.

He had no idea he'd soon be on the country's deadliest flight in 2004 – the deadliest flight in Missouri since 1973. He didn't know his plane would be one of four to go down in Missouri in October, a period that left 20 dead and only three survivors. And he didn't know that he, the oldest on any of the flights, would be one of those three. He was just flying to a medical conference.

John had taught at the Kirksville College of Osteopathic Medicine for 23 years, and while there, he won multiple teaching awards for his excellent relationships with students. Clark Ator was one of those students.

Clark attended the same Church of Jesus Christ of Latter-Day Saints in Kirksville as John and his wife, and the two began playing basketball and attending church events together. But it was Clark's generous personality that really drew John to him. Two years later Clark became a doctor, and when one of John's students couldn't find a physician to do rounds with, Clark would always offer his services. Clark later joined the staff of the Kirksville College of Osteopathic Medicine and became a regional assistant dean in Utah with John.

The first leg of John's flight took him into St. Louis. Seven other employees from the college's regional offices around the country gathered to board the plane to Kirksville. John said hello to Mark Varidin, another of John's former students who was now the regional assistant dean in Florida.

John walked up the tarmac's portable staircase and into Corporate Airlines' 19-seat turboprop jet, Flight 5966. There was a one-seat row to the left of the aisle and a two-seat row on the right. John chose the emergency row on the right. Here he could stretch out his 6-foot-1-inch frame in the extra space.

As he sat down by the window, Wendy Bonham, his assistant from Utah, leaned over from her seat left of the aisle.

"We've got assigned seats, and I'm not sure that's yours," she said. John peered around the plane.

"I'm the last one on, so I don't think it will matter," John replied.

They were in the air at 6:45 p.m.

Flight 5966 had 10 people traveling to the seminar in Kirksville, eight of them from the college's regional offices. Two photographers and a history teacher were also on board. The 13 passengers came from Texas and Utah, Michigan and Ohio, New York and Florida. One of those 13, sitting less than 10 feet from John, was 39-year-old Clark Ator.

Up front, the two pilots were beginning their 14th hour on duty and sixth flight of the day.

This can't be happening

Three women carried on a lively conversation near the front of the plane, but the roaring engine prevented John from hearing much. He turned his attention out the window.

Patches of fog passed by in the darkening night, and

John thought of a time 17 years earlier when Karen had been flying into Kirksville. The cloud cover was too heavy then, and the pilot had to turn around.

John heard the landing gear extend and snapped out of his thoughts. His daughter, Janelle, and grandchildren were waiting at the airport. John tried to reach in his pants pocket for his Listerine strips. He couldn't reach them with his seat belt on and decided to wait until they landed.

He crossed his legs and leaned over to tell Wendy about Karen's foggy flight.

BANG!

Before he could open his mouth, there was a loud metallic crash like a car tearing into a tin shed. People screamed. This couldn't be happening, could it? People were talking a moment ago. No sudden loss of altitude. Just a crash. Seconds later, a series of staccato bumps. No one screamed now; they didn't have the breath.

The plane rattled. The lights flickered. John gripped his armrests. More jolting knocks. More loud thumps. Then nothing. The pilots had radioed Kansas City's regional control tower at 7:27 p.m. to say the flight was going fine. According to the National Transportation Safety Board, the plane crashed 10 minutes later in a wooded patch four miles from the airport. Visibility on the ground was excellent, but a thick cloud cover hovered 300 feet above the airport. It's possible the pilots didn't see the trees until it was too late.

The Terrain Awareness and Warning System, a device that alerts pilots to obstacles in their path, such as trees, will be required on all commercial planes with six seats or more by March 29. Before the crash, Corporate Airlines had installed the system on two of its 11 planes. John's flight was not one of them.

John woke up to a smoky cabin. Papers, luggage and clothes were strewn everywhere. A single person groaned. John took a breath. The haze singed his nostrils and burned his eyes. There was a weight on his lap, and he looked down. A woman in a red sweater and a brown leather jacket lay across his knees. Blood covered her arm and hand, and she wasn't moving.

Was he the only survivor? That couldn't be.

He looked to his left and saw light pouring in from an opening. He had to get out. He moved the woman and fell to the ground. His hip was broken. He struggled across the aisle.

Wendy's voice rang out.

"Dr. Krogh! Dr. Krogh!"

She was alive! If he could stand on the wing outside, maybe he could pull some people out. There was hope. But when he stuck his head out the opening, his heart sank. The wing was gone, and the plane was lodged 8 feet off the ground in a patch of oak and hickory trees. His hip screamed at him, and he made the only decision he could. He threw himself out.

Falling eight feet, he landed on his head. Perhaps this is when he broke his back and ribs. Flames from burning debris tickled his feet, and he immediately crawled away on his back. The 69-year-old man with a broken hip, a broken back and broken ribs mustered all his upper body strength to distance himself from the fire. He saw another figure appear at the opening and tumble out. He'd later learn it was Wendy, who would also survive. He struggled on 25 feet through a rose thicket that tore at his skin until he couldn't continue.

John looked up through the thorny bush at the fuse-lage stuck in the tree.

BOOM!

The plane spit plumes of fire toward the heavens. The canary-yellow leaves of autumn scattered about the ground became, for a moment, illuminated by the burst of flames. Molten plastic rained down, burning his legs and feet.

Minutes passed, and the explosions slowed. The night crackled with small fires. Less than a foot from John's face, a mouse scurried across the thorny branches. This whole thing didn't make sense. He had lived 69 good years. So many people on the plane had lived only half that.

The situation slowly took hold of John. Tears trickled down his cheeks. Mark Varidin left behind a wife and child. Clark left behind a wife and seven children. John lost it.

He sobbed and sobbed. For the people he knew: Mark and Clark. For the people he didn't: Richard Sarkin, Steven Miller, Judith Diffenderfer, M. Bridget Wagner, Toni Sarantino, Kathleen Gebard, Matthew Johnson, Paul Talley, Rada Bronson, Kim Sasse and Jonathan Palmer. He cried for their families left behind. He cried for the years they would not live. Lying in pain in a patch of thorns in the middle of a northern Missouri field, John cried for everything.

More than 20 minutes passed before John heard rustling.

"Confirmed sighting of downed aircraft," someone said.

"Over here, over here," John managed to squeak. His voice came out no louder than telephone-conversation level. Finally, someone stumbled across his bloody body, and rescuers gathered around him.

Troy Mihalevich, a flight paramedic, leaned over John.

"I used to wrestle with your son, Dr. Krogh," he said.

John was safe now, but his emotional journey had just begun.

Part of the pilots' log book, recovered only 15 feet

from the burning wreckage, remained intact after a large portion of the plane's body was destroyed. Pieces of the manifest scattered for 5 or 10 feet around the area, and the pages that weren't incinerated are being used as evidence in the pending lawsuits. (Courtesy of Al Maglio/Kirksville Daily Express)

A Guilty Conscience

In a dark room filled with beeping machines at Northeast Regional Medical Center in Kirksville, John tried to sleep. His conscience, however, would not allow him to. When his eyes shut, his mind opened to the crash.

Debris floating around the foggy cabin. Light pouring in from the left. The bloodied woman across his knees and the balls of fire shooting into the sky.

He could picture it all. His faith told him to pray.

Please God, give me the strength to endure.

During the day, John's psychiatrist Dr. Andrew Lovy just listened. John talked through what had happened, and the doctor nodded. It was good to talk, the doctor said.

But couldn't John think about something else for just a minute? What about the cabinets and crown moldings and fireplaces that awaited him back in Utah? He longed to think of that again, to dream of the next project. But his mind wouldn't allow him such a reprieve.

Two weeks after the crash, Travis Lee, a respiratory therapist, visited John's room for a checkup. When Travis mentioned the crash, John sniffled then choked up. He reached up with his hand, latched onto Travis' neck and pulled him into an embrace. John sobbed and stammered, "If only I hadn't broken my hip, I could have helped them."

John's fingers dug into the therapist's neck. His voice caught as he tried to get his breath. He sobbed on Travis's shoulder. If John could hold onto him long enough, maybe things would be different.

"If only I hadn't broken my hip, I could have helped them," he repeated. "If only I hadn't broken my hip."

John didn't want to let go. He couldn't let go.

Please God, give me the strength to endure. Give me the strength to endure.

A couple of days later he sat down with Dr. Lovy. Up to this point, John had done most of the talking. It was good to get it out, right? But John had gotten it out. He had talked about it, and still the blanket of guilt choked him.

He hadn't sat in his assigned seat. He had kept his seat belt on instead of taking it off. He had crossed his legs seconds before the crash. One doctor said this caused his left leg, not his head, to take the brunt of the impact. Plus he was the oldest person on the plane by 15 years.

There were so many reasons to say "if only," so many reasons to ask why. Why did he survive? Why did Clark, 30 years younger, die? If only he hadn't broken his hip, maybe he could have ...

But when this session started, Dr. Lovy didn't just listen.

"How long did it take you to get out of there?" the doctor asked.

"Just seconds," John said.

"How bad was the smoke?"

"It was bad. It burned my eyes, burned my nose."

"If you were able to bring the people to the opening, what would you have done?"

"I guess I would have thrown them out."

"Do you think they were already dead? Would they have survived the fall? How would you have dragged them away from the flames?"

John didn't say anything else. He let the doctor's words roll around in his head. On November 12, three weeks after the crash, John, with a walker rolling in front of him, limped out to a motor home where his two sons, Benjamin and Frank, were standing.

The two packed the walker into the motor home's closet, helped John into the vehicle and began the journey 1,200 miles back to his home in Utah. The doctor's words continued to replay in John's mind.

The Road to Recovery

It was December, two months removed from the crash. John sat up from the sofa, walked to the TV and turned off the 10 o'clock news. His left leg hitching with each step, he walked toward the staircase of his Utah home.

He passed the windows that looked out on the snow-capped mountains. He limped up the stairs and into his bedroom where the windows looked out over the valley. He crawled into bed and pulled the covers up around his neck.

John had talked with Clark's wife, Karlene, the day after Thanksgiving. The autopsy showed no smoke in Clark's lungs. He died on impact.

The weight was lifting from John's shoulders. With his wife beside him, John turned out the lights, closed his eyes and pictured it all again.

Knotty wood around a fireplace in the basement. That's what the house needed next.

all hail the queens

Misty Huber, University of Kansas

Alexus calls me to say she's stuck in traffic on her way to Lawrence from Kansas City, Mo., and she'll be a few minutes late to our 6:30 p.m. interview. This is my first time talking to Alexus Panache. She directs the "Alexus Panache Show," a once-a-month drag show at Jack Flanigan's Bar & Grill, 806 W 24th St., hosted on Wednesday's alternative lifestyles night. Before today I had only talked to her male alter ego, Dan Fulk, a freelance makeup artist for Estée Lauder and M.A.C cosmetics.

I arrive at Jack Flanigan's Bar & Grill at 6:35 p.m., surprised to see that Alexus is already there. "A queen is never late," she tells me. "Everyone else is just early." She is wearing a green sleeveless t-shirt, baggy shorts and flip-flops, with a flawless French-tipped pedicure. She has comedy and tragedy masks tattooed on her upper arm. She and another performer, Montana, are eating Sonic. They're already in heavy makeup and false eyelashes, preparing for tonight's show, but they tell me they aren't even close to ready. We sit down at a table as the two dig into their fast-food bags.

Alexus tells me she got into drag on a dare from a group of friends. She did theater in high school, and became interested in makeup, entertaining and dancing. "Drag is just another form of theater," she explains. I notice she keeps referring to me as "honey" or "sweetie." She went through many looks before creating Alexus Panache. She picked the name from the "Dynasty" character Alexis Carrington, played by Joan Collins, and panache, which is a French word for "pizzazz." She did her first show in April 2001. Now she does the drag shows at Flanigan's, and occasionally at Tootsies, 1822 Main St., Kansas City, Mo. Still, she says, drag is more a paid hobby than a lifestyle. Alexus is only a small part of Dan, she says. As Alexus, she says she's a little cattier and more fabulous. She likes glitter, glamour and looking pretty.

Alexus tells me a stereotype she faces is that people think she wants to be a woman. She also says she doesn't do drag for a sexual kick, and she doesn't do sexual things with men as Alexus. Montana tells me there's even a stigma in the gay community that all queens are whores. This perception of immorality seems strange when I find out Montana does drag on Sunday nights and gives all the profits to the Kansas City Free Health Clinic, 5119 E. 24th St., Mo.

Montana chose her drag name from a character in the 1991 movie Soapdish. She's been doing drag for 16 years. At age 21 Derek Dyer, Montana's male name, was working at a gay bar in Kansas City, Mo., where he met drag show director, Miss Sandy Kaye. "She did a Judy Garland you would not believe," Montana says. Derek was fascinated that men could look like women. He moved to San Francisco, where he made a living just doing drag, but missed his family in the Kansas City area. He moved back and is again working with his "drag mother," Miss Kaye, and managing an apartment complex. Montana does drag two to three times a week in Kansas City, Mo. She says there is no difference between her and Derek. "I'm the same person on the inside," she says. "There's no emotional change."

Beauty is Pain
The girls have converted the women's bathroom into their dressing room. The smell of hairspray is thick as Montana fluffs a wig on a plastic foam head. Alexus keeps her stage makeup in a huge electrical box; inside are M.A.C

cosmetics and Ben Nye stage makeup. "Cover Girl is to cover a girl, not a boy, honey," she says. They keep their costumes in large blue plastic storage bins. Because the clothes they need are made to fit women's bodies, they have to make a few modifications, such as buying strapless tops to accommodate their wider shoulders, or making their own drag clothes, as Alexus does.

The drag transformation is painful, but you get used to it, Alexus says. Demonstrating how she creates cleavage, she grips the sides of her chest with one hand, and pinches them together. She tapes her faux cleavage with clear packing tape before she stuffs. Drag queens also have to tuck their male genitalia between their legs, and if they're wearing something skimpy, they use duct tape to hold it in place. I wince, but Alexus just shrugs. To avoid shaving their legs, some queens wear up to 10 pairs of pantyhose, Alexus says, but she can get away with a pair of dance tights covered with a pair of nude fishnets. She also glues her heavy jewelry to her skin to keep it from falling off during her dance routines.

Three GQ-esque young men show up to help Alexus and Montana set up their stage. Brandon Prusa, Ulyssus sophomore, says he's helped with all of the shows since he met Alexus last year at Flanigans. He's gay, but not an aspiring queen, he says. Alexus and Montana hang black and red curtains to create a backstage area, while singing to No Doubt's "Just a Girl." Still in their male clothes, they are stapling brightly colored fabric to the curtains. Alexus jokes, "Don't make me get butch." In not much longer than an hour, they have set up a stage and catwalk on the dance floor, complete with a pole.

At about 10 p.m., two more performers arrive, almost in full costume. Desiree Luv is a voluptuous 24-year veteran who does a lot of character drag, invoking Tina Turner and Patti LaBelle. She tells me there's an art to female impersonation; one that's transformed into a beauty competition. She is the only transsexual of the group. She says she has always felt very feminine and as a child everyone always thought she was female. The difference between her and the other girls is the lifestyle, she says. Desiree lives as a woman, she has size 38 C breasts from hormone therapy, but hasn't had sexual-reassignment surgery. She performs in drag shows six nights a week and runs a party bus, called the Mudslide, in Kansas City, Mo. Her transformation to drag takes less time, just 20 minutes.

The queen next to her is tall and slender Channing LaRue. She's been doing drag for almost seven years. Several years ago she was a theater and music student named Andy at Carnegie Mellon University in Pittsburgh. Andy became a music teacher during his coming-out period in 1997. He soon quit teaching and began bartending, and now he is a hairdresser. Tonight as Channing, she describes drag as her "Aha!" moment. She had always wanted to perform, and within a year was doing drag one or two nights a week. She tells me her character, Channing, is a senator's wife with a background in ice skating.

The girls banter and joke while getting ready in the dressing room. It's an easy, relaxed atmosphere. The last of the performers, a sassy, dark-skinned Milano queen, named Iman Mykales, shows up shortly before showtime. She complains she got lost on the way from Kansas City, Mo. Iman makes her living on drag shows, doing four to five shows a week. She holds 11 titles, and is the reigning Miss Gay Kansas City, she says. She started 10 years ago, as Michael, on a bet from her friends. "And then began the drama," she says.

Show and Tell

It's almost 11 p.m., and the crowd starts to pour in. It's mostly gay men, some lesbians and straight women, and a handful of straight men. "The heteros come because they've never seen this before, except on Ricki Lake," Alexus says. A few people sneak into the dressing room, and everybody is eager to meet and greet the queens. Their celebrity status is obvious. I expect to be asked to leave the dressing room, but the queens seem to have forgotten I'm there. Desiree walks out topless in pantyhose and a girdle and I can only think two things: yes, her breasts are real, and they're bigger than mine. Alexus is in a top and pantyhose. They're singing and dancing to "Hey Ya" by OutKast while putting on their finishing touches. They tease each other and gossip. Iman's recounting an episode from earlier that week. "And I was like, I will whoop your ass and then put you in drag," she says to Desiree and Channing. Montana wears an outfit just for mingling with the audience before the show. I ask her what she uses to stuff, and she pulls a prosthetic breast covered in fabric out of her bra.

I take my place next to the catwalk. Alexus comes out from backstage in a black bustier and pants with one sequined-denim leg and the other rainbow-colored fringe. She also wears a blonde, shoulder-length wig. The buxom queen is the undisputed star of the show. People push to the front of the catwalk for a chance to put dollar bills in her top. Alexus also emcees the show, heckling the audience more than they heckle back. The show is a cross between a lip-synched concert, a beauty pageant, a pole-dancing show and a comedy club. Alexus announces Desiree, who shocks the audience in a fluorescent, multicolored cat suit and neon yellow pigtails.

Next is Montana, donning a black leather jacket, black

sequined bustier and faded jeans. She has long silver talons and stilettos. She looks a bit like Madonna, with a Farrah Fawcett-inspired feathered mane. Alexus changes backstage into a slinky black dress with a hot pink shawl around her waist, and short brunette hair. She introduces Channing, about whom she jokes is just back from the Republican National Convention. Channing comes out in a bright green can-can dress and a long, blond feathered wig. During her routine, she strips to a neon orange and green ice-skating dress with sequins, and then twirls down to an even skimpier neon yellow fringed skating dress.

Alexus portrays Iman as a bad girl. "She's foul and she will cut you," Alexus warns the audience. Iman walks on stage in jeans, a sleeveless denim zippered top and plenty of bling-bling. The first half of the show wraps up with a slow song from Desiree to "I Believe in Miracles," by Whitney Houston. She's in an off-the-shoulder evening gown and adorned with fist-sized sparkling earrings.

At intermission, in the dressing room, I'm surprised to see Channing out of costume. I had almost forgotten the performers were men. Desiree is shaking her Tina Turner wig, making sure it's secure. The mood is subdued; the girls are getting into their next outfits, or silently rehearsing. They help each other get into costume and fix their hair. The quiet lasts only as long as intermission.

Iman starts the second half a seductive dance to "T-Shirt and My Panties On," by Adina Howard. She wears flashing jewelry that light up, a red body suit with red boots, a blue ripped T-shirt and a high ponytail that makes her resemble Naomi Campbell. The most important aspect of the show is the interaction with the audience. Alexus doesn't speak over the crowd, but rather to them, asking questions and commenting on select patrons' clothing or sexuality.

No one seems to mind even the harshest teasing. One girl is yelling Alexus' name, but Alexus can't see her. She yells back, "Are you pretty?" And then after a moment, "No, you're not because nobody said anything." After Montana's rendition of "Walking on Sunshine" in a yellow and pink swimsuit and leather jacket, Alexus announces Rock the Vote voter registration. She's not campaigning for Kerry as much as she's calling for the ousting of Bush. Next is Channing in another ice-skating outfit, this one blue. Her eyelids are heavily glittered and her routine includes an exhausting number of back kicks and twirls. The event everyone seems to have been waiting for is the pole-dancing competition. Young topless men are picked from the crowd. They strut down the catwalk and dance on the pole while the audience cheers and boos to vote for its favorite. One contestant reveals he's not wearing any underwear to the delight of the crowd. The show is winding down as Desiree, dressed as Tina Turner, performs an ambitious "Proud Mary." Out of breath, she announces Alexus, and the audience once again crowds the stage. In a white, sleek asymmetrical dress, Alexus ends the show with a fast-paced finale.

The queens and their entourages gather their costumes and makeup in the dressing room, while several fans come back to congratulate them on their show. I ask how long it will take to get out of drag, and they all tell me fewer than 20 minutes. "I like to put it on, but I love to take it off," Montana says After almost eight hours at the show, I wonder how these provocative performers can do this night after night. I slip out quietly, knowing it will be a long time before the girls will get past their fans.

Know your vocab

Drag Queen/King: A person, usually homosexual, who dresses in exaggerated clothing and makeup of the opposite sex. Drag is a form of performing art.

Cross-Dresser: A person, usually heterosexual, who dresses in clothing of the opposite sex, sometimes as a sexual fetish.

Transsexual: A person who switches sex through hormones, surgery or both.

© The University Daily Kansan 1996-2005

Consumer Magazine Article: Investigation & Analysis

the face of AIDS in africa

Joanna Mayhew, Boston University

Shifting the Shame

"The culture is promoting AIDS; no question about it," Susan Aradeon, Ph.D. said, shaking her head. "As long as the norm is multiple partners, there will be AIDS."

For this reason, Aradeon, Senior Behavior Change Communication Specialist for the Benin Integrated Family Health Project (PROSAF), lists "promoting contraception to prevent multiple partners" as one of her organization's main objectives in Benin.

PROSAF, a contractor for USAID, was created in 1999 and is located in the Borgou-Alibori Department of Benin. In the year 2000, the department had an AIDS prevalence rate of eight percent – two times the estimated percentage for the country. Still – "I don't know why it's not higher; I don't believe it's not higher," admitted Aradeon, revealing a slight northeastern-American accent. The most probable reason it is not higher is that, in the past, commercial sex workers did not frequent Benin because there was no money in the country. And by the time these workers came, Population Services International (PSI) had widely promoted condoms, according to Aradeon. So, ironically, Benin has potentially benefited by being a poor country.

One part, about a fifth, of the PROSAF project is behavior change. This section, Aradeon's, has its work cut out for it. The Beninese culture not only has deep-seated traditions and norms, but it also a communal culture. Therefore, in order to change the mindsets of individuals, PROSAF first has to change the beliefs of groups.

"We promote family planning to keep the man inside the house," said Aradeon, swiveling in her roller chair to face me. Her office was airy and quiet – everyone else had left for the day. "We're promoting contraception so that the husband doesn't go to other women."

The Beninese believe that a man should not have relations with his wife from the time she is showing in pregnancy until the baby is grown. Traditionally, people thought sperm would kill the unborn baby, said Aradeon. Each ethnic group has a different length of time that should be adhered to after birth. The longest is among the Yoruba – they believe the couple should not have sex until the baby is three-years-old. Islam states that the couple should wait for two years, except to consummate the birth at 42 days after delivery.

Historically, women also returned to their families when pregnant, and this is still frequently practiced. They often stay there until the baby is old enough to come off their back, or about two years.

"People here believe a man physically has to have lots of sex," said Aradeon, as we walked outside past a row of shiny PROSAF SUV vehicles to her car. The setting sun was painting the sky a mélange of rusty colors. "The women believe it too," she continued as she drove. If both believe it, and a man's wife is often gone for up to two years, the result seems obvious. "He's going to have multiple partners. People have to use condoms."

A few moments later, a loud "Shit!" erupted out of Aradeon's mouth. With all dashboard warning signs blinking, her car had lurched to a stop – approximately 10 feet outside of her gate. As it was almost dark outside, she placed orange triangular warning signs behind and in front of her car. "Life is never too easy," she said with an exasperated sigh as we walked into the house.

And as for the consideration of men waiting without sex for their wives to have the baby – "They don't believe it. They think it's unacceptable to assume a grown man can stop from having sex."

Aradeon knows what she is talking about. Though she has only lived in Benin for three years, she spent 25 years in Nigeria and is married to a Nigerian. "That's why I know so much about the culture – I'm right," Aradeon said, in a matter-of-fact tone that strangely gave no hint of conceit. "I say things others aren't saying."

Abstinence does result from these "after birth" traditions, but in a different sense. Abstinence within the marriage takes place – the abstinence that exists when a man is running around with other women. And as the object of getting married in Benin is to have children, a couple gets pregnant as soon as they tie the knot. Therefore, a couple begins being "abstinent" right at the start of their marriage.

PROSAF promotes contraception to solve this problem – so that a husband can continue having sex with his own wife without inevitable pregnancy. This promotion comes in various forms – ranging from theatrical plays to radio spots to interactive sessions on AIDS. In each medium, PROSAF pushes condoms, as well as other contraceptives, over abstinence.

"We've done a lot of promotion of condoms," said Aradeon, disappearing into her bedroom momentarily. I glanced around the large living room. The tidy white-tiled area was comfortably sparse – decorated only by a couch set, coffee table, chandelier light, and blank white walls. "Couples have to start using them when the epidemic is really bad in a country," she said, in a loud voice that traveled through the empty room. "They won't use them if they have a bad rap. We want to normalize them so people will use them."

PSI has been trying to "normalize" condoms for some years by promoting them through radio and television. Religious groups often make the accusation that people haven't been sensitized enough to abstinence, but they are not using these media, according to Aradeon.

"Mass media works," said Aradeon as she emerged from the bedroom. She had changed from her business skirt and blouse to a typical simple Beninese dress – a colorful, cool, and comfortable one-piece that falls like a nightgown. Her gray hair was elegantly swept up into a tight bun.

PROSAF airs various messages through many rural radio stations, as well as in Parakou. These messages air in all different languages – French, Bariba, Fulani, Dendi. "If you want to reach people, radio spots are very important; they get information out – but they don't change attitudes."

Abstinence wouldn't work because asking a Beninese man to abstain is like asking him to be "effeminate," said Aradeon. It seems completely abnormal not to "satisfy." For the young people, PROSAF encourages them to "delay" until they have a partner rather than "abstain."

"Delay doesn't mean sex is bad – abstinence does."

And faithfulness? "Fidelity isn't a product, it's an attitude. People have never heard of it." For this reason, fidelity wouldn't have been successful even if promoted over the media, said Aradeon.

"It's unrealistic to ask people to be faithful. The key is to reduce the number of partners," she paused before dejectedly adding, "But they don't understand that."

I asked Aradeon what she thought about a sight that

had often bothered me in Parakou. At the entrance to the city, a big Prudence-brand condoms sign boasts "l'amour sans risque," love without risk. But, having grown up in the United States, I knew that there was still a risk – maybe small – with using condoms.

"It's better to tell people it's without risk than to say that condoms are 'without risk, except in the case of such and such,'" replied Aradeon, just as the room was enveloped in darkness – the electricity had been cut. I had become accustomed to these frequent cuts soon after moving to Parakou. Aradeon had adapted to them, as well – she continued talking as if nothing had happened. "Public-health wise, you are protecting them much more by pushing condoms."

Very few condoms break; millions are used without breaking. We only hear about the few that do, according to Aradeon. As far as contraceptives being dangerous, childbirth creates a much higher risk. "And contraceptives are a choice." We choose to get in the car when there is a bigger risk in that, she reasoned.

"I think it's a moral imperative to advise them that it is without risk," Aradeon stated firmly. With that, she finally made a move toward a light. She carried in two bright fluorescent lamps that accentuated the whiteness of the room.

PROSAF has organized various plays, in French and Bariba, advocating condoms. One, titled "Spacing our Children," toured for eight months starting in September of 2000. Another, "Condoms for Prevention of AIDS," was performed along with a "pre-test" and a "post-test." PROSAF discovered that before the play, 50 percent of the audience knew condoms can prevent AIDS and 25 percent considered loyalty or abstinence. After the play, 100 percent understood condoms can prevent the disease and 75 percent considered loyalty or abstinence. The play also emphasizes "parent-to-child" transmission rather than simply mother-to-child transmission. PROSAF wants people to understand that fathers can give it to their children by first giving it to their wives. "Hopefully that'll make them think," said Aradeon, getting up and motioning me towards the raised dining room.

The organization also runs other plays that try to reduce the fear and stigma of those living with AIDS. For example, in one called "Fighting AIDS," which recently finished touring in secondary schools, the actors are portrayed as eating out of the same bowl as those who are HIV-positive – without getting infected by them.

Aradeon hopes to soon begin a new phase of awareness – through interactive sessions in various villages. The information content would include discussions on AIDS, human sexuality, human sexual response, traditional norms they have retained, sexual norms that are being passed down, whether these norms are positive or harmful, and whether it is desirable to pass the same norms down to the next generation or to change them.

She originally had the vision for these groups because she saw the young actors from the plays change their mindsets towards sex. Why? "They were immersed by the information."

Therefore, the setup for these sessions will be four groups of 15 to 20 people who get together twice a week. They will have 15 meetings of two-and-a-half hours each – the equivalent of a six-day workshop. Aradeon wants them to absorb the information and share it with others.

PROSAF does not aim their radio broadcasts, plays, and interactive sessions at a single group of people in the population. "There is an underlying belief that if you don't change the men's mindsets, you can forget it," she said. "But it takes two to tango."

As far as "peer educators" in schools, Aradeon thinks the concept is ridiculous. "Twenty kids trying to change the minds of 2000? Bull shit! It won't work."

PROSAF does have an ultimate focus as far as education, though. They want people to know two methods of contraception and two symptoms of STDs for their own sex.

"We're trying to get the community to change something," said Aradeon, passing me a big bowl of sticky rice and vegetables.

'Trying to get the community to is exactly what PROSAF is up against – the community. Collectivism dominates Beninese culture – "It's pervasive," said Aradeon, in between mouthfuls. "It's very hard to change if people don't want you to. People in Benin are raised to respond to collective pressure."

When you ask men to reduce their number of partners or use contraception, you are asking them to change a behavior that is linked to their identity.

"Look at the goddamn map!" interjected Susan suddenly, with her fork raised in the air. I gave her a questioning look, and she clarified. "AIDS started in the States!" In the 1970s and 1980s, AIDS blossomed in the gay community and spread throughout cocaine circles. "But it didn't spread into the middle class. Why not?"

I responded to her question with a second puzzled look.

"Because men having multiple partners after marriage is not at the core of their identity in the States," said Aradeon. American men are not placing their social relationships at risk, not diminishing themselves, by not chasing other women. In Benin, to some extent, men are.

Pressure exists for women, as well. When a married Bariba woman returns to her home town for a ceremony or other special event, she is devalued if no man is "interested" in her.

"It's not easy. People have to choose between a health risk and a social risk. The two are in conflict; you can't have it both ways," said Aradeon, wiping the sweat from her forehead. With the electricity still non-existent, the heat was stifling. "And in a collective society, it's very hard to put your identity at risk" Therefore, PROSAF aims to change people's collective behavior rather than their individual behavior.

The choice between a health risk and a social risk is further simplified by the fact that the Beninese people do not understand the AIDS disease.

"We believe the science in our bodies without question," said Aradeon. Raised an atheist in a New Jersey suburb of NYC, she had no science in high school. But, everything she knows about science she has always believed "on faith" of her society, regardless of never learning it herself.

People in Benin believe in sorcery or fetishes for the same reason – their society does. They don't understand science and viruses, said Aradeon.

"And the AIDS virus is a smarter-than-hell virus. It survives by hiding." AIDS can even hide for up to ten years before ever rearing its ugly head.

"But we can understand a disease hiding in a body; people here can't." Aradeon paused as her "home help," a shy girl of about 18, appeared to clear our plates and serve dessert – mangos. As they were in-season, mangos had become a staple food for me. I didn't know how I would ever part with them in a few months. I eagerly dived into the fruit as she continued, "Even the well-educated have a hard time comprehending."

Benin's collectivist society is in transition. The former society had many more social controls, but now taxation, education, jobs and consumer goods are all individualized. These are all causing a breakdown in the traditional power of elderly people in the villages, said Aradeon.

However, people are leaving old communal pressures only to find new ones away from their village. "Fundamentalism wins – replacing old control with new control." The victory of fundamentalism is obvious in the rapid growth of structured religions like Islam in Benin – where their lifestyle is decided for them.

"They don't grow up making decisions; decisions are made for them by family and community." I nodded my agreement – testimony of my time here – and filled my glass with water for the sixth time. It was a vain attempt to make up for all the fluid I was losing to perspiration. "They find security in clear decisions; we find it in choice," she added.

Westerners are brought up to confront everything in front of them. The Beninese, on the other hand, are taught not to question anything society tells them, said Aradeon.

The collectivist society in Benin also brings with it a different moral control system. The system is regulated by fear – of what would happen to you if do something wrong – but more dominantly by shame – that you would be spurned by society and bring shame on yourself and your family if you do wrong.

The "glory and shame" culture had puzzled me since I had arrived in Benin. I had seen it played out in numerous different scenarios throughout my short time in the country. The culture programs people to first and foremost do anything to bring glory to themselves; and secondly, if not equally as important as the first, to avoid doing anything that will bring shame on themselves.

The shame aspect is confusing because shame is not brought on a person by a wrongdoing; shame is only brought when the person's wrongdoing is discovered.

In the West, people feel guilt for doing something wrong. "Very different," Aradeon stated simply.

An example of this is if somebody brings new jeans for everyone in their village. That person will receive glory for the deed, even if everyone suspects the person stole the jeans. However, if it is found out that the goods were stolen, then the act is wrong and that person is shamed – but not until the act is uncovered.

The same holds true along the line of AIDS. A majority of the population is sleeping around, whether married or unmarried – and, under the surface, everyone knows it. But, if it is disclosed that a person has AIDS, that person is shamed – because his or her promiscuity has been revealed.

Though I had often found this culture, which is so different from the West, confusing and therefore frustrating, Aradeon was more positive. "I'm trying to use it. It's not the way I was brought up," she said, holding out the palm of her hand to concede the fact. "But there's good in it."

Aradeon, through PROSAF, is trying to change how and why people are morally sanctioned. She wants to change what people are shamed by – for example, change the shame of being HIV-positive to the shame of having unprotected sex.

"That's exactly what we're trying do – shift the shame." Aradeon wants to establish "shame sanctions" for people who do things that are negative health-wise and "praise sanctions" on those who have positive habits.

This same strategy would be used with family planning. Instead of a man being shamed by having few children, as is tradition, the man would be shamed by having too many kids to bring them all up correctly, she said.

Aradeon has had these ideas for behavioral change since 1992. "I knew the culture," she repeated. She began working for USAID in 1993 – or more specifically for PATH, Program for Appropriate Technology and Health, under which she is currently employed while working on the PROSAF project. She had no formal training in behavior communication before being signed on with USAID. "I just read everything." With an unpretentious grin, she added, "If you have a Ph.D., you know how to read."

Aradeon had a myriad of jobs before joining USAID – ranging from a Peace Corps teacher to a BCC officer in the Pacific to a university professor of archeological history. "I'm a career changer," she said, shrugging her shoulders with a smile. Though involved elsewhere, she had always wanted to do something with behavior communication. "And now I'm doing it," she said, staring past my shoulder. "I'm really lucky."

Her eyes quickly snapped back into focus as she returned to her shame-shifting idea. "So that's what I'm trying to do. We have to change what's a 'good person' – but it's too hard to do as individuals."

The goal of changing groups of people at a time was hard for me to understand. As a Westerner, I have heard the phrase, "One person at a time," said innumerable times – as a kind of idealistic way of reasoning that you can't change the world overnight, but every person and every step towards the goal counts. I realized I had no idea how you would realistically go about changing the minds of groups. So I asked Aradeon.

"To be honest, I don't think we know very well. My personal aim is to try to find better ways."

The dramas work well with groups because people see everyone else react. People see that others have the same misconceptions as them. Take the play where the people are eating out of same bowl as AIDS victims – people realize that others thought it was possible to catch the disease through that, too.

In the West, there is a mindset that people need to talk about things – bring them into the open – for change to occur. So Western agencies often try to use that same method in Benin. "But people here can't talk about sex. People will start talking about contraceptives after they are all using them – not before." Through the dramas, people can learn together without being in a threatening atmosphere, said Aradeon.

Aradeon's outlook for the future is mixed. She began by saying, "If I'm honest, it's hopeless. Because family planning is the core of identity – and, historically, to have successful family is to have lots of kids."

But this idea is fading, she later said. Beninese society is in transition. Ten years ago in Benin, sex meant placing sperm inside a woman. Now, people do not hold to that belief. Instead, they are starting to think condoms are a good idea – though she added that of course they do not always use them. They may not, but the statistics are positive. In the Borgou-Alibori Department, the 1996 statistics showed that less than six percent of people used contraceptives. In 2002, there was 11 percent contraceptive use, and the numbers are even higher now. The tradition of after-birth abstinence has also broken down quite a bit.

"It takes time to change these ideas," said Aradeon. She believes change happens in about a half generation

– a 25 year-old mother passes on new information to her niece, rather than her daughter.

"But if you are waiting 10 years for change with AIDS, the epidemic is getting deeper and deeper into society."

Aradeon does not believe, as others I had met did, that people need to know somebody with AIDS in order to change. "If they did, I'd give up."

But, she admits people need to know "a lot." They need to know they are at risk with multiple partners. And, if they want to be faithful in marriage, both members of the couple have to make that choice – and even then there is a personal risk.

"With the sexual practices, though, there is no reason to think that AIDS won't escalate – rapidly."

Her confusing responses were more confirmation to me of the complexity of AIDS – and that there is no clear answer for the future of Benin.

Aradeon adjusted her thin glasses and glanced anxiously around the room. "What time is it?" The lack of electricity always makes it seem later than it is – but we had been talking for a while. It was already past 10. Not wanting me to walk in the dark, and having no functioning car to drive me home, Aradeon offered to let me spend the night.

I thanked her for her generous offer but declined it. As I gathered my things, Aradeon continued, saying, "Too often, you don't respect the people you're trying to change. You have to respect them. Why should everyone have to live like you?" She chuckled quietly before adding, "In our case, because they'll live better!"

She walked me to the door of her circular house. "And there are too few people involved in AIDS work who really understand the local culture – so it's a great opportunity."

We paused in front of her small gazebo as she called

for the young girl who had served us dinner. Aradeon insisted that she walk me to the road, where I could find a motorcycle taxi. I stared up at the sky as we waited. The clarity of the innumerable stars made me immensely grateful for the power cut.

"I love my work, no question about it," said Aradeon softly, next to me in the darkness. "Who could ask for a better job?"

Acquiesce

"Your sickness is common in the country right now," the long unnerving silence that followed the statement was finally broken by, "The sickness is called SIDA."

The gravity of what I was witnessing hit me like a punch in the gut. I was sitting in the back of a small bare classroom as Martha Koetsier told her newest patient, Esther, that she was HIV-positive. I could only see the woman's left side. Esther was a beautiful lady who looked about 25 but was actually over 40. She had two traditional Bariba scars – a semicircle curving in towards her mouth on each cheek. She wore a green-and-black light nylon scarf over her head and yellow flip-flops a size too small.

As I watched the consultation, I couldn't help feeling guilty that I knew exactly what sicknesses and social rejection Martha's last statement implied, and that Esther did not. As Paul, a local co-worker of about 24, translated Martha's French into Bariba, Esther's face remained unchanged. She kept her soft brown eyes focused on him and nodded with a "Toh," meaning okay.

Martha locked her concerned aqua blue eyes, accentuated by her blue-beaded necklace and blue dress, on Esther with a clenched jaw as she asked, "Do you know of the sickness?"

"C'est la mort," Esther bluntly replied in French – It's the death.

Esther did not know the details of AIDS – how it's contracted, what it does to a person's immune system, how far-spread its impact is in the world – but she knew the bottom line. It would kill her.

As much ignorance as there is in Benin surrounding AIDS, Martha usually finds that people are at least aware of the fact of looming death.

Even as she spoke the morbid words, Esther remained unsurprised and unperturbed. She shed no tears and raised no objection. She simply accepted her fate.

I felt like jumping up in her place; I wanted to argue for her, "But how? Why? This isn't fair! I had plans for my future! This can't be happening to me!" But I sat still in the uncomfortable child-size chair and tried to swallow her resignation.

Esther's blood had been tested the day before at HEB, Evangelical Hospital of Bembereke, the governmental zone hospital in the town of Bembereke, in the northern half of Benin. HEB is considered one of the best hospitals in the country, and Martha's AIDS counseling and awareness project is a branch off of the hospital. Esther had come to seek help at HEB because she had been struggling with a variety of problems for over two years – periodic diarrhea, weight loss, body aches, and sores in her mouth and vagina.

Martha had started this meeting in her temporary schoolroom office with the test results. "Yesterday we tested your blood and found a little problem. It's a little complicated so we invited you here to explain." Martha now follows this protocol about 10 times a month – the rate at which she is receiving new patients.

She had then gone on to ask Esther some background questions – age, family situation, occupation. Esther didn't know how old she is but had already had 10 children, three of whom died. The youngest is eight. As most HIV-positive children die before the age of five, her little ones are safe. She lives in N'Dali, a town about 45 minutes away, at her brother's house. As there are no house numbers or street names in Benin, Martha took about 20 minutes to get an idea of exactly where the house is in order to follow-up on Esther. For a living, Esther sells pounded yams, a staple food for every Beninese. She is married, but her husband lives in Banikoara, about four hours north of N'Dali.

Separation during marriage is a norm in Benin. A wife only stays with her husband for certain periods of time. Once a woman is pregnant she will often go back to her family until the baby is finished nursing. A woman will also return to her family when she begins menopause – because men believe that if they sleep with a post-menopausal women they will get "a disease." And, as in Esther's case, a woman will return to her family when she is sick. Esther told Martha she plans to stay with her family.

This division in the home usually leads the husband to find other women – Esther's husband had two other wives, but she was the first. Bariba culture names the second wife "Nissi," which literally translated means "jealousy."

"Now I'm going to explain the sickness you have," continued Martha after gaining little solid information from Esther. "We found you have a little germ. This germ is a little complicated; it causes you to stay sick for a long time." She went on to explain that Esther's white blood cells are not able to fight against the sickness; that they no longer have a defense against the sickness.

As Paul translated to Esther, I wondered if she even understood the term "white blood cells" – the type of knowledge I took for granted. I was later told by Martha that Paul does not translate her literally when it comes to explaining AIDS. He has worked for her long enough that he understands what she wants to communicate, but he is also Bariba and knows how to put it in terms that his people understand. "He just does it in a way that she'll get the point," Martha told me.

This was the moment Martha had hit Esther with the word "SIDA."

After Esther's acquiesce to imminent death, I anxiously wondered where Martha would launch. The beating fan above seemed deafening. She went with a positive route – if that was possible, considering the circumstances.

"There are medicines to help you with this sickness, but not to cure it. However, this doesn't mean you will die tomorrow. We can help fight the sickness."

Martha went on to explain that Esther would have to take an antibiotic – Bactrim – every day for the rest of her life. She said that these tablets would increase her resistance against easily getting infections. She added that, if it were okay, they would like to stop by her home from time to time to check on her. Martha told me that these home visits not only speak value into people's lives but also help her to know what kind of situation they live in – how much money they have and how many people they have to help care for them.

"There are things that you can do to help yourself, too," Martha continued, with a comforting smile. She explained the necessity of changing her eating habits a little bit – basic routines that any Westerner would have been taught from a young age. She told her she must cook her food well before eating, or else she will get bad diarrhea; if she eats uncooked food, she must clean it well before eating. She should fill her diet with vegetables, fruits, beef, and eggs.

She must also sleep with a mosquito net. And, if she gets a small infection or cut, she must take care of it quickly. Martha slowly explained that usually small problems like this would go away within a week, but for her, now, it could become a big problem if not treated.

Martha then moved on to a more sensitive subject — sex.

"The disease usually comes when two people are sexually involved," she said, "I don't know how you got it, but it is possible the other people involved have it." Martha later told me that she rarely tries to discover exactly how a person contracted SIDA. "It doesn't concern me now. The person could have been infected for eight or nine years already."

With Esther sitting expressionless, Martha continued. "If you sleep with other people you could infect them, too. Does your husband come to visit often?"

"No," Esther slowly shook her head.

I thought of her husband's two other wives. I wondered how many children they both had. AIDS could have already infected a half dozen people in this one family.

"It's necessary to check if he has it. The only was to find out is to look at the blood. He could have the disease for a long time before becoming sick. You have to tell him that you have a disease that he might also have."

Esther spoke softly, for the first time in minutes. "I don't have enough energy to go."

Martha urged that it was important for somebody to take a message to him. "I don't know if that will happen,"

Martha confided to me later. She told Esther that her disease not only concerned her, but also concerned her whole family.

"It's often that if one person in the couple has it, the others will have it." Martha had a simple yet truthful way of putting things.

Pen in hand, she asked Esther for the name of her husband and his location in Banikoara. Esther said his name was Zachary, but she didn't know his last name. Sadly, this could either be true or false. Either she had ten children by a man she only knew by first name, or she was trying to protect him from shame.

Martha closed her session by emphasizing that Esther must take her medicine each day. She told me that most people take the medicine until they start to feel better. Then they assume they are cured and quit the medicine, only to have their sicknesses come back with a vengeance. "You will be tired a lot; you will not have good health."

She told Esther not to spend her money on Fetish healers, but instead to spend it on good food. Money management is a tough subject to teach in Africa. Culture in Benin does not allow much room for saving. If you have any money, your family and friends expect to have access to it – either to borrow or take. Nothing stays in one hand for more than a few days.

Martha asked Esther if she had any questions. The elegant statue swept her eyes downward to signal a "no."

"Do you have diarrhea now?"

"Not now, but I recently had it for a month."

"So, it's already begun," Martha muttered dejectedly to me in English.

Esther was told to come back in the month. For the medication, testing, and consultation, Esther had to pay

5,000 CFA – about 10 US dollars. Each successive visit would only cost her 1,000 CFA, just enough to cover the medicine.

As they got up to leave, Esther let out another "Toh." She shyly smiled at Martha and gave a half curtsey as she said, "Ka somburu" meaning, "Good work."

Mystified, I watched her carefully walk out the door and up the dirt path. A slim, dark silhouette against a blinding sun-lit landscape; a woman unmoved by the fact that her world had just shifted beneath her.

The Whole World Mourns

I gritted my teeth and tried to ignore the smell as I removed the soiled diaper. The odor was so overpowering it dominated the large cement living room of the orphanage. This job was pushing my limit. At home, I would at least have the clean comfort of disposable Luvs diapers and wet wipes. Not in Africa. Cloth diapers for the babies and panties for the toddlers – both washed by hand. During the day, most would go without either, leaving their presents on the floor.

Though a Canadian runs the orphanage, Margaret Bevington, who has been there since 1957, she wisely keeps it a little "Africanized." If the children get used to complete cleanliness and are then taken in by a bush family, they will no longer have resistance against diseases easily picked up on the dirt floors.

I was changing Boni, the youngest baby in the orphanage, before laying him down for a nap. He was lucky he was so darn cute – milk chocolate complexion, toothless smile, pudgy arms and legs, and a little Afro on top. If not, he might have gone out the window along with his stinky diaper.

I spent about 10 minutes trying to decipher how to get the new diaper on – the material, safety pins, and nylon lining much too large and awkward for his little bottom. After deciding that it wouldn't completely slide off, I carried him over to throw his old diaper into the designated bucket, dreading dealing with it later.

I picked up a few toys and put them back on my way to Boni's bed. By the time we reached it, I regrettably discovered that he was wet again. I headed back to the "changing area" – namely whatever free chair I could find. No sooner had I gotten the next diaper clipped on than Boni went to the toilet again. Three diapers in less than three minutes. Unbelievable. Definitely just to test my patience. I shook my head at Boni, and he responded with his usual laugh – mouth fully open and sounds coming out, but no movement. I couldn't help but laugh at the adorable way he mocked my situation.

When I finally laid him down in his small rickety wood crib – dry for the time being – I heard a line I had heard numerous times over the past couple months. "Make sure you peg the mosquito net down tight. Cover all the corners." Margaret was completely overprotective of Boni. He had separate diapers, towels, blankets, milk, water, and food from the rest of the children. She had a hard time letting me do anything for him; she wanted to be sure everything was done her way.

I couldn't blame her, though. Boni had been premature – born seven months into his mother's pregnancy. She hadn't made it through the delivery; so Boni had been dropped off by the family at the orphanage. He had been on the verge of death when he arrived at Margaret's door – just skin and bones. She had spent weeks feeding him through an eyedropper around the clock.

He had now been at the orphanage for six months and had made outstanding progress. He had rounded out and was now a completely healthy and cheerful baby. He also seemed to be Margaret's favorite, but she would never admit to it.

When I arrived at Margaret's the next week, after fighting my way through her petting zoo of 8 goats and 12 chickens outside, I was shocked to find Boni gone. As I heated water for morning baths, I asked Margaret where he had gone. She seemed busy moving things around the kitchen crowded with baby bottles and laundry and said, "Oh, yes, Boni's gone." For the second time, I asked where. "Oh, his family came and took him."

"They did?" I said, surprised. I hadn't heard any news of this beforehand. "Was that expected?"

"No." Margaret didn't seem to want to talk.

As I watched the kettle boil, I was suddenly filled with sadness. I realized that in my short time in the orphanage, Boni had managed to worm his way to the center of my heart. I was happy that he was home, but upset that I hadn't been able to say goodbye. I also knew that nowhere else in the world could offer love and care like Margaret could.

I thought of Margaret, who had saved his life and been a mother to him since birth. "How do you do that?" I asked, amazed by her. "How do you raise them and then just let them go?" Margaret, always unaffected and tough after 46 years of doing this, replied with "You just do. You have to."

"But how do you keep them without becoming attached?" Margaret gave the first half-smile of the morning, revealing the deep wrinkles surrounding her glistening brown eyes, as she responded, "Well, that's impossible."

Still seemingly distracted, she left the room and me with my thoughts. I couldn't imagine having her life. The job of raising these children would be hard enough in itself, but to then entrust them to a new family or back to their own family...I would never last in her profession.

One week later, I returned home after another morning of dodging urine puddles, serving bouille, and playing peek-a-boo with the kids. I paid my motorbike-taxi driver, thankful to just be alive after the way he had torn through the city. I was preparing a salad as Mary, my co-worker and next-door neighbor, stopped in to say hello.

She kindly asked me how the kids were and how my morning had gone. I sadly told her it was much quieter – I had said goodbye to another baby, Waru, who had been picked up by his new family.

"Did Margaret ever tell you the truth about the little one?" She asked, hesitatingly.

"What do you mean? Who? Boni?" I asked, confused. At an affirmative nod, I fumbled with words, "Well, yeah, she told me his family came to get him..." I trailed off as I saw her look down and away. I suddenly felt dread clutch my chest. "No way," I shook my head emphatically. "Don't tell me...don't tell me...he died?" My pleading was to no avail; she nodded affirmatively.

"I'm sorry, Joanna. He died a week and a half ago. I thought she must have told you by now."

My heart seemed to stop at the words ringing in my ears. I looked down as my eyes filled with tears, blurring the tomatoes I was chopping into a wavy sea of red. It couldn't be true; I must have heard wrong.

"But how?" My voice cracked at the words. I wasn't sure if I wanted to hear anything, but it was worse not knowing. "Why didn't she tell me?"

"She knew how attached you already were to him. She thought it would be too much for you…" She spoke cautiously, as if tiptoeing on thin ice. "I'm sorry to just throw that on you. But I thought you needed to know the truth…"

Anything else she said flew past me. As she turned to go, I wearily thanked her for telling me; that it was better I knew.

I sat through lunch like a zombie; then sat through work useless. My mind was consumed with little Boni. And with questions. How did he die? Why? Had he been sick for a long time?

Whether Margaret had wanted me to know or not, now I did. I needed to see her.

When I reached the small blue-framed house, I found her parked outside in her rusty red 1970s station wagon. She had loaded up all the kids in the back and was headed for the market. At 71-years-old, she was still too independent to let anyone else do her shopping for her. She invited me into the front seat and poured herself some water out of an old dust-covered Coke bottle.

Surprised to see me, she bluntly asked why I had come. Margaret wastes no time. Not knowing how to bring the painful subject up, I explained to her that I was going to be away that coming weekend and wouldn't be able to make it that Friday to help.

"You didn't have to come all this way to tell me that. You could have just called."

Right. Good point. With no way out, I launched.

"Well, actually, I, uh, wanted to talk to you about something," I said slowly, knowing I was on the verge of tears for the fiftieth time that day. She gave me a nudging 'get on with it' look.

"I know about Boni. Mary told me. And, I just, uh, I just wanted you to know that I know." I let my elegant statement rest at that.

Margaret let out a long sigh. "Poor Boni."

With those two words, she promptly turned her head to look outside the window. She did her best to hide from everyone, but I could see her cheeks start to wobble. Soon tears found their way down to her chin. I was completely taken back. The toughest lady I have ever met was now broken before me.

My heavy heart went out to her. "I wish you would have told me. I understand you had good intentions, but I wouldn't be in Benin if I wanted to protect myself from this type of..."

"It's too hard," she said, interrupting and trying unsuccessfully to gain composure. "When little babies die like that, it's too hard for me to talk about it." Suddenly it made sense. It wasn't for my sake that she withheld the news of Boni's death; it was for hers. She couldn't bring herself to speak the heartrending words. "And his family did come for him," she said, trying to justify herself, "They came for the body."

I asked how it happened, knowing it was hard for her but also knowing I needed answers.

"Had he been sick?" I asked, trying to start somewhere.

"No," she said, frustrated, "He wasn't sick at all." She painfully recounted what had happened, interrupted periodically by kids in the back asking irrelevant questions, tugging at her silvery hair, or reaching for water.

Boni hadn't had any signs of sickness. "Perfectly healthy." Ten days ago she had put him down for a nap, but he had carried on crying. She had picked him up just in time to see his eyes roll back and his body flop unconscious. She had tried to take him to the dispensary, but her unreliable Renault 4 had a flat tire. She had quickly begged a neighbor to take them. But, after arriving at the nearest government dispensary, they had been told that nothing could be done for Boni.

I interrupted. "What do you mean, nothing could be done?" I asked incredulously.

Well, for some unknown reason, the dispensary did not have any medicine that day. I asked if this happened regularly and was told it does.

So, the nurses had sent the dying baby on his way. Margaret had then rushed him to the next-closest dispensary. Before anyone there was available to see them, Boni was gone.

Margaret had no more to say. She looked drained. She had probably played those few hours over and over in her mind. I wiped away the tears that had been pouring quietly down my cheeks. She offered to drive me back. We rode in silence. I flatly thanked her at the end of the short trip and told her I'd see her the following week.

For the next few days, I felt as if my life had been thrown into a tailspin. I couldn't stop crying; I couldn't think of anything but poor Boni. It wasn't fair that his life was cut drastically short. He had been saved at birth; now for what purpose?

I was overwhelmed with an amount of sorrow I have never felt before. My chest seemed to carry one hundred tons of weight on it. I was heartbroken over Boni, but somehow I sensed it was bigger than him. I was crushed by the fact that this occurrence is so common here. Life is a gift quickly taken away from many in Benin. Children often die before the age of two for simple reasons – cold, flu, dehydration. It was as if I could suddenly feel all the suffering surrounding me. And I didn't know how to carry that load. I felt lost.

I spent time praying to and questioning God. Suffering in the world is one of the hardest things to comprehend. Why are innocent babies dying when all that would save them is a simple antibiotic?

I felt as if God was saying, "I'm letting you hear my heartbeat." He had a purpose for Boni's life, and He too is heartbroken by the tragic shortening of the joyful child's time on earth. He was allowing me, just for a time, to weep with Him – to feel His pain. I was struck by the verse, "Sorrow not as those without hope." (I Thess. 4:13) It didn't say not to sorrow; mourning was necessary. But because I knew that God's love outweighs all the confusion, there was still hope in the deepest darkest place of sadness.

Sages used to say that when one life is saved, the whole world rejoices. When one life is lost, the whole world mourns. They said this to illustrate that groups of people don't die – individuals do. And each one counts.

The infant mortality rate is almost 10 percent. But that didn't matter. Boni was not a statistic; he was a life. And he was dead. To me, his death represented every death.

The heaviness did not last forever; I slowly found my smile again. But, something has changed within me. No longer will I be able to hear of poverty-stricken people dying without pausing…and remembering. The whole world mourns. No matter who it was – regardless of race, religion, age or status – the world is not the same without that person.

The following Friday, I sat feeding one of the toddlers on the orphanage's cold gray floor. Sabi, about 17 months old, had been abandoned by his family for superstitious reasons. As I tried unsuccessfully to get him to eat rather than throw the chopped-up spaghetti, he reached his stick-like arms out towards me with a single word – "mama."

I realized I didn't understand Boni's death, and never would. But I knew one thing. Sabi and the others were still alive – and needed love.

I reached towards Sabi's outstretched arms and, as I picked him up out of a heap of stray noodles, hugged him close – wet bottom and all.

the withlacoochee: a river in balance

Sarah L. Stewart, University of Florida

The bird swoops low over the pontoon boat, offering passengers a fleeting head-on glimpse of beady eyes and a hooked bill. Captain Mike leans over the side of the boat, straining for a better look before it crosses the river and disappears into the cypress trees on the other side.

After consulting a worn field guide, he's pretty sure it was an immature Mississippi Kite. It's the first time he has seen this migratory bird in flight, he tells his passengers, his satisfaction audible as if marking a mental checklist. The boat hasn't yet left its cracked cement ramp, and already nature is showing off.

As Captain Mike Tracy, certified eco-tour guide, steers the 24-foot boat upstream at two or three miles an hour, he begins the story of the Withlacoochee River in his rich, showman's voice.

The Withlacoochee, or "little great river," gouged its path 17,000 years ago through primarily limestone beds. On its 157-mile northward journey through seven central Florida counties, it drops just 18 feet from its headwaters in the Green Swamp to a spot just north of Yankeetown where it empties into the Gulf of Mexico.

As he speaks, Captain Mike's brown eyes scan the river banks. He spots a turtle sunning on a branch just above water level, the first of many on today's route. The four passengers at the back of the boat, all of retirement age, leave their seats for a closer look. Turtles can only absorb sun through their skin, Captain Mike says, which explains why its head and legs are extended from the shell.

"They kinda look like Superman trying to fly," he says with a laugh.

The boat nears a spot where Captain Mike and his first trip of the day saw an alligator. He trains his binoculars on the bank, hoping to fulfill his passengers' requests to see Florida's most famous reptile.

"Well, he went hidin'," he says. "Little bugger." He sounds like he feels stood up.

"You little stinker. We'll have to find some other ones."

***

Beaches, rivers, lakes, swamps, springs. Second to sunshine, water is probably Florida's most sought-after commodity. In an effort to improve the quality of this resource, the Florida Department of Environmental Protection and the Environmental Protection Agency developed a program to analyze and collect data on the level of pollutants in Florida's waters. This program, the Watershed Management Basin Rotation Project, divides Florida's waters into 52 basins and places each of these basins into one of five groups. Each group undergoes a five-year assessment.

In the first phase, the FDEP analyzes data from the past 10 years to develop a list of waters within each basin that are potentially impaired by contaminants. Group 4, which includes the 2,100-square-mile Withlacoochee Basin and four others, entered this rotation in 2003. Of the 151 water body segments identified in the Withlacoochee Basin, 24 were listed as potentially impaired.

In the second phase, which is nearly complete for the Withlacoochee, the FDEP creates a list of verified impaired waters based on a detailed, 18-month analysis of data from the past seven-and-a-half-years. Confirmed impaired waters contain levels of certain pollutants higher than are permissible for the water to fulfill its designated purpose, such as for drinking or recreation.

These impaired waters then enter the final three phases

of the program, aimed to bring the contaminants in these waters to acceptable levels. The FDEP first develops a Total Maximum Daily Load (TMDL), a determination of the maximum amount of a given pollutant a water body can absorb and still maintain its designated uses. Once it adopts a TMDL, it develops and implements a plan of action to meet that TMDL. At the end of five years, the process restarts.

Florida's current system of water-quality assessment is a model for other states. Improving water quality, however, requires responsible management of land and water, says Tom Singleton, the FDEP's Withlacoochee River basin manager. He cites Homosassa Springs as an example, where a large volume of visitors has decreased water clarity and sea grass growth.

"We're kind of loving these resources to death," he says.

A suit brought by environmental group EarthJustice that challenged Florida's adherence to the Clean Water Act of 1977 resulted in the Florida Watershed Restoration Act of 1999. The act required an overhaul of the FDEP's management of the state's waters, part of which included a revamped method of assessing water quality. Thus, the basin rotation program began in 2000.

"The old solution to pollution is dilution," Singleton says. The rationale: When dispersed through enough water, a pollutant is too diffuse to cause a problem. This theory is valid, but only to a point; continue on this course, and eventually there will be too many contaminants present to offset their effects.

"We used to think that just because we couldn't detect something, it couldn't hurt us."

***

Captain Mike rises from his seat behind the steering

wheel, walks to the front of the boat and steps over the gate bearing "Best of the Best" stickers from the Citrus County Chronicle every year since 2000. He stoops out of sight for a moment, then stands, holding up a juice glass full of river water.

In the river, the water is a dark tea brown; a result of the tannic acid that dead leaves release into it. This darkness, however, is exacerbated by a layer of black muck nearly a foot deep in some places on the river bottom, Captain Mike explains. Fifty or sixty years ago, white sand covered 90 percent of the river bottom. But that was before the river had a problem with hydrilla, an invasive species. In order to stop it from clogging the river, the state uses herbicides to kill the hydrilla, which over several decades has formed muck on the river bottom.

But for some swirling particles and a slight pinkish brown tinge, the water in Captain Mike's glass is surprisingly clear.

"Oh," he adds, hoisting the glass a little higher. "Anybody want a drink?"

***

In the late 1990s, 45,000 fish died in a single fish kill in Lake Rousseau, a man-made lake not far from where Captain Mike leads today's tour. The culprit? In part, insufficient dissolved oxygen, the most frequent water-quality problem in the Withlacoochee River Basin. It is a factor in 14 of the 24 water bodies on the potentially impaired list.

But, Singleton notes, an oxygen deficit can occur naturally. In the slow moving, often shallow waters of the Withlacoochee, sunlight encourages growth of vegetation. These plants use oxygen that would otherwise be dissolved in the water.

Though the FDEP does investigate the causes of an

oxygen deficit, "we tell folks not to get too excited," Singleton says.

The second most common impairments in the Withlacoochee Basin; an overabundance of nutrients such as nitrogen in the water and mercury in fish, concern the FDEP
more than low dissolved oxygen levels. Both are likely to
result from human activity and threaten environmental
and human health.

Excess nitrogen can cause aquatic vegetation to bloom
excessively, choking waterways and killing fish. In drinking
water, it can cause reproductive problems, as well as cancer
and blood disorders in adults and children. In wildlife
mercury can cause slower growth, abnormal behavior,
decreased fertility and death. Human consumption of mer-
cury-contaminated fish, which is the most common form
of mercury exposure, can cause brain and nerve damage.

Historically, point-source pollution, such as industrial
waste and sewage dumping, received the most attention.
That type of water pollution is now basically under control,
and now the major source of water pollution derives from
ground runoff and the air, Singleton says. This type of pollution is more difficult to control, since everything from
using fertilizers (which contain nitrogen) to waste burning
(which releases mercury into the atmosphere) to cars brak-
ing (which leaves cadmium on the roadway) contributes to
this diffuse-type of water pollution.

The Withlacoochee and other water bodies face a real
threat from this non-point source pollution. Singleton
recalls when he worked on water quality in South Florida
and some fish developed ulcers, multiple sets of scales and
fins and other abnormalities. They determined cadmium
and zinc were the principal culprits.

Two portions of the lower Withlacoochee River, where

Captain Mike leads today's trip, have been verified as impaired for dissolved oxygen and mercury. Compared to others around the state, the basin as a whole has a relatively low number of impairments. Development has not yet encroached on the Withlacoochee as much as it has in other parts of the state, Singleton says; in many places, the river remains largely unchanged from 100 years ago.

"[The Withlacoochee] gives one a sense of how things used to be," he says. It helps people "understand how far other places need to go to improve water quality."

***

The older women on Captain Mike's boat shudder when he tells them that March is the ideal month to see snakes on the Withlacoochee. Fresh from hibernation, often they lay unmoving on the river banks.

"We do have a lot of snakes," he says. Forty-four species in Florida, to be exact. He chuckles. "Only 44!"

Just five of them are poisonous: the diamondback, pigmy and timber rattlesnakes, the coral snake and ("the most dangerous snake of all") the water moccasin. Moccasins will not only chase people and bite them in the water, Captain Mike says, but "they've also been known to climb into boats and bite people."

His comment hangs for a moment.

"So we stay out of those areas," Captain Mike continues. "People tend not to come back when them things happen."

Around a few more bends in the river, a cypress tree extends through a deck built over the river. It is massive not in height but girth, and its weathered gray bark contrasts the feathery spring green of its needles. These trees grow about one inch in diameter in 40 years, Captain Mike says. One like this could be from 1,000 to 1,500 years old.

These trees are Civil War veterans. They have seen floods, freezes, and hurricanes; have stood quietly for centuries as the river and its ever-changing traffic flows past: alligators, river otters, Indians, pontoon boats, and, more recently, airboats.

***

Sitting inside his home along the Withlacoochee, Ron Johnson can't carry on a conversation when the louder airboats pass by. In his five years living there, Johnson estimates there has been a 30 percent increase in the amount of airboat traffic on the river.

As a spokesman for a group of several hundred trying to make the airboats quieter, Johnson has pitted himself against a well-organized airboat lobby.

After three years of County Commission meetings, petitions, and working with state representatives, senators and even the governor, a measure went before the Citrus County Commission on April 12 to require airboat noise be no more than 90 decibels at 50 feet. Ninety decibels is about the amount emitted by a garbage disposal or an electric drill; extended exposure to noise over 85 decibels causes hearing damage. Similar legislation recently passed in neighboring Marion County.

"It's grassroots politics. You've just got to keeping hammering after it," Johnson says. For him, the need to quiet the airboats is obvious.

"If you lived on the river, you'd know the answer to that."

But airboaters argue that the "90 at 50" limit isn't practical.

"Have you ever made a margarita?" asks Bob Hoover Jr., president of the Citrus County Airboat Alliance. "Well, your blender just did 95 decibels!"

Hoover's organization favors making mufflers mandatory, which would help the noise problem, he says. Once a boat reaches a certain RPM, however, the propellers produce the majority of the noise. Quieter propellers cost more.

"I don't know where 90 came up. It seems like that's the magic number," Hoover says. "And it's not feasible."

The County Commission agreed. The measure failed, three votes to one.

***

The first alligator, no longer than a person's arm, clings to a small branch just above the surface of the water. The sun glints off its reptilian eye. Motionlessly, it watches as Captain Mike guides the boat slowly past.

A few feet away, two more come into view. Captain Mike's gators have not let him down. Each gator is slightly larger than the one before it. The mid-March sun seeps into their leathery hide, and not a blink betrays their stillness.

"Are you sure they're real? They're here all the time?" asks one passenger, a well-manicured woman of about 65.

"I'll be glad to let you off any time you want," Captain Mike responds. The woman laughs and declines the invitation. He explains that although people want to see the gators move, he doesn't like to disturb them.

Just past the gators, the boat nears a dead end. Captain Mike executes a three-point turn and retraces his path. But for a faint vibration of the seats, there's no indication that the four-cycle Yamaha motor is even running. The boat eases past the gators once more, closer this time. Eva and Skip, two visitors from Kentucky, scramble for their disposable camera.

A whirring noise filters through the cypress trees, distant at first then growing more insistent.

"Here come the airboats," Captain Mike says.

Within a minute, what sounds like a giant fan turned on high has drowned out the bird calls emanating from the tree canopy. Captain Mike and his passengers watch as its source appears from around a bend in the river.

An unsmiling man of about 60, wearing sunglasses and black ear muffs, sits in the driver's seat of the purple-glitter striped airboat. He slows when he sees Captain Mike's tour, and a throaty "chug-chug-chug" replaces the whirring. Captain Mike's boat bobs in the wake.

With a splash, the second gator falls from its perch. It struggles to regain its balance, reaching with one scaly arm and then another to climb back on the log. Its hide glistens after the dip in the 63-degree water.

The airboat picks up speed and disappears downriver. For a moment Captain Mike and his passengers are silent. High in the trees, the birds resume their song.

"It's amazing the birds are still chirping," Captain Mike says. His tone turns to disgust. "We're just losing so much along our waterways from just normal stuff, without having to do crap like this."

stream cleaning

Mike Burden, University of Missouri

A pool table, two prosthetic limbs, three propane tanks, 11 refrigerators, 173 tires, a keg, a toilet, two messages in bottles and three televisions. Items in a scavenger hunt? No. This is a small sample of what Missouri River Relief hauled out of the Missouri River in one day on one of its major river cleanups.

The trash in Missouri's waterways is an eyesore and causes wildlife habitat destruction, while toxic materials such as cigarette butts threaten aquatic life. But discarded kitchen appliances and couches aren't the only form of pollution drifting down Missouri's waterways. Every day, hundreds of millions of gallons of wastewater from sewage treatment plants flow into the Missouri and Mississippi rivers and Missouri streams without being disinfected for bacteria. Chemicals and metals from lawn care, farming, industry and mining also end up in Missouri's water and can endanger aquatic life and human health.

But the pressing financial issue facing the state now will be disinfecting wastewater to make waterways safe for swimming. The Missouri Department of Natural Resources has developed new standards for Missouri's waterways to bring the state closer to the 1972 Clean Water Act goal of making all waterways fishable and swimmable. The standards are on their way to the state attorney general's office and must be approved by the Environmental Protection Agency by April 2006, or the EPA will set the standards for the state.

The standards will hold 22,000 miles of Missouri waterways, including the Missouri and Mississippi rivers and 14 streams in Columbia, to a swimmable standard. This means that the water entering natural streams must have less than 200 colonies of fecal coliform, the bacteria in human and animal waste, and less than 126 colonies of E. coli per hundred milliliters of water. Currently, approximately 5,000 miles meet this swimmable standard. Also, the settlement calls for any wastewater facility within two miles of a classified waterway, or one that flows year-round, to disinfect the water leaving its plant.

The impetus for the upgrades was a December settlement between the EPA and the Missouri Coalition for the Environment. Ted Heisel, president of the coalition, says it was tired of the state dragging its feet on complying with the Clean Water Act.

Trent Stober, president of Columbia-based MEC Water Resources, says the cost for the regulated community to meet the new standards could be in the billions. "People are going to have to pay higher sewer rates, and I am concerned about that," he says.

In Boone County, 35 million gallons of wastewater flow into Perche Creek, Grindstone Creek, Hinkson Creek and other waterways. Only 13 of 126 wastewater facilities in the county are monitoring their effluent for fecal coliform. In the entire state, only a third of the nearly 3,000 facilities do the same.

Tom Ratermann, general manager at Boone County Regional Sewer District, says the district will have to invest $300,000 to upgrade 43 of its facilities to comply with the new standards. The estimate is based on the money needed to purchase the equipment and doesn't account for operating costs. The district's annual operating budget is $1.5 million. "Rate payers pay for those changes," Ratermann says. "Is that the best bang for your environmental buck? Are we prepared to spend the money for the 12 people who swim in Hinkson Creek?"

Whether they are huge facilities pumping hundreds of millions of gallons of wastewater into the Mississippi

River, such as the Metropolitan Sewer District of St. Louis, or small wastewater lagoons such as the one at Green Hills Mobile Home Park in Columbia, all facilities have the same three options. They can demonstrate that they already meet the standard. They can prove people aren't swimming in their local waterway, and therefore they won't have to disinfect. Or they can disinfect their wastewater to bring bacteria levels to the swimmable standard using chlorine or ultraviolet radiation.

The Green Hills Mobile Home Park pumps its wastewater into Perche Creek after passing it through a lagoon. Fred Burks, the owner, says he was informed of the new standards.

"Right now we're not exactly sure how we fall into it," Burks says. "If I have to go to a chemical type of treatment, I've had estimates of $30,000 to $50,000 just to have the system put in." He says he'll have to pass the additional costs on to his renters.

Behind the curve

Are Missourians ready to pay for cleaner water?

Some visitors to the Grindstone Nature Area agreed that the standards are needed, and most are willing to pay additional money to achieve them.

"I think it would be worth it," Justin Dijak, a cook, says. "My first instinct is 'finally [government is] spending money on something productive.' Especially on the conditions of the streams I've seen."

"If Missouri had adopted better standards sooner, we wouldn't have to play catch up now," Courtney Kerns, a natural biologist, says. "As to the cost to me, I would prefer that more of my taxes go to the environment."

But some people in the business of wastewater are worried about that cost. "I cannot meet these standards today," says Mary West, the director of Moberly Public Utilities.

Although many municipal operators are concerned about the cost, environmentalists point to the fact that this law has been in place for more than 30 years, and states were supposed to comply by 1983. "I don't know why Missouri was allowed to ignore federal law for the past 21 years," says Ken Midkiff of the Sierra Club.

Thirty-one states, including Missouri neighbors Kansas and Illinois, have established the fishable and swimmable standard. Sharon Watson, communications director for the Kansas Department of Health and Environment, says the financial impact on Kansas businesses has been minimal. This is because for the past decade, KDHE has taken a proactive approach and required facilities discharging into their streams to increase the amount of disinfection in their system or make other upgrades to reduce the bacteria.

So why is Missouri behind the curve? Recreation on the water generates millions of dollars each year, and Missouri has some of the most pristine national waterways, including the Eleven Point, Jack's Fork and Current rivers.

Thousands of volunteers across the state are removing the trash dumped in the rivers and streams, but the Missouri Department of Natural Resources, the agency charged with protecting Missouri's natural resources, has only a handful of people conducting chemical tests across the state's water bodies.

John Ford is one of them. He has spent the past 28 years wading in Missouri's waterways, cooling off after watching birds from the banks of a stream in his spare time and collecting samples for the Department of Natural Resources. In his sojourns through the water, Ford has twice contracted illnesses from bacteria. He samples streams near wastewater discharge plants to detect if the effluent flowing out of their pipes is depleting oxygen from the water and threatening sunfish, bass, frogs or any of the other critters that call the waterways home. For data on bacteria harmful to humans such as fecal coliform and E. coli, MDNR relies on the United States Geological Survey's 66 water quality monitoring stations around the state.

"To do a good job we would need about 28 staff," says Scott Totten, the soil and water protection division director with MDNR. "We have eight."

Missouri does have a State Revolving Fund that is used to help cities pay for environmentally friendly upgrades. But through the next year, President George W. Bush plans to cut the national budget for this program from $1.1 billion to $750 million. This means that federal backing for Missouri's fund will decrease from $30 million to $19 million. This leaves MDNR more dependent on the fees they receive from granting business permits.

"When budgets get cut, we have to get permits out the door, and that is more important than monitoring," Totten says. Between 60 and 70 percent of MDNR's water pollution program and 100 percent of its storm water management program are paid for by permit fees.

Getting the trash out takes time, energy and cultural change, but reducing the bacteria requires cash and information. MDNR estimates that 911 facilities around the state will need more than $300 million to upgrade their facilities to make more waterways swimmable.

Beyond the storm drain

For paddlers such as Joel McCune, water quality issues are a daily concern. He grew up paddling on the Big Piney and Buffalo rivers in northern Arkansas.

"My first memories are on the water," McCune says.

When he is not working on his master's degree in parks, recreation and tourism at MU, he is paddling his canoe in Finger Lakes, Gans Creek or other local waterways to train for the upcoming U.S. team trials in white-water slalom. McCune says sewage treatment is improving but not at the rate that it needs to, and the biggest problem is addressing nonpoint source pollution – pollution from multiple sources, such as agricultural and urban runoff.

"As long as we can turn on the lights, flush the stool and turn on the faucet and get water, we don't really care," says Bob Broz, a water quality specialist at MU Agricultural Extension. Broz says the community needs more watershed stewardship. "How do my actions affect someone else or the environment is the big question we need to ask," he says.

Last year, Representative Dennis Wood (R-Kimberling City) sponsored statewide legislation to provide an opportunity for unincorporated areas to do just that. His bill would allow areas such as Harg outside Columbia to access the state's revolving fund for wastewater upgrades.

"Water knows no boundaries," Wood says. "What's under your property today is under mine tomorrow, and you have no right to pollute it. We can't afford not to protect our water."

Volunteers and clean-water advocates across the state and especially around Columbia, which boasts the highest concentration of stream teams in the state, are taking action to achieve these goals. They are directing their efforts at the nonpoint source pollution. The EPA reports that storm water runoff is "one of the most significant sources of contamination in our nation's waters." This is especially the case in waterways such as Hinkson Creek, the backbone of Columbia's streams.

Where does the pollution come from?

Rain washes off the sidewalks, through the parking lots and down the streets and carries with it antifreeze, lawn chemicals, tons of trash and anything else that lies on the thousands of acres of impervious surface around town.

"Rampant residential development is a big problem,"

says Scott Hamilton, an urban conservationist with Show-Me Clean Streams. "We need to enforce stricter standards on developers clearing the ground. People need to realize that the storm drain right by their house flows directly into the streams."

Most of the water drains directly into Hinkson Creek, which meanders 11 miles through Columbia, collects 60 percent of the raindrops that fall on Columbia and is currently listed as an impaired waterway due to this nonpoint source pollution.

"What's going on in Hinkson Creek is going on in every city in Missouri that size and all over the country," said Leanna Zweig, a fish kill and pollution investigator for the Department of Conservation. "We're all downstream from someone else."

That is the message that Mona Menezes, the storm water outreach coordinator for Columbia, is trying to spread. After growing up on the Niangua River, Menezes now works to educate citizens by organizing stream clean ups, holding lawn-care seminars and other efforts. She says many Columbians believe storm water is treated at the wastewater treatment plant and that a watershed is a type of building.

In her own neighborhood, Menezes received a report on a woman picking up her dog's waste in a plastic bag and dumping it into the storm drain. Recently, she contacted a man who poured leftover wood stain in the drain and explained to him that the water ends up in Rock Bridge State Park.

"Every cigarette butt, plastic bag and other trash that isn't properly disposed of ends up in our city's streams," Menezes says. Fifty percent of the trash she has collected in streams has been plastic bags such as the ones used at Wal-Mart.

Menezes has led the charge to place the blue decals

that read "No Dumping/Drains to Stream" on the storm water drains around Columbia. Her volunteers have placed more than 400 of the decals around the city, and she says eventually they hope to have one on every drain.

She leads stream cleanups around Columbia at least twice a month during the warmer months. In March, she gathered the Fun City youth group at Flat Branch Creek. When the kids weren't distracted by tossing rocks or looking for frogs, they filled 32 red mesh bags with plastic Bud Light cups, Twix wrappers and other trash.

Menezes is also coordinating a healthy lawns program with Hamilton. Their program will be city-wide this summer. According to EPA reports, pesticides from lawns create three times more chemical waste in waterways than agricultural production. Together, Hamilton and Menezes are trying to educate the community about how to have a beautiful and watershed-friendly lawn.

Hamilton will host a rain garden workshop April 9, and he says there are already a dozen people who want to install the gardens this spring. Rain gardens use native wetland plants such as cattails to absorb and treat rainwater in yards. "Somebody could install one in one weekend," Hamilton says.

He also invited Jeff Zimmerschied to speak to people interested in watershed-friendly lawn care earlier this month. Zimmerschied is a former Monsanto employee who has transformed his career from convincing people chemicals are good to demonstrating how to care for land without them. He now owns a natural lawn-care company. "It isn't what you know but what you are willing to learn," he says. "People have been trained by TV to spray, spray, spray, and most homeowners don't take the time to read the label."

Below the surface

Farmers in Boone County are taking action, too. Ken Struemph administers the Special Area Land Treatment Program in Boone County. The aim of SALT is to improve water quality through farming practices. Struemph says in the past three years farmers have added 400 feet of stream bank stabilization, modified 1,300 acres of pasture, installed eight ponds and more in an effort to improve soil and water quality in the upper Hinkson watershed. Farmers can get 75 percent of the cost covered through the program, which has an annual budget of $464,000. Much of the funding comes from the one-tenth of one percent sales tax in Missouri that goes to parks and soil conservation.

For private landowners, there is the Environmental Quality Incentive Program through the Natural Resources Conservation Service. It is designed to fund projects that preserve wildlife habitat and reduce nonpoint source pollution, emissions, soil erosion and sedimentation. Taken together the practices can improve water and soil quality.

So what's the best way to look at water quality now? Until Missouri comes into compliance with the new standards, there are visual cues to look for to help determine whether a particular stream is a good place to splash around in.

"A lot of people call me and ask if it is safe to swim, and basically I tell them if the water is turbid and muddy, that's a bad time to go swimming because that means there is a lot of surface runoff, and bacteria is coming in," Ford says.

Hamilton looks at the critters living in the stream to determine its health. A few weeks ago he found only mosquito larvae and worms living in Flat Branch Creek — indicators of unhealthy water. Crayfish, mussels, mayfly larvae and stonefly larvae are usually good signs that the stream is fairly healthy. Hamilton says to monitor by checking bugs because they reveal the presence of pollution.

Although Missouri's water isn't always clear, one thing is: improving it will require cultural change and lots of cash, and the effort will affect everyone from environmentalists to industry leaders, farmers to factory workers, and paddlers to homeowners.

Here's how to start protecting Missouri's waters in your own backyard:

1) Plant native plants such as bluestem, which do not require synthetic fertilizers or pesticides.

2) Install a rain garden to collect and naturally filter runoff from your yard.

3) Mow properly. Zimmerschied suggests mowing on the tallest setting when grass is 3.5 to 4 inches long. Leave the clippings behind to provide nutrients to the grass and soil.

4) Clean up pet waste and garbage. When it rains, these pollutants wash into storm sewers that drain directly to local streams.

5) Join a stream team to help clean up trash, and learn how to conduct basic water quality tests.

6) If you choose to use chemicals in your yard, consult an expert and use them sparingly.

7) Work to preserve wooded buffer zones around streams that provide shade and absorb nutrients and sediment from surface runoff.

8) Take your car to the car wash, where water is reused several times before they send it to the sewer system for treatment.

First Printed in the Columbia Missourian

over medicated

Brad Parker, University of Missouri

Sara's* drug use began in the sixth grade. She was fidgety at school, so her doctor diagnosed her with Attention Deficit Disorder (ADD) and prescribed Ritalin. She used the drug until she was a sophomore in high school. During her sophomore year, she spent three or four months supplementing her prescribed dosage with another three or so pills at night to help her study before voluntarily giving up the medication altogether.

"I got great grades," Sara says. "But I'd stay up for three or four days straight. When I stopped taking it for two or three days, I'd crash."

During her senior year of high school, Sara's doctor prescribed a different medication for her. Sara does not know why there was a switch, but her doctor began prescribing Concerta – an encapsulated, time-release drug designed to circumvent the Ritalin abuse that had become prevalent nationwide in the previous year or two. Still, Sara and her friends discovered how to cut open the capsules, scoop out the medication and snort it like cocaine to get a buzz.

Sara had a prescription for Concerta until her sophomore year at MU. She was supposed to take one or two pills per day, depending on how much studying she had to do. Instead, she irregularly took pills to help her focus and saved the others to crush and snort for fun on the weekends.

Snorting the stimulants allows them to enter the bloodstream more rapidly and in a greater concentration through the nasal membranes. It also magnifies the common side effects, including headaches, jitters, tics, moodiness, insomnia, stomachaches and loss of appetite.

After Sara gave up her Concerta prescription because she felt that she didn't need it anymore, she would use her friends' medications, including Adderall. It is a more powerful medication that provides a stronger buzz when abused. When those highs were not enough, she and her friends started using cocaine.

Sara's slide into drug abuse characterizes a growing concern about college students illegally using Attention-Deficit/Hyperactivity Disorder (AD/HD) medications – including Ritalin, Concerta, Adderall, Dexedrine and Metadate – as a study aid or party drug.

Variably referred to as ADD, ADHD and AD/HD over the years, the diagnosis Attention-Deficit/Hyperactivity is now contained in the American Psychiatric Association's Diagnostic and Statistic Manual, Fourth Edition, an evidence-based listing of mental disorders. This reflects the different forms the condition can take. As an umbrella term, AD/HD can describe individuals who either exhibit symptoms of inattention, hyperactivity or impulsivity, or both.

A study published in the January/February issue of the Journal of American College Health reports AD/HD drug abuse might be approaching the prevalence of cocaine and marijuana use. On the campus where the researchers conducted their study, 17 percent of the 179 surveyed men and 11 percent of the 202 surveyed women abused prescription stimulants. Nearly half of the surveyed students – 44 percent – said they knew others who used stimulants for academic or recreational reasons.

People sometimes refer to AD/HD medications as "academic steroids" or "smart drugs" because they improve concentration. By increasing levels of the neural transmitter dopamine in the brain, the medications help people with the disorder combat the restlessness and inattention that often results in unfinished assignments, daydreaming and sloppy work. In small doses, they give people with normal dopamine levels an almost superhuman ability to concentrate.

Academic performance seems to be a secondary motivation for abuse, says Dr. Paul Robinson, associate clinical professor of child health and director of adolescent medicine at MU. "I think the primary motivation is recreational," he says, based on interviews with his patients. "I think it's to get a high."

Sara says she does not know anyone in college who actually needs AD/HD medication. "I'll be honest," she says. "I didn't need it. I grew out of my ADD like most people do. It was more recreational than academic — maybe even all recreational."

Many college students heavily abuse Adderall because it provides the strongest, longest high and the fewest unwanted side effects, Sara says. "It's extremely prevalent," she adds. "I know people who use Adderall more than anything else."

Elizabeth Burns, program director for Boonville Valley Hope, says prescription drug abuse in general is increasing in the area. She says many current and former MU students seek rehabilitation at Valley Hope, a 65-bed treatment center for people with chemical dependencies. Painkillers are the most commonly abused prescription drugs among college-age people, she says, with ADD medications next on the list.

Robinson says students often try to work the system to get unnecessary prescriptions. "Kids are coming in and acting like they have ADD so they can get high on the medication or give it to their friends."

Doctors are on the lookout for those pretenders,

however. And physicians and psychologists should work together to prevent misdiagnosis, Robinson says. Some learning disabilities and health problems, such as lead poisoning and sleep disorders, have symptoms similar to AD/HD. Therefore, diagnoses should follow a thorough review of a patient's history in addition to psychological and medical testing.

"Too many people make the diagnosis without all of the proper information," Robinson says.

Because of the changing attitudes in American culture toward mental health, there has been a jump in diagnosis for mental health-related problems, Burns says. She also cites an increase in advertising among pharmaceutical sales companies as a reason that people are going to their doctors and demanding specific drugs.

"The problems lie with the individuals who have the propensity to have addictive personalities," Burns says. "That biological predisposition coupled with mood-altering medication creates a more likely scenario for drug abuse."

Burns offers the example of students who take illegal drugs, such as cocaine, then complain of mood swings and trouble concentrating. Doctors diagnose them with AD/HD and prescribe stimulants without realizing they actually are compounding a problem, she says.

Sara acknowledges there are legitimate uses for the medications. "You need Adderall and Ritalin for the people who really need it, but there will always be people around to abuse it," she says. "People are going to abuse drugs no matter what."

Taking a small dose of the medication – half a pill – helps focus, Sara says. In recreational settings, however, people take larger dosages to over-energize their bodies for a day or two.

"When you need it, you become centered," Sara says. "When you don't need it, you become unbalanced, energetic and hyper."

Sara says taking too much of her medication does not lower inhibitions or cloud memory. "It's like living in fast-forward, but you're fully aware of everything that's going on.

"You want to go to sleep, but there's nothing you can do to get to sleep. Once you do get to sleep, it's for really short periods until the drug gets out of your system."

Some AD/HD patients abuse their prescriptions. The typical result of abuse in those who are diagnosed with disorder, and in need of medication, is sleepiness — not the usually desired effect. It is more common, however, for them to give away or sell their pills and risk the consequences of not treating the disorder (if they actually have it), says Dr. Robinson.

Sara agrees. "A lot of students get a prescription so they can sell it," she says, adding that Adderall fetches about $5 per pill among students. In a pharmacy, the price is about $3 per pill.

Both ends of the transaction are illegal. Methylphenidate (Ritalin, Concerta or Metadate) and amphetamine (Adderall or Dexedrine) are controlled substances that present a high potential for abuse. Possessing those drugs without a prescription is a Class C felony, which carries up to a seven-year jail sentence. Unauthorized sale and distribution are Class B felonies, which can earn five to 15 years in jail.

Robinson says the risks associated with taking larger dosages of AD/HD medication seem minimal, and those who actually have the disorder are more tolerant of the drugs than recreational users are.

Robinson does not know the long-term consequences

of abusing AD/HD drugs. "My thought is that it would be the same as that of any stimulant: weight loss, depression when coming down from the drug, cardiac arrhythmias and other similar things," he says.

"One of the problems is that drug abuse in this population is almost never a 'pure' event," he says, speaking of the adolescents and young adults he has interviewed in his office. "Most who abuse stimulant drugs also abuse many other substances, including – perhaps – marijuana, tobacco and cocaine, which are equally dangerous."

Sara knows firsthand that problem behaviors tend to group. "People who use ADD medication recreationally use other stimulants along with it," she says. "And people who use another stimulant like cocaine replace it with Adderall when they can't get it because it's a similar high.

"If you want a better high, you go to the narcotics. You can meet people who will lead you into that other stuff, but you need to have strength to say no to it."

Although the AD/HD medications are not addictive for those who take them according to their prescriptions, the greater dosages achieved through snorting increase the likelihood for psychological dependency in abusers, Robinson says.

People who find themselves addicted to prescription medications can start on the road to recovery by being honest about their drug usage, Burns says. Then she advises a medical checkup because of the drugs' physical effects. Joining a support group and exploring outpatient or residential treatment are the next steps.

Addiction to prescription drugs is something that needs to be taken seriously and treated, she says. "It requires a lifestyle change."

Sara says everyone around a recreational prescription-drug abuser suspects or recognizes the problem. "Once you come clean with your friends, if they're real friends, they'll help you quit."

To head off abuse and addiction, there are controls on prescriptions, Robinson says.

Prescriptions for AD/HD medications cannot be written for refills, meaning patients must request new prescriptions from their doctors every time. If patients request a new, 30-pill prescription in fewer than 30 days, doctors will begin to ask questions about misuse.

Burns says it is also important for past or recovered abusers to notify their doctors about their previous prescription drug abuse.

"There is often an unaddictive alternative available, but doctors have to know that normal drug treatment could be problematic," says Burns.

Now a senior in MU's College of Arts and Science, Sara has not used drugs – prescription or otherwise – for approximately four months, and she is confident that she will stay clean. She says the one or two positives are not worth the huge number of negatives.

"No more for me. I'm done," she says. "My body is tired, and I've grown up. I'm not trying to rebel anymore."

Prescription drug abuse statistics

Attention-Deficit/Hyperactivity Disorder is a medical disorder that affects people of all ages. The most recognizable symptoms include distractibility, impulsivity and hyperactivity. The growing problem with AD/HD prescription drug abuse is explained in terms of the statistics below.

• 17% of 179 surveyed men and 11% of 202 surveyed women reported illicit use of prescribed stimulant medication.

• 44% of surveyed students said they knew students

who used stimulants for academic or recreational reasons.

• Students reported time pressures associated with college life and stated stimulants increased alertness and energy.

• According to the Drug Enforcement Administration, methylphenidate (Ritalin) production increased about 900% from 1990 to 2000, then 40% from 2000 to 2002 (introduction of Concerta and Metadate). Amphetamine (Dexedrine and Adderall) production increased 5,767% from 1993 to 2001.

• Recreational stimulant use is more frequent among 18- to 25-year-olds than any other age group.

• Babcock and Byrne (2000) found 16% of students at a Massachusetts public liberal arts college had tried methylphenidate recreationally, and 31% thought Ritalin was abused on campus.

• 3% of surveyed students had been or were diagnosed with AD/HD. About 3% had a prescription for AD/HD medication.

• 40% of students who had prescriptions had used them illicitly.

• Of abusers, 37% of the men and 29.2% of the women knew students who would provide them with stimulants.

• 22.3% of surveyed students said stimulants were used illicitly on campus.

• Insufficient sleep, combined with academic and social pressures, might lead college students to seek energy boosters and study aids.

• Illicit use of stimulants already might be approaching that of cocaine and marijuana.

Additional Percentages from the study:

63% preferred to take stimulants orally.

27% took stimulants during finals week.

21% took stimulants with other drugs.

15% took stimulants before tests.

15% took stimulants with alcohol.

14% thought stimulants helped their academics long-term.

12% took stimulants when they partied.

12% preferred to snort stimulants.

First Printed in the Columbia Missourian

Consumer Magazine Article: Service & Information

look familiar?

Erin Rietz, Ball State University

Every girl needs a fairy godmother. In the classic
fairy tale, Cinderella needed the enchanting assistance of a
helpful little lady to create the beautiful gown that would
bring out her inner princess as she attended the ball of her
dreams.

Although Angie Abrams-Rains may not possess such
magical powers, this bubbly Ball State journalism instruc-
tor serves as the fairy godmother to high school girls across
east central Indiana through her passionate devotion to an
organization she founded less than a year ago. '

When teenage girls find the demands of the high
school prom to be too much, they can turn to Abrams-
Rains' project, the Great Gown Giveaway, for help.

Last spring, Abrams-Rains perused a Web site for The
Princess Project, an organization based in San Francisco
that collects and distributes used prom dresses to area high
school students. Soon after, she began to get ideas.

The Princess Project has helped more than 2,000 girls
in the last two years, and Abrams-Rains wanted to help.
She and graduate assistant Amie Morehead considered
sending some of their old formal dresses to the charity, but
instead they decided that the project was such a good idea
that they would start their own version in Muncie.

GOWN GATHERERS UNITE

Little did they know how quickly the Great Gown
Giveaway would grow. Abrams-Rains and Morehead
enlisted the help of two other women from the Department of Journalism. Christi Girton, another staff member,
and Jennifer Woods, a journalism undergraduate student,

joined the effort, and the group members almost immediately began having meetings to establish the role of the organization.

The Great Gown Giveaway would seek to provide girls with all of the components they need for the prom, the women decided. They planned to open the service to all east central Indiana high school students, but the women mainly focused on Delaware County from the beginning.

Abrams-Rains smiles widely with an excited twinkle in her eyes as she talks about every aspect of the Great Gown Giveaway. "I just think that every girl deserves to go to prom," Abrams-Rains says. "I think every girl should have that one night to feel great about herself."

Girton and Woods both attest to Abrams-Rains' fervor for the project and say that it is her enthusiasm that drives the group's success. They hope to eventually expand to the surrounding counties, particularly Jay and Randolph. Girls interested in obtaining a dress from the organization are not required to produce proof of financial need – all Great Gown Giveaway requires is to see a student ID, and the dress each girl chooses is hers to keep.

"You could be the wealthiest person in the town, but as long as you think you need a dress, that's all that matters," Abrams-Rains says.

FREE PRESS, 50 DRESSES

The original plan was to begin collecting dresses in time to donate them in the spring of 2005. However, a reporter from the Star Press learned about the project last spring and wrote a story about it that the ladies say gave them a head start. "It just kind of blossomed all at once from that," Abrams-Rains says. "We got about 50 calls just that first day from people who wanted to give us dresses."

Following the publication of the article, the Great Gown Giveaway prom dress collection began to form. Mainly because of the free publicity, the ladies say they were able to help girls from five area high schools obtain free dresses for their proms.

"It was just amazing that even through a small story in the newspaper so many people would pick up on it," Girton says. "With our lack of promotion at that point, it was great to have so many people get wind of it."

Following such a quick and successful start, the women were excited to make big plans for their second year. Although Abrams-Rains says Morehead left the group due to time constraints, the three remaining members began to set goals for a Spring Extravaganza that would be held before the 2005 prom season.

"Basically at the extravaganza the girls can just show up with a school ID and we can fit them all with the whole works," Abrams-Rains says.

NOT YET NONPROFIT

The group hopes the extravaganza will include not only dresses, but also everything else that makes up the traditional prom ensemble such as accessories, shoes and even hair and make-up tips from area businesses. "It's kind of like a bridal show for prom stuff," Girton says.

Despite all of the early success and plans, however, things have not been trouble-free for the women of the Great Gown Giveaway. Girton says they held a callout for dresses and accessories earlier in the fall but only collected a few dresses. Also, sudden illness within the organization has slowed down the group's progress and brought some initiatives to a temporary halt.

The women say one of the most frustrating problems

is lack of financial stability. Although they received some donations following the Star Press article, much of the money was used while filing for nonprofit status with the government – recognition the Great Gown Giveaway still has yet to receive.

Abrams-Rains says some would-be donors have committed to helping out, but not until the nonprofit status has been obtained.

Woods says the organization has had its problems this year, but everything will pick up soon enough. "Once we get that nonprofit status, I think things could start falling into place," Woods says. "It's really like a domino effect."

Abrams-Rains already has plans for the money once the organization receives it. She says the organization would like to have the ability to hold more fund-raisers and actually buy dresses in the odd sizes that are hard to come by. Also, Girton says she hopes to get more money so that the women can promote the organization more heavily.

The women of the Great Gown Giveaway plan to have a second callout sometime this spring semester, and they are looking for a variety of donations from the public.

DONORS, DON'T DISCRIMINATE

Abrams-Rains says people and businesses can donate any type of formal dress, shoes, accessories, gift certificates for hair and make-up appointments, or even just their time – volunteers will be needed to ensure that the Spring Extravaganza is a success.

The Great Gown Giveaway will not turn down any kind of donation. Girton says that although the women may not be able to give away dresses unsuitable for a modern-day prom, they would take them off anyone's hands.

Abrams-Rains, who currently keeps two large racks of dresses in her home's guest room until the organization can afford a storage facility, says she has some dresses that were probably worn in the '70s and '80s.

"We've got some horrible dresses," Abrams-Rains says. "But then again, we've got some gorgeous, some absolutely amazing dresses."

Although Girton insists that Abrams-Rains has spearheaded everything, her own excitement for the project is based on a feeling of satisfaction in helping others. "Just seeing how happy it made the few people we have helped already has made it all worthwhile," Girton says.

"We don't want them to think it's a hand-me-down or a gimme. We just want them all to have that special experience."

First Published in Expo Magazine

you can refuse booze!

Dana Schmidt, Iowa State University

Let's face it. If you haven't been offered alcohol by now, chances are you soon will. Deciding whether to drink is a big decision and when you've seen the most popular girl in your school or the cutest guy in your math class take a sip at a party; it's hard to resist the temptation. Here are some tips from teens that've been in your shoes to help you refuse alcohol.

Just Say "No." You've undoubtedly heard this phrase before, but in many situations it's all you need to do. Jessica H., 18, from Aberdeen, S.D., was 16 years old when she was first asked to drink alcohol. She had gone to a classmate's house after school just to hang out. "I didn't know the person very well and she ended up having alcohol there and asked me if I wanted some to drink," Jessica H. says. "I said no. A simple no was all it took for me."

Laura, 17, from Strafford, N.H., says she's also been pressured to drink. "It's a little intimidating when you have a peer asking you to do something you really don't want to do. It's nerve racking to say no, but after you've said no, people will usually leave you alone."

Be Confident. If someone senses you're hesitant in saying no, he or she might pressure you even more. "Everyone loves to take advantage of a weak person and boss him or her around," says Jawad, 18, from Owing Mills, Md. "If you don't cave into peer pressure, you will be a strong person and no one will be able to bring you down."

Also, if you're confident in saying no, the people pressuring you know you've already made the decision not to drink, so they might be less likely to keep pressuring you, Jessica H. says.

Give an Excuse. Okay. So saying no and being confident might not always work. If that happens you can give the person a reason why you don't want to drink. "Most people that I know are fine with someone not drinking, but if they keep insisting you could just say you're driving tonight or you're allergic to alcohol," says Kaleb, 17, from Red Bay, Ala.

Juli, 18, from Stowe, Vt., suggests you say, "My parents will kill me!" or "I hate beer. It tastes like piss." If you're in a sport at school, you can tell them "My coach will kill me!" or "I have a meet tomorrow so I can't," Jessica H. says.

Remember, you can always just tell the person you're not in the mood and ask for some soda instead, Jawad says. Even if you don't like soda, you can ask for something else to drink, such as water, milk, or juice.

But beware when someone offers punch or Kool-aid that has been sitting out on a table. Lots of times people will spike punch by adding some alcohol or even dangerous drugs to it. Never leave your soda can or glass of juice unattended because someone may try to put something in it. If you forget and leave your glass sitting around, just ask for a new alcohol-free drink.

Also, prepare a couple of excuses before you go to a party. That way you'll be ready if you're offered alcohol.

Leave the Situation. It's natural to feel alone and uncomfortable when it seems as if you're the only one not drinking at a party. Jessica B., 17, from Bloomington, Minn., says it's important you feel comfortable in every situation you're in. "My mom always tells me if you don't want to slip, don't put yourself in a slippery situation. If you don't feel safe at a party, than don't go."

If you do decide to go to a party and the people there

keep pressuring you and telling you that if you drink, "It'll be lots of fun," or "It'll loosen you up" or if they keep telling you how fun it will be for them to see you get drunk, find a way to leave the party. You can call your parents to come pick you up or have a friend who hasn't been drinking take you home.

"Your parents will understand if you call them and tell them you want leave the situation," Juli says. And she should know. When Juli was a freshman in high school she frequently carpooled to school with a girl from her town. One night before driving to a school event, Juli's friend suggested they go out to dinner. "When we got there her friends were sitting there smoking and drinking. I decided to leave and called one of my classmate's mothers. I didn't know the classmate very well, but her mom came and picked me up."

Find a Support System: It may seem as if you have to drink to be cool, but that's not true. You're a cool person – a way cooler person – if you choose not to drink because that means you can have fun without being intoxicated. Because you're such a cool person, there will be plenty of other cool people like you – people who choose not to consume alcohol – who you can hang out with. It's important to have friends and to surround yourself with people who share your same viewpoint about drinking. Having friends who don't drink is the best way to resist pressure because you can support each other and remind each other of your decision not to drink. "If you have friends who will only be your friends because you drink with them, than honestly you're too good for them," Laura says.

Juli knew a friend who felt as if she was the only one in her school who didn't drink, so Juli suggested she start a Students Against Destructive Decisions (SADD) chapter at her school. The girl, who attended a school of 150 students, had 10 people show up at the first meeting. "[The group] will help you be with people who have the same feelings as you do," Juli says.

It's tough to say no when you're pressured to drink alcohol – especially when it seems as if everyone else is doing it. But you can stay strong and resist the pressure if you really want to. And remember, someone who pressures you to do something you don't want to do really isn't a friend. Real friends accept you for who you are and respect your decisions.

Alcohol-Free Alternatives

The weekend is finally here and you've got nothing to do. Here are some ideas teens from the SADD National Leadership Council have for having alcohol-free fun:

Karaoke Night: Like singing and dancing? Then get some of your friends together and have a blast performing your favorite tunes for each other. To make things even more exciting, have your own American Idol contest where each week you vote off your friends until only one is left. Take the winner out to a movie or have all your friends chip in to get her a CD of her favorite group.

BYOB: No, no, no. BYOB does not stand for Bring Your Own Beer. It can stand for anything you want it to stand for, such as Bring Your Own Banana (to make banana splits, of course) or Bring Your Own Board game. Be creative and come up with your own fun BYOB night ideas.

Movie Marathon: Do you and your girlfriends think Chad Michael Murray is really cute? Then grab some popcorn, sodas, and your other favorite munchies and have a movie marathon night where you watch all the movies he's ever been in. Or, if you want to see lots of cute actors and not just Chad, have each of your friends choose her favorite movie and watch all of the movies in one night (or one weekend).

Play Dress Up: You're never too old to play dress up, so grab your friends and have some fun. Decide on a theme, dress up in funny outfits, and go out to dinner. You might get some weird looks from people, but you and your girlfriends will have a blast dressing silly for the evening.

Make a Difference: Spend your Saturday helping your community by volunteering at your local hospital, children's club, homeless shelter, or any other organization in your town. Lots of organizations everywhere need volunteers, gather your gal pals and choose a group! You will not only have fun —you'll be helping someone in need.

hoops and hollers

Basketball, Buffets, Booze and Bracket Busting
Adam Wright, Arizona State University

A Vegas son rises

It's 6:30 a.m. in Las Vegas, and Danny Bogen isn't sure whether his day is starting or ending.

He stretches, wipes the corner of his mouth and hits on a 12. The dealer turns over a face card and takes Danny's chips before his brain can even do the math.

Danny finally gets up from the blackjack table where he spent the night and decides to catch some winks.

On his way to the elevator he runs right into his father.

Most fathers would be disappointed to find their son just making it to bed at sunrise with an empty wallet after a night of craziness. But instead, Norm grabs Danny by the arm and steers him toward their home for the weekend: the sports book at the Golden Nugget.

Danny and Norm arrive at "the book" around 7 a.m. to find hundreds of fans wearing jerseys and hats, dragging coolers of beer and food, and holding piles of betting slips. Hundreds of potential dollars worth of paper slip into pockets and wallets as sports fans settle into seats in front of three huge TV screens. It's three full hours before the first game starts, yet March Madness has officially begun in the City of Sin.

Who needs the Super Bowl?

The first weekend of March Madness marks one of the biggest weekends of the year in Vegas. Starting March 17th with the first round, 64 college basketball teams battle their way toward the national championship. Fans can watch and bet on every single game. Some of those thousands of fans will leave town with a few "thousands" of their own.

Unlike the Super Bowl, where fans must wait to see who's playing before booking reservations, college basketball fans can expect at least one of their favorites to make the field every year. Jeremy Handel, public relations manager for the Imperial Palace, says the hotel starts receiving reservations for rooms during March Madness as early as fall of the previous year.

The Imperial Palace, or "the I.P." as it's affectionately known, devotes its bars, 230 individual TVs and 12 big screens to fans and gamblers. The bets and odds are listed on dry-erase boards behind the tellers.

The I.P. harkens back to the old days of Vegas; when the emphasis was on gambling rather than shopping and shows. The I.P. is loaded with card and dice games as well as countless slot machines and video poker. After the basketball games are over, the blackjack dealers become "Dealtainers" as they perform and deal cards dressed like Michael Jackson, Barbara Streisand and others.

Downtown, the Golden Nugget sets up a sports book in its main ballroom, which is enclosed by frosted windows, giving sports fans the feeling of being in a fishbowl looking out on the rest of the casino. Multiple big screen TVs as well as numerous smaller sets broadcast every game simultaneously.

Before each game, an announcer asks the crowd to cheer for the game they want on the main TV. The game that receives the loudest cheers is shown on the main TV, and the audio is pumped through the sound system.

The "Nugget" stations two tellers in the ballroom so bettors can place bets without leaving the room. Between games, hundreds of people often stand in line to place bets. Meanwhile cocktail waitresses cruise the room and serve drinks and delicacies, such as hot dogs and sandwiches, all weekend long.

The book at Caesar's Palace, one of the nicest and biggest in Vegas, has booths with individual TVs as well as big screens on the walls. Additional big screens list the bets, spreads and odds. The chairs are large and comfortable. The dark colors and cool lighting evoke a calm, luxurious mood.

Don't ever look away

It's 10 a.m.

The beers are flowing, and 4th-seed Maryland is about to tip off against 13th-seed UT-El Paso. The spread for the game is Maryland by 7 points.

Danny places his bet on UTEP because he likes betting against his dad and he knows just how much 7 points can be in the tournament. He also knows UTEP's shooting guard Chris Craig can shoot the lights out from anywhere, at any time.

The fans are fresh and rowdy for the first game, drinks are flowing and the announcer in the Golden Nugget sports book is keeping the crowd pumped up.

Maryland builds an 11-point lead with just 10 minutes to go in the game. The room starts to relax and Maryland bettors start thinking about cashing in their slips and hitting the nearest buffet.

Before anyone notices, UTEP rips off a 7-point run capped by a Chris Craig lay-up and Maryland's lead is cut to 4.

The spread is now in serious danger. The gamblers tense up. Palms get sweaty, knuckles turn white.

Some games are quite upsetting

Picking an upset is one of the best ways to make money because the odds are always longer. One place to look for upsets in the NCAA tournament is in the 12-5 game between the 12th-seeded team and the 5th-seeded team.

Since 1990, the 12th seed has upset the 5th seed 22 times, which translates to a 37 percent winning percentage. This upset has occurred at least once every year since 1990 except for the 2000 tournament.

Although a 16th seed is rarely as competitive as a 1st seed, by the 12-5 game the teams are much more evenly matched. The 5th seed is often overconfident and has a tendency to forget just how good the team they're facing in the first round might be.

In seven of the last 15 years, the 12th seed has beaten the 5th seed in two or more of the four games.

Money time

After Chris Craig buries a 3-pointer, the game is tied at 81 with 1:39 to go.

Danny and his brethren who picked the underdog start screaming. They know that if UTEP loses by no more than 6 points, they'll all still win big.

Bettors for the favorite start praying for overtime, because only in overtime can Maryland rebuild its 7-point lead and cover the spread.

UTEP fouls Maryland's D.J. Strawberry, who drains both free throws to put Maryland ahead 84-81 with just 47 seconds left.

Vegas is holding its breath.

There's still enough time for Maryland to extend the lead…or for UTEP to win.

UTEP scores.

84-83.

Maryland fans are just hoping to squeeze out a win at

this point. They'd be heartbroken if they lost their bets and their team in the same game.

Maryland makes two free throws.

86-83.

14 seconds left.

It's high noon. It's a showdown. Get the ball to the gunslinger, Chris Craig.

If UTEP misses Maryland advances and the spread is covered.

If they tie the game, Maryland bettors have a chance to beat the spread.

Maryland fans, Maryland bettors, UTEP fans and UTEP bettors, all in the same room, all with different hopes on the outcome, all with their butts on the utmost edge of their chairs.

The ball is in-bounded; Craig comes free, gets the ball and puts it up for the tie.

The shot is blocked.

Maryland fans exhale, but UTEP's Jason Williams picks up the ball with time left on the clock.

He passes back to Craig, who throws up a prayer at the buzzer, and it hits nothing but…

…nothing. It's an air ball. Fans cry for a foul, but none comes. The game finally ends.

Maryland wins by 3, but the spread is covered. Soon the floor of the room is also covered…with torn betting slips rendered meaningless by UTEP's inability to give up and go quietly.

But Danny and those who bet UTEP are winners of their first bet of the weekend.

That's how it goes in this town.

Beers pop open. Fans settle deeper into their seats,

take a deep breath and get ready for the second game. One down, 31 more to go.

A Bettor's Primer

Although betting in the sports book is a major step up from your yearly office pool, it's still one of the simplest bets in town. There are no cards to count, no little ball bouncing around on a circle of numbers, no cherries to line up, no bluffing – and you never need to wear sunglasses like the poker players on TV. It's simply feeling your hunch and placing your bet with a teller.

The first thing to know is the point spread or line, which is the number of points the favorite is expected to win by. It's also the number the experts know will compel half the bettors to bet for the favorite while enticing the other half to take a chance on the underdog. By betting on the favorite, you give the underdog the lead before the game starts because the favorite has to overcome this hypothetical lead for the bet to be a winner.

Here's an example. The New England Patriots were favored to win the 2005 Super Bowl by 6 points. The bet at the casino would look like this: Patriots –6/Eagles +6. Before the game even starts, you have to view the game as if the Eagles are already up by 6 points. The Patriots won by only 3, meaning that in Vegas, they lost by 3. The Patriots won the Super Bowl, but anyone who bet on them with the point spread lost the bet.

Another bet is the money line, which eliminates the point spread. Whoever wins the game, no matter if by one point or 100, wins the bet. This bet comes with odds. The lower the odds, the more it has a chance of happening.

The bet is written in the sports book like this: Suns +240/Spurs –280. This means the Spurs are favored. A

$100 bet on the Suns would win $240. You'd have to bet $280 on the Spurs to win $100.

Most casinos offer futures bets, which deal with games that are, well, in the future. For example: Let's say you bet $5 on the Washington Nationals (300:1) to win the 2005 World Series this coming October. If by some miracle they actually do, you'll win $1,500.

Betting the totals, also known as the over/under, doesn't require you to pick a winner. Instead, the casino sets a number of total points that two teams will score. You simply decide whether the teams' combined final score will add up to "over" or "under" the set score.

For example: The Suns beat the Jazz 136-128. The total was 264, definitely over the point total that any casino in the world would have set. If you'd bet the "over" on this game, you'd have been the big winner.

The parlay bet is one of the most exciting and lucrative bets in Vegas. Bettors pick two or more games, and if they all win, the winnings compound. The more games you pick, the higher the odds. A five-team basketball parlay at Bally's pays off at 20 to 1. If you bet $5 and win all five games, you get $100. Unfortunately, if just one team loses, you lose the whole bet.

Consumer Magazine Article: First Person

daddy's girl

Nicole Williams, Arizona State University

March 10, 2005 3:45 p.m.

Southwest Airlines Flight 251 from Phoenix to
Portland, Oregon isn't full. I have three seats all to myself.
Chunks of salad cling to the back seam of the middle seat
– a previous passenger's lunch. When I sit down I smell
Chinese food, and sure enough two rows back someone is
cramming down Panda Express.

The plane takes off. Soon we fly over the red bluffs
of the Colorado Plateau. The pilot says those of us seated
on the left side of the plane will be able to see the rim of
the Grand Canyon. The recycled air circulating inside the
plane makes my eyes sting.

It's my last spring break as an Arizona State University student. I'm going to graduate in a few months, and I
should be celebrating by traveling to Mazatlan or Cancun
or Rocky Point, the Mexican resorts that attract so many
ASU spring breakers. Instead, I'm going to visit Wayne
Williams, my father, a convicted child molester currently
incarcerated in Oregon.

I haven't seen Dad in nearly two years. I know I have
to go through with this planned visit, but it bothers me
that I am going to visit him at all. Why should I give
him the privilege of seeing me? It's like saying, "Hey, you
haven't been there for me in the past 21 years of my life,
but I'm going to visit you in prison."

Why do I feel this is a battle and I'm the one surren-
dering and he's the one winning? I want to turn the plane
back. It's going to be awkward tomorrow.

I'm going to ask my father if he molested my nine-
year-old stepsister.

I don't even want to know the truth. Yet again, I need to know the truth. Something inside me tells me that if I just ask him, he will deny he's a pedophile and it will all go away. So I will ask him and I will write a story about it for a journalism class. I have everything packed. I have my tape recorder, notebook and laptop; everything but the audio CD of his sentencing, which was sent to me a few weeks ago by the Deschutes County Circuit Court. I have not been able to bring myself to listen to it yet. I left the CD in Arizona

***

Nicola

…You were the one in my life that made life worth living when sometimes I wasn't doing very well. I will always remember and cherish these special times between you and I. These are the few little years that made you and me who we are as father and daughter, that I will always thank our heavenly father for…

Dad

***

My father is one of about 234,000 sex offenders in America, according to the Bureau of Justice Statistics. The bureau says one in four children fall victim to inappropriate touching by a sex offender. Eighty-five percent of the predators are known to the victim.

In November, 1994, 10 years before my father was sent to prison, Oregon voters approved Measure 11 in the Oregon State Legislature. The measure boosted mandatory minimum sentences for serious sex crimes. In 2004, Dad was sentenced under Measure 11 to six years in prison with no chance of parole for sexually abusing my stepsister. For the past six months, he has been serving his 75-month prison sentence in Two Rivers Correctional Facility in northeastern Oregon, in the isolated town of Umatilla, which is just across the Columbia River from Washington.

***

Nicola

…I'm finding that I have so many things I want to say and talk to you about, but I seem to get lost in all my thoughts and feelings. I pray that you and I still have time to spend together in this life. We've got a lot of catching up to do… so much unfinished business. So many things too, that we never had the opportunity to discuss, so we might have a better understanding of each other's feelings. You and I have been robbed of times that can never be caught or relived again, but I am thankful that not all has been lost…

Dad

***

I was the first person in the family he wrote from prison. When I received that first letter in August, 2004, I felt as if it was the only time he'd ever tried to show me he cared about me. And yet he spelled my name wrong. Nicola instead of Nicole.

***

I don't have very many memories of my dad. I remember times we went fishing. Rubber boots, hair in a pony tail, Levi jeans. I went fishing for the snacks; chips, jerky, sandwiches and candy. But I mostly went as an excuse to be with him; to be with my dad. I also remember a lot of time spent with our animals. One year Dad decided we were going to incubate chicken eggs; we put the incubator in my bedroom. Thirty-two baby chicks hatched in my room that year.

I remember Dad leaving for work in the mornings. He was a logger. He loved cutting timber in the Oregon forest;

he was one of few fathers I knew who actually enjoyed what he did for a living. He would tiptoe into my bedroom just before he left and almost instantly I would wake up, but pretend I was still asleep. He would tuck the covers under my shoulders and all the way up to my chin so only my tiny face was peeking out. Then he would kiss my forehead and shut the door again. I would hear the rumble of his old Ford truck warming up while he packed his gear and power saws for work. He would pull the truck out of the carport and coast down our gravel lane. I would open my eyes just to watch his headlights dance across the top of my bedroom ceiling. Then the white lights faded into the early morning darkness. I would fall fast asleep after he left. I hadn't thought of it until now, but this memory of my father leaving me is the most vivid of all.

***

Nicola

…I wish for your sake that I wasn't in here so that you wouldn't be sad. I want to turn your sad into glad by saying I'm doing better in here than out there. What I'm experiencing in here is priceless for me. I will be a better person when I get out. I will know who I am again…

Dad

***

We lived in the country when I was little, in a small town called Marcola, Oregon. I loved our house. It was the last house on Railroad Lane. It was a large gray house with a weeping willow tree in the front yard and an old red barn near the back of the property. The tire swing in the large maple tree was my favorite place.

My parents split up in the summer of 1992. My father slammed my mom against the refrigerator, and she left him. She moved my brother and me into a two bedroom apartment in town. I shared a bed with my mom. I was eight years old. I felt my world had flipped upside down, right on top of me. I wanted my parents to stay together and I couldn't understand why they were apart. I felt punished.

After my parents divorced, my father lived alone in the gray house with three bedrooms and two bathrooms. After my mother, brother and I left, the house was completely empty, only a bed in the master bedroom. No other furniture. My father sold most of the animals and so he had all the property to himself.

There wasn't much to do around our father's house during our weekend visits. My father usually slept most of the day. My brother Garrett and I entertained ourselves and created adventures on the unkempt property. Our favorite game was searching for buried treasure with homemade pirate maps. I was always Captain Hook and Garrett was Smee.

Dad kept his change in a large glass beer pitcher in his saw shop around the back of the house. The shop smelled of gasoline and wood; sawdust was scattered on the floor. One weekend my brother and I decided to have a treasure hunt with my father's coins. We stole the pitcher and buried it near the back of the abandoned chicken coop. We drew a treasure map of the riches; an "X" marked the spot in the back of the coop where the treasures lay.

It wasn't until a few weekends later we re-discovered the money. We were playing around in the overgrown chicken coop once again when we spotted a shiny quarter in the back of the coop and remembered our adventure from before. We uncovered the loot and never told Dad. He never questioned where we found the funds to pay for our smorgasbord of candy that day, he just slept.

In 1994, my father married a woman named Rhonda who already had two children from an earlier marriage. I suddenly had a three-year-old stepbrother and a one-year-old stepsister. I was 10, Garrett was six. Then three years later, when I was 13, my half brother was born. I was never close with my father's other family. I never felt welcome in their home.

***

March 11, 2005 8:10 a.m.

My mother, Dawn, and my stepfather Doug take me to Two Rivers Correctional Facility. The drive to the prison seems long and boring. Train tracks run parallel with the highway for almost 10 miles. The Columbia River flows along the highway too. The river is murky and still.

Doug has been in our lives for the past nine years. He's been more of a father to me then my real dad ever was. Doug was there for the dance recitals, the plays and the swim meets. Doug was there to help me with my homework. Doug checked under the hood of my '91 Honda Accord my freshman year when he and Mom dropped me off at college. Doug handed over the "in case of an emergency" credit card. If it were up to me, Doug would be my dad.

But he isn't.

I have a sick feeling in my stomach. I don't want to see my father. I just want to leave it all inside for no one else to know about. But I have to do this. I have all the questions written down; I know exactly what I want out of this visit with my father: ANSWERS. I'm sick of having a loser father. I'm tired of being ashamed. Didn't he think for a minute that sexually assaulting my stepsister had consequences for my brother and me?

My mom asks me what I might talk about with him.

"I don't know." I say, looking out the window.

"Once you're in there you'll know what to say. He's your dad; conversation should come natural. You both have plenty to talk about," Doug says.

"I think you'll feel a lot better when this is all over." Mom says. "I remember the day you were born. I was sick, so I didn't get to hold you right after birth. The nurse was cleaning your newborn body and you were screaming. Your dad always said you were the loudest baby in that hospital. The nurse handed you over to him in a neatly wrapped bundle. You were still screaming at the top of your little lungs. Then he said your name. 'Nicole.' He started talking to you and suddenly the screaming stopped and the tears disappeared. He says he thinks this happened because he used to talk to you through my belly. You knew the voice in that hospital room was the same voice you'd heard in my womb. Your dad and you have always had a connection, whether each of you has seen it or not."

***

March 11, 2005 9:23 a.m.

We're nearly at the prison. I can't find a place to rest my hands and the orange juice I had an hour ago has gone sour in my stomach. My eyes burn and my head pounds. I wonder what the room will look like. How will I gather the courage to ask my father if he hurt my stepsister? Will he deny it? Was he wrongly convicted? Will we make up for lost time?

I think about the CD back home and what it might say.

I realize I've never had a one-on-one conversation alone with my father before. My brother, Garrett, has always been right there with us, he always cleared the dead air of silence. My father and brother have always been close; joined at the hip, working on some odd job together, going hunting, talking football… anything as long as they were together. When I first tell Garrett I'm going to visit Dad in prison, it surprises him. The first thing he asks is if he can come along.

I tell Garrett he can't come with me, because Garrett is 17 and a minor and Dad had committed a crime against a minor, so Garrett isn't allowed to visit him. Garrett is angry and jealous.

"This isn't fair," Garrett shouts. "Dad never once tried anything with me! He didn't even think about it! Why am I the one being punished? I want to see my dad and he wants to see me. This whole thing is stupid."

"Are you okay?" I ask.

"Tell him 'Hi' for me; tell him that I love him," he says, fiddling with the TV remote.

I can tell Garrett is bothered and jealous he can't come with me. To make him feel better I ask him to help me recall memories about our dad growing up.

"Remember how Dad always walked around the house only in this underwear?" I ask.

"Remember that time you wanted a drink of Dad's Squirt and you took a drink out of his spit bottle instead?" he asks.

"Ugh, yeah, he always wore jeans with a Skoal ring in the back pocket."

"With Budweiser suspenders," my brother adds.

I don't mention the memories I have of Dad missing every dance recital of mine and making every football game of Garrett's. I leave out the part about Dad never helping me with my swim stroke but always showing Garrett what went on under the hood of a truck.

**

Nicola

…I miss you Nicola and I have for a long time. I hope

from the things I have written to you, you can understand how much. I just hope, now that you're older, we can talk about things that are already molded…

Dad

***

March 11, 2005 9:30 a.m.

We arrive at the prison. I walk across the empty visitor's parking lot, leaving Doug and my mom back at the truck. I'm doing this alone. I worry I will not keep my composure. I worry I will not confront him about the crime.

I walk into a red brick building with low vaulted ceilings. There are green holding lockers to my right where I must leave my tape recorder and list of questions. I'm not allowed to bring anything with me, but it's OK because I know what to ask. I pass through a metal detector three different times before the two correctional officers take me over to get my hand stamped. I walk down a hallway to an outside door. I'm held in a retaining cell until the next door opens and I follow a breezeway toward a much larger building that smells of fish. The officer tells me it's Fish Friday.

I'm led into a visiting room with white walls and 10 rows of chairs lined up on the black floor. Couples face each other in some of the chairs. There are makeshift coffee tables made from wooden boxes painted black. Artwork created by prisoners is tacked on the walls. The names of the artists are tagged under each work of art - the drawing of the American flag, the sketch of a lion, the painting of a mountain landscape.

The officer tells me I may hug and kiss my father, but only when I first see him and when I'm about to leave. I can only hold his hand, no other touching is permitted.

He says I may purchase a snack or a soda from the vending machines but I'm not allowed to share them with my father. He says I can buy a separate snack for my father, but once I've handed it to him I can't take it back. He emphasizes again I may not share. I feel guilty I didn't bring any change.

I start crying.

The officer hands me a square of tissue torn off a roll of toilet paper. He says to sit tight and wait for my father. I wait 10 minutes. I want to bolt out of this room and never look back. Then my father enters through the back door of the visitor's dayroom. I break down to another level. I sob.

My father has lost some weight and I can tell he's been working out. He has a well-kept, trimmed beard. I remember that in the summers, he would always have a dark tan, which he attributed to his Indian roots. He would shave his full beard off, to keep cool and he would always slim down. In the winters he would grow the full Grizzly Adams beard back and gain weight in his gut.

I'm surprised to see how old he looks. His hair has been receding since he was in his early 30's, and now it has thinned to a peppered black and white fluff of hair above the forehead and sideburns. Behind his '70's-looking glasses, his dark brown eyes seem foreign. I really don't know this man sitting in front of me. I just know he's my father. He wears dark blue jeans with orange letters 'TRCI' patched on the left thigh and a blue collar shirt, and worn-out brown shoes.

"You're the last person in the world I ever thought I'd see in here," he says.

I can't believe it either. This time the officer brings me the entire roll of toilet paper. My father asks about Garrett. He asks about Mom. I chat. I smile. I cry. But I can't bring myself to ask if he hurt my stepsister.

My father tells me that as a child, he grew up with an alcoholic father and a working mother. He took care of himself. Sure, he always had a warm bed to sleep in at night, a hot meal and Christian discipline, but he never had any emotional support or love. This relationship has happened between us too. I tell the bearded stranger in front of me that I hate seeing him in here. He needs fresh air in his lungs, the breeze on his cheek, wide-open space. He doesn't belong in an isolated prison in Oregon.

Now I have to share the toilet paper roll with my father. We only have 10 minutes left to our visit, I know because I keep looking at the clock above my father's head. I feel sorry for my father. I didn't expect this, but I hope that time will stop just this once and we can stay in this place forever using this time to catch up. But I need to ask him the question that's been burning a hole in my mind since the day I found out. I need to ask him if whatever is recorded on the CD from his sentencing is true.

My throat constricts. Then the guard says visiting hours are over. Dad tells me not to worry about all the little things in my life right now. He tells me to live in the moment and never take life for granted. He tells me to forgive and forget. He tells me to talk to God every day.

I reach across the black box and hug my father. I tell him for the first time in 10 years that I love him. As I line up to leave the room, my father blows me a kiss.

In the breezeway I smell Fish Friday and I know that my father is on his way to eat lunch and I wish I were joining him.

As I make my way across the empty parking lot once again, I notice just how nice of a day it is outside. The light wind is crisp and the sun is warm on my arms and face.

I need the safety of my mother's arms. I melt into her shoulder. We laugh because I've smeared mascara all over her shirt. She tucks my hair behind my ear. I tell her I never asked my father if he is a pedophile.

My mother says she knew I couldn't do it.

"Are you okay?" she asks.

"I wasn't a reporter in there. I couldn't ask my question, I was just his daughter. I don't even know who that man is in there, Mom."

"I know," she says. "I knew when I asked you earlier that it was going to turn out like this, I'm just glad you came all this way to see him. This is good for you."

My father never molested me.

How could he be a pedophile?

***

March 18, 2005 9:51 p.m.

I am back at ASU. I don't talk about my spring break. I still dread listening to the CD from the court. I need to hear my father's confession, but I can't push the play button.

I wonder if he had wanted to abuse me, and that's the reason he stayed away from me when I was little. I need answers still, and the CD is all I have left, since I couldn't bring myself to ask my father anything during our visit. Finally, I ask my roommate to help me out by pushing the play button.

The prosecutor states the facts.

"The victim in this case was the stepdaughter of the defendant… It was reported that on approximately five or six occasions the defendant had the victim rub lotion on his penis and on at least one occasion it was reported that he licked her breasts."

I hear my father's voice.

"Everything written on this paper is true but one

thing," my father tells the judge.

"I have to admit being a sinful, malicious, piece of dirt is not a good thing when you find out that's what you've been. I'm a very sinful man. I've caused a great sin towards my whole family, not just to the family I can't go back to. I have a lot of people in this world who love me. I'm thankful there are some who are able to forgive me... I never once threatened my daughter; I never once terrorized my daughter. There was never any verbal abuse, there never was any physical abuse, and there definitely was sexual abuse."

My father's voice breaks, he sounds remorseful. But then in a roundabout way, he blames my stepsister for what had happened. "She was curious about me," he said, "and I didn't realize what was going on. I never realized my sexual feelings for her until she was seven years old. I treated her as my first daughter Nicole... I helped with her bath, helped her go to the bathroom."

He had fallen in love with my stepsister.

"I never once went against her will," my father tells the judge. "I never once made her do anything. We had a very loving precious relationship... I don't feel good at all about what I've done. I miss my daughter, and I know she misses me... Sexual abuse is nothing I am proud of. It's hard to explain the relationship that we had for a few years."

Then my father feels sorry for himself. "My depression comes to a point where you don't feel anything any more. You just want to die. You want to commit suicide; you want to end your life... You get so wrapped up in your depression. Where it comes from I don't know... When you get depressed you lose your feeling about anything, the only thing that made me feel alive in these depressive states of mind was pain. Why I don't know, I just didn't feel anything else. And it's not in my heart, but in my mind. If I could give my heart out there and show it to everybody in this world, you might be surprised what's really in my heart. I never wanted to hurt anybody. Never."

The judge pronounces the sentence in a monotone.

"You'll be sentenced to 75 months. The post prison supervision is 120 months… You'll be required to submit to DNA testing. You're also going to have to register as a sex offender. That will be for the rest of your life. I recommend that, as conditions of post prison supervision, you have no contact with the victim or her immediate family. I recommend that you have the standard sex offender conditions, no contact with minor females."

***

March 19, 2005 11:20 p.m.

I cannot explain why I still love my distant father, but somehow, under the roof of the medium security prison, I felt as if we finally understood we needed each other as father and daughter. But how do we sustain a normal relationship?

My father's confession to the judge plays over and over in my head. I'd put off listening to the CD because on some level I knew I couldn't have visited him if I'd heard the confession before.

My father did unspeakable things to a defenseless child, and yet I feel I need to be strong and love him for who he is. He has to live the rest of his life knowing what he did was a sin. He'll also have to live the rest of his life knowing that I will never fully trust him, and will never leave him alone with my children when I have them.

***

After the prison visit, I receive another letter. He spells my name right this time.

Nicole

...I am here to help you find truth and understanding. I will never tell you what to believe, that is between you and God alone. I will tell you what is in my heart and how I feel and all I know about my relationship with God. I will give you things to think about but will never tell you what to believe! I love you Nicole Marie. Thank you so much for your letter. Thank you too for coming so far to see me. Love you forever...

Dad

***

I know the answer now.
My father is a pedophile.

everything decided forever

Jennifer La Lima, Hofstra University

Everything seemed like silence, until I heard myself scream. The phone was still off the hook gripped between my hands, my knuckles pressed against the laundry room floor. Kelly had hung up minutes ago on the other end. Kathleen, my best friend, had been killed. Kelly was so sorry to be the first to tell me.

I ran from the phone, practically sliding into the staircase where my mother had stopped short in fear. "They think something happened to Kathleen," I said, feeling nothing but the abrupt and complete halt of time.

Hoping to hear her mother's upbeat voice, I called Kathleen's home phone. It was a detective who answered. I don't even remember breathing as this stranger quickly told me the story that would break my heart forever: Kathleen had been killed by her boyfriend, Tom, at her Columbia University dorm.

The following afternoon, Tom's body was found in pieces after he jumped in front of an uptown subway train. Kathleen's picture ID was in his pocket. "Fear" was spelled out in graffiti on the subway station wall.

This couldn't be happening.

The voices on the news that night had never seemed so strange, as they murmured simple tidbits of a person and a life they knew nothing about: "Kathleen Roskot, 19, was found covered in blood, beaten and stabbed on her dorm room floor…a magazine featuring Jack Kerouac covered her face…Kathleen Roskot was allegedly killed by her boyfriend…Kathleen Roskot, an Ivy League student, mourned here today by family and friends."

Did they know that Jack Kerouac was one of her favorite writers?

Kathleen's name and yearbook photo were everywhere. It was a journalist who first notified Kathleen's parents that something had happened to their daughter. Eager to get a story, a reporter rang their phone to ask how the Roskots felt about the murder of their daughter. Another journalist knocked on their door. To them, it was a story. To the Roskots, it was the beginning of the rest of their lives.

That night, I was in so much disbelief that I called her dorm room.

I got the Rolling Stones: "Pleased to meet you, won't you guess my name?" Her answering machine sang "Sympathy For The Devil," as usual.

"Hey this is Kathleen; I'm not here right now. Leave a message and I'll get back to you, thanks. Bye." I left one. Looking back, I don't know what I was thinking.

I cried the rest of the night in a way that purged the youthful innocence we'd all still held onto from high school. I was unable to comprehend, in the moment, that everything happening around me implied something that was forever. The phone calls. The TV announcing her death, over and over again, like it was the first time every time. I didn't understand the story she was being reduced to, and I certainly didn't understand journalism. I just sat in the dark with the TV light in my eyes, barely seeing, as I watched the video of her covered body being carried away.

I searched through my box of old journals to find the one that Kathleen and I had shared in our senior year of high school. We would write entries together, or read to each other what we had written. Our journals were mostly jumbles of quotes scribbled on post-its, detailed stories of everything that we did that weekend and our latest philosophies on life itself. We loved to read, we loved to write and we loved to tell stories – the same stories – again and again, like they had never lost their original zing. Kathleen told a story like it was the most enthralling thing you'd ever hear. At her funeral, many of her close friends reminisced about her unique, joyful voice, as well as her hysterically contagious laugh.

In the journal, I came across a letter Kathleen had written to me before we began college. The letter began with a Jack Kerouac quote: "It made me think that everything was about to arrive – the moment when you know all and everything is decided forever."

I stopped reading.

Suddenly these words had a new and heartbreaking meaning.

"We may go far," she wrote, "but we'll never forget." The letter overflowed with her words of remembrance and inspiration. She recounted the memories of the Bay Shore childhoods we were about to leave behind, and projected her wishes for the lives that were before us as young adults. She had always had a handful of best girlfriends, to whom she brought unyielding loyalty and esteem. She was the girl who could always entertain herself and all others at any place, any time. She was the girl who could talk lacrosse with the boys, while each of them secretly wondered if they just might be in love with her. She was the spirit that you could feel enter the party before her flip-flops could flip-flap through the door.

That was Kathleen. . .

As the news continued its attempt to answer the unanswerable question of "Why?," Cosmopolitan magazine prepared to cover Kathleen's story in its June 2000 issue.

There is nothing that Cosmopolitan magazine reminds

me of more than picking up Kathleen for the beach. Picking up Kathleen for the beach went the same way every time. I'd drive up to the front of her house knowing she'd be ready and waiting on her front lawn, in the sun. My backseat would be littered with every imaginable beach essential, while Kathleen's preparation consisted of a few things: a water bottle, sometimes a towel, a Cosmopolitan magazine and a big, old book.

In June 2000, I stood in the grocery line and picked up Cosmopolitan. Her photo and story filled pages inside.

For a while after her death, conversations would run through my mind from when Tom, the California wrestler and former Columbia student, returned to New York. Kathleen knew Tom only from her circle of college friends. I remember her telling me about this mysterious, intelligent person whom she had met through her friends. Tom told her within days of meeting her that he thought he could love her. A stranger to Kathleen, Tom immediately connected to her profound feelings about life itself and her love for Kerouac.

Many times, when I would call Kathleen at her dorm, she would put him on the phone so we could get to know each other better. He would often speak to me about California, since I dreamed of living there one day. He would describe it as beautiful, peaceful and wonderfully laid back. When I finally met Tom, he seemed pensive and obviously enamored with Kathleen.

In the days after her death, I fantasized about Kathleen coming to me one day when I was much older. We'd both be married, with small children. She would tell me that she had a very important reason to disappear for some time. She would say she was so sorry she had to leave everyone. Other times, I would just dream about everything I wanted to say to her when we could finally be together again. If there is a heaven, I've prayed enough times to know that she will be the one waiting at the gate to meet me, with her long brown hair and flip-flops. And we will be 19 again.

I've found that when you speak of someone who has passed in such a violent way, you often get a reaction as though you've just spoken about a ghost. This reaction makes my heart sink every time, because it's a reminder that her name is sometimes associated more with fear and the way that she died, than with the life she lived. To me, she is the same unequivocal girl. I can still hear her laughing, with life exuding from the tips of her red painted toes and silver toe rings, to her bright and knowing eyes.

*Specialized
Business
Press
Article*

gripping reality

Kerrin McNamara, Humber Institute of Technology

Rain made a slushy mess of the Toronto streets leading to Jackman Hall at the Art Gallery of Ontario. Still, a crowd trudged through the drizzle to see Peter Raymont's Shake Hands With the Devil. The documentary was fresh off an award-winning run at the 2005 Sundance film festival.

The theatre hushed the moment the lights turned down and Gen. Roméo Dallaire appeared onscreen, revisiting Rwanda ten years after witnessing the genocide. When the lights came back on, the audience erupted in a standing ovation. A man's emotional victory over his haunting past was a cinematic triumph.

At a post-screening gathering, Raymont admitted between sips of Merlot the success of Shake Hands, and subsequently all documentaries, started with this subject.

"The film is good because he's great. It's not me," he says. "I was just like a witness."

Luck accounts for the poignant scenes, like when Dallaire agrees to visit the memorial with hundreds of skulls. Or when he recounts how the bodies were piled at the morgue.

Without Dallaire, there is no film.

How do you convince people, emotional and vulnerable, to let a camera intrude in the darkest corners of their lives?

Just finding a person can prove to be a challenge. Alex Anderson, a documentary filmmaker and a program director at the School of Image Arts at Ryerson, says access to subjects is key. Although anyone can contact the person they want to film, gaining their trust is another story.

"Say I was going to make a film about young people on the streets of Toronto. I'd go in there looking middle-aged and all concerned and they would resist me. There are some stories young people can get better access to no matter how much experience the older filmmakers have, but you've got to make the access."

Making the connection and getting permission is the first big step, but in a documentary the stories are real. These people may be considered actors but their scene never ends. Creating a lasting relationship with them is what Peter Raymont did with Roméo Dallaire. To do that, he had to take a hands-off approach to directing the film.

"Donald Brittain used to say a documentary director should 'Get a good subject, get a good crew, and get the hell out of the way.' So I did that. I got the best crew in the world. I didn't interfere very much. My main role was being Dallaire's buddy, keeping him going, and maintaining that trust. He wasn't communicating with the cameraman or the soundman. He locked his eyes on me. My job was to keep nurturing that relationship."

Erin Faith Young used this mentality in her first film, Hardwood. It follows the director, the son of a former Harlem Globetrotter, as he examines his family, including his absentee father. The critically acclaimed film grabbed a nomination at the 2005 Academy Awards for Best Short Documentary.

"My role while I was there was to make sure everything was easy and flowing smoothly," she says. "The director doesn't have to think about where the dolly is or if a location is booked. I even remember Hubert (the director) leaving the Vancouver shoot saying it was the best shoot he'd ever had. I felt that way too."

It's strange how the director aims for the emotional in

a documentary. Western culture doesn't handle strong emotion very well. When real emotions are at stake, the director must create a sensitive atmosphere, even if it's not what they're feeling. Anderson came across that on a shoot once.

"I was interviewing a famous historian in Britain named E.P. Thompson. He's a practiced speaker, tells really good stories, and he was talking about World War II and being part of a campaign to support the partisans, people fighting against the Nazis. We were just talking about the period and he must have been thinking of people who had died. All of a sudden he just stops and starts to cry. I'm sitting there thinking, 'Oh great, now what am I going to do?' I realized later we were all so intently listening to him, it was so quiet, and he was talking about something painful while the camera was on him that he just got overwhelmed by the intensity of the moment. It just goes to show you that you don't even have to be talking about anything particularly personal. The camera sometimes acts as an accelerator to truth."

The camera can also be detrimental to gaining personal insight. Anderson has experienced both sides of the documentary filmmaking experience in her career.

"The hardest film I ever had to do was a film about Che Guevara. Nobody wanted to talk about him because they were scared. It was the least satisfying film because I had to convince everyone of my intentions and they always doubted me. They were never truly forthcoming. Everyone was so cagey because I was talking about somebody who'd been misinterpreted so many times. People weren't going to let me do my interpretation. There was nothing I could do about it. I couldn't be nicer. I couldn't be more honest. It was just impossible. Sometimes you come back from shooting and you have no film."

"I heard through contacts about this one person and I went to see them without a camera. I knew if they were in my film their life would be very uncomfortable, so I didn't put them in. I could've insisted. I don't know if they would have said yes. I didn't go there because I already knew I couldn't protect them. It's not worth it if it's going to make their life very difficult. It's my code of ethics. You leave and they have to stay."

But the payoff of trust can be plenty. After weeks of preparation and filming Roméo Dallaire in Rwanda, Peter Raymont used patience and quick-thinking to create one of the most poignant scenes in the film.

"We made a list in Toronto of places we'd do, and with the morgue he kept saying, 'Let's go tomorrow. Let's go in a couple of days.' I figured he didn't want to go. So on the last day he said, 'Let's go to the morgue.' We frantically phoned the hospital and asked if we could come and they said it was okay, so we went. That footage you see is pretty much all we shot. He walked in there, told us what he remembered seeing and he walked away. It's a very powerful moment. One of the strongest things in the film as he walks down that alleyway with the lights, all alone. When he walks away you know, okay, let him go but keep the camera running. Let him go, let him be alone. You just have to be sensitive enough to know when to push and when to pull back. If you get too pushy, the film's over. The trust is lost."

Young says it's a Catch-22; the camera has to stay rolling as long as possible but you can't lose their trust.

"We're not paparazzi. We're not there to shove this camera in their face and get the real raw story. You're not going to get good stuff that way. If they get emotional and walk away, you keep the camera rolling for a bit. If they get upset, you respect their feelings and turn the camera off. You can always start again."

These unscripted moments are so important to a personal documentary. When it's real life, there's no way of knowing what will happen.

"It's luck, it's instincts, it's coincidence and I guess it's having done this for 35 years," Raymont says. "You've got to be good to be lucky."

But Young knew this, even on her first film.

"If you set it up right in your treatment, it just happens. Nothing was forced here. When we put the camera in front of Hubert's mother to tell her story, we didn't say 'Okay, can you cry now?' and 'Can you get emotional about when he left you and how much you love him?' It wasn't like that at all. I think when it's an emotional story that's hard to tell, people are suddenly willing to open up. Your emotions are very vulnerable and it just happens."

She recalls a scene from Hardwood that just "happened."

"Hubert asked his brother to write a poem for the film and he could film him saying it. He hadn't prepared and he didn't write anything until the morning we were going to shoot it. He got up, wrote something down and came to the shoot. We were sitting in a park and just had the camera on him, and he started to read the poem for the very first time out loud. It was incredible. It was this beautiful and expressive poem, and he got very emotional. That's one of the most touching scenes of the movie. It wasn't planned at all. We just wanted him to read something, a poem for his dad. It was amazing. I think it's luck or fate. It's meant to happen. He had to get that off his chest and it happened in just the right way."

Those moments make documentary filmmaking

one of the fastest-growing genres. Since Michael Moore's acclaimed Bowling for Columbine, documentaries have taken off. Just look at the top 10 highest grossing documentaries of all time. Columbine sits at number two, out-grossed only by Moore's own Fahrenheit 9/11. Six of the top 10 were made post-Columbine. Moore set off an unprecedented return of the documentary to the big screen, inspiring young filmmakers to grab their cameras and find a story. It's a movement that excites Anderson.

"We have students who are interested in a documentary career. It's a recipe for an interesting life, if not a completely lucrative one," she laughs. "But I think it's an interesting life, making films about people you find more interesting than yourself."

john bubala

Developing relationships with vendors is 'key to survival'
for this family man and independent restaurateur
Abigail Bains, Northwestern University

"Sleep is overrated," says John Bubala, co-owner, chef, purchasing manager and head dishwasher of Thyme, a French-American restaurant in downtown Chicago.

After a late night hosting a wine-tasting dinner, the exuberant multi-tasker is back in the office bright and early. With so many responsibilities at the restaurant, Bubala usually finds himself catching a few winks between 1 a.m. and 7 a.m., when he rises to take his children to school.

By 8 a.m. Bubala sits in Thyme's basement office, which is tucked behind the extra stores of dried goods and wine, where he surfs the Internet and gnaws on an unlit cigar.

For the first hour of his day, he responds to customer inquiries – the restaurant is a popular location for business meetings and wedding rehearsal dinners – and scans his favorite websites, such as SuperChefBlog.com, ChowHound.com and SauteWednesday.com.

Thursdays are important days in terms of preparing for the weekend, and this one is no exception: Bubala eagerly is awaiting the arrival of Slow Food organic products for that organization's dinner, which will be held at Thyme the following Monday. He plans on testing some menu items over the weekend, but thus far only a few organic turkeys have been delivered.

An hour later the first delivery of the day arrives. Removing the packaging, Bubala sniffs the fish.

"Just like the ocean," says the deliveryman from the Fortune Fish Co. "Just like the ocean," Bubala agrees. The two laugh at some private joke as Bubala sets the fish out to prepare gravlax later that afternoon. A moment later he gingerly climbs the steps to meet another purveyor. "Thursday's check day!" he yells behind him.

"If you don't manage your sales reps, they will ruin your life," he adds.

Bubala, who has purchased from the same vendors for the past seven to 12 years, emphasizes a weekly schedule for payments and deliveries. Over the years he has developed friendly working relationships with his suppliers, so when his produce purveyor is out shopping, the vendor will think of Bubala and occasionally bring samples of new produce for him to try.

"That's the key to survival – the trust and relationships you have with your purveyors," Bubala says. "You want someone who's looking out for you." Without that trust, he says, operators will end up spending all of their time at the office, making sure purveyors are not taking advantage of them. "How much can you do by yourself and still live a normal life?" he asks.

"You have to help your purveyors keep their costs down by ordering smart," he adds. "You have to have their best interest in mind."

That not only fosters goodwill but also may keep prices down, since purveyors often have a range of prices they offer to customers. "If you can save two percent on everything, that really adds up," he notes.

But symbiotic relationships are more than just a financial consideration for Bubala. "Some guys won't pay the extra pennies for the face," he says. "In some instances paying a little more is worth it."

With his wine list in hand, Bubala moves into the room that doubles as storage for liquor and restaurant odds and ends, such as CDs, chairs and lamps. Stooping a little to avoid the low ceiling, he sets aside a few bottles of wine, which the bartender will bring up that evening when the bar is restocked. As Bubala scans the room, he scribbles notes to himself, muttering along the way.

"You talk to yourself a lot in this business because that's your double-check," he says.

He says he imagines all of the chefs he has worked with standing behind him as he goes about his day, making selections, taking tasting notes from them and interpreting those notes in his own way. Bubala attributes his development as a chef to the many great cooks he worked with throughout the years – those who were willing to instruct a man who was more than willing to learn.

Bubala got his start in the restaurant business as a busboy at Willow on Wagner, a neighborhood tavern that was known as the Pink Flamingo during Chicago's Al Capone era. At Michigan State University he studied hotel and restaurant management and helped open Bennigan's restaurants in the area.

After graduating, Bubala moved to Boston, where he worked with Bennigan's, Morton's of Chicago, the Boston Harbor Hotel and, finally, the Four Seasons Hotel, where he met chef Michael Kornick. The two returned to Chicago and opened March 6 in 1993. Bubala was chef de cuisine at the restaurant but always knew that he wanted to have his own place.

"It was a great opportunity to learn how to fix things yourself," he says, speaking of his knowledge of rough plumbing and minor electrical work. "If you don't, you'll forever be paying through the nose," he adds.

Now, as purchasing manager for his own restaurant, which he opened in 1998 with his childhood friend Ben Jennings, that's exactly what Bubala tries to avoid. On a chilly winter morning, Thyme feels only slightly warmer than the street outside.

"You're not just purchasing food; you're purchasing gas, electricity and water," Bubala says. "Purchasing is not only getting the best deal but also managing things you can't control, like the prices of gas and electricity." So rather than heat the entire building for the several hours when he and accountant/translator/"gate keeper" Armie Arguelles are the only people in the building, the two come bundled up and don't turn on unnecessary lights.

Bubala also cuts costs by fixing things on his own. "It's all about labor," he says. "That's the most expensive thing now." Instead of calling for assistance every time something breaks, Bubala has collected spare parts of machinery he can use in a pinch. He gestures toward a backup motor in the corner of another storage room: "I could lose $15,000 one night for a $250 motor," he says. And in his opinion it's better to invest a little cash to avoid a big disaster.

He moves into the dried-goods storage and then the freezer, making notes along the way. Bubala does the majority of his purchasing between the months of May and October – the height of the growing season for most produce. Since the Chicago environment is not conducive to year-round growth, he tries to order fresh foods directly from more temperate climates during the rest of the year.

Sometimes, though, he says, good produce can't be found. That's when it is important to remember that "'frozen' is not a bad word," he says. "Neither is 'canned.'" Out-of-season berries, for example, don't have the same taste as the real deal, Bubala says, so rather than using tarter fruits, he opts to freeze raspberries from his friend's farm and use them all year long.

At noon Rob Royce, Bubala's sales representative from

Edward Don & Co., arrives as usual. The two reminisce about their shared past, from their business relationship at Marche to when their wives were pregnant at the same time, emphasizing again how important relationships are to Bubala and his business.

"John knows that if he's out of something on a Friday night, we'll stick something in a cab or however to get it to him," Royce says before the two get down to business. Bubala requests a few kitchen staples and quickly peruses the company's catalog. He decides to visit Edward Don's outlet store rather than make any impulsive purchases at the moment, and Royce exits as quickly as he entered, like clockwork.

Normally, Bubala would eat his packed lunch now, but today he plans to meet a friend, a former meat purveyor, in Chinatown, so he gets back to work, advising his carpenter as to which locks to buy and raiding the freezer for gravlax ingredients.

"Most purchasers don't taste anything," he says. "How can they? It came in a box. That's the hard thing when you have a separate purchaser from the chef."

For Bubala, his personal connection to the ingredients is of the utmost importance. "I think a lot of people gravitate toward independents because they know the person checking everything in the morning is the person tasting everything at night."

Before he gets underway UPS arrives with several Slow Food packages, none of which contains what Bubala was hoping for. Instead, there are only books, pamphlets and a few tomatoes. He sighs and returns to the basement kitchen to prepare the salmon for next week's menu. Gravlax completed, Bubala grabs a sack of lobster bodies and goes upstairs to the restaurant's open kitchen to prepare lobster stock for the evening.

By 1:45 p.m., about the time he usually would be leaving work to pick up his children from school, he is careening down the highway toward Chinatown, rattling off a 15-item list of wines to a purveyor on his cell phone. After all, there's no point in wasting time in the business day, he says.

Though his friend can't make it to lunch, Bubala enjoys a quick meal of dim sum and heads back to Thyme to catch up with the employees, who filter in over the next few hours. Typically, Bubala spends the afternoon with his children, returning to the restaurant at 5 p.m., in time to eat a staff dinner, his favorite time of the workday, and start cooking.

As he enters the restaurant, set to trade his purchasing-manager's cap for his chef's toque, Bubala readies himself. "We've prepared ourselves as best we can," he says. "Now is when the X factor comes in: the customer."

At A Glance

NAME: John Bubala

AGE: 41

EMPLOYER: self-employed; own two restaurants--Thyme and Thyme Cafe--with childhood friend and partner Ben Jennings

TITLE: owner, chef, purchasing manager

LENGTH OF TENURE: seven years at Thyme

CAREER MILESTONES: being invited to a lunch event by chef Charlie Trotter; meeting chef Freddy Girardet at one of Trotter's lunches

PROFESSIONAL ASPIRATIONS: to have a good, honest legacy through my work and someday own an oyster shack on the dock in Nantucket, Mass.

HOMETOWN: Glenview, Ill.

PERSONAL: married; three kids
FAVORITE PASTIME: playing with my children and perusing my cookbook library

apprentice
house

Apprentice House is the future of publishing...today. Using state-of-the-art technology and an experiential learning model of education, it publishes books in untraditional ways while teaching tomorrow's future editors and publishers.

Staffed by students, this non-profit activity of the Department of Communication at Loyola College in Maryland is part of an advanced elective course and overseen by the press's Director. When class is not in session, work on book projects is carried forward by a co-curricular organization, The Apprentice House Book Publishing Club, of which the press's Director also serves as Faculty Advisor.

Contributions are welcomed to sustain the press's work and are tax deductible to the fullest extent allowed by the IRS. For more information, see www.apprenticehouse.com.

Student Editors (2005-06)

Jerrell Cameron
Meghan Connolly
Katharine Dailey
Kinzee Ellis
Natalie Joseph

Dana Kirkpatrick
Ann Marshall
Joanna Walsh
Alison Wright
Kevin Zazzali

Printed in the United States
47331LVS00003B/62